CATHEDRALS
OF STEAM

By the same author

Railways

A Short History of Trains

Driverless Cars: On a Road to Nowhere

The Story of Crossrail

Railways & the Raj

Are Trams Socialist?

To the Edge of the World

Engines of War

Blood, Iron & Gold

Fire & Steam

The Subterranean Railway

On the Wrong Line

Down the Tube

Broken Rails

Forgotten Children

Stagecoach

The Great Railway Disaster

The Great Railway Revolution

CATHEDRALS OF STEAM

How London's Great Stations
Were Built – and How They
Transformed the City

CHRISTIAN WOLMAR

Atlantic Books
London

First published in hardback in Great Britain in 2020 by Atlantic Books,
an imprint of Atlantic Books Ltd.

10 9 8 7 6 5 4 3 2 1

A CIP catalogue record for this book is available
from the British Library.

Hardback ISBN: 978-1-78649-920-2
E-book ISBN: 978-1-78649-921-9
Paperback ISBN: 978-1-78649-922-6

Map artwork by Jeff Edwards
Endpaper image: Detail from *The Railway Station* by
William Powell Frith, 1862. (*Photo 12/Alamy Stock Photo*)

Printed in Great Britain by Bell and Bain Ltd, Glasgow

Atlantic Books
An imprint of Atlantic Books Ltd
Ormond House
26–27 Boswell Street
London WC1N 3JZ

www.atlantic-books.co.uk

Dedicated to my wife, Deborah Maby, with whom I was in lockdown during the coronavirus pandemic for nearly the whole period of writing this book, and who put up with me dodging the housework. Also to Sir John Betjeman, whose writing I sadly cannot match, but whose enthusiasm I can.

CONTENTS

List of Illustrations   ix

Maps   xi

Acknowledgements   xiii

Introduction   1

  1.   Starting slowly   7
  2.   The railway in the sky   19
  3.   The first cathedrals   43
  4.   A modicum of order   71
  5.   Breaching the City walls   91
  6.   Upstaging King's Cross – or not?   109
  7.   Southern invasion   139
  8.   The three sisters   163
  9.   The workers' station   199
10.   A terminus too far   217
11.   London's unique dozen   233
12.   Settling down and dodging the bombs   259
13.   Round London with Sir John Betjeman   277

Appendix I: Timeline for the opening of London's
   terminus stations   305
Appendix II: Passenger numbers in the year to 31 March 2019
   at the London terminuses   307
Select Bibliography   309
References   313
Index   323

ILLUSTRATIONS

SECTION ONE

1. Part of the London & Greenwich Railway, which opened in 1836. Line engraving by A.R. Grieve. (*SSPL/Getty Images*)
2. Spa Road railway station by Robert Blemmell Schnebbelie, 1836. (*The Picture Art Collection/Alamy Stock Photo*)
3. The London terminus of the Brighton and Dover Railroads, 1844. Colour engraving by H. Adlard after an original drawing by J. Marchant. (*SSPL/Getty Images*)
4. Camden Town Engine House, London, July 1838. Coloured lithograph drawn by J.C. Bourne. (*SSPL/Getty Images*)
5. Primrose Hill tunnel, 10 October 1837. Wash drawing by J.C. Bourne. (*SSPL/Getty Images*)
6. Nine Elms station, London, 1838–1848. (*SSPL/Getty Images*)
7. Bishopsgate station, 1862. (*Bridgeman Images*)
8. Cannon Street railway bridge leading to Cannon Street station, c.1880. (*Sean Sexton/Hulton Archive/Getty Images*)
9. King's Cross station, c.1860. (*Hulton Archive/Getty Images*)
10. Illustration of the dust heaps in Somers Town. (*The Print Collector via Getty Images*)
11. Erection of the roof of St Pancras station, 1868. (*SSPL/Getty Images*)
12. Construction of St Pancras station cellars, 2 July 1867. (*SSPL/Getty Images*)
13. The Midland Grand Hotel and St Pancras station, c.1880. (*Hulton Archive/Getty Images*)
14. Midland Railways Milk & Fish Depot, c.1894. (*SSPL/Getty Images*)
15. The Doric arch at the entrance to Euston station, 7 September 1904. (*SSPL/Getty Images*)
16. The Great Hall at Euston station. (*History and Art Collection/Alamy Stock Photo*)

SECTION TWO

1. Liverpool Street station, c.1885. (*Paul Popper/Popperfoto via Getty Images/Getty Images*)
2. Paddington station, c.1900. (*Paul Popper/Popperfoto via Getty Images/Getty Images*)
3. Broad Street station, 1898. (*SSPL/Getty Images*)
4. Fenchurch Street station, 1912. (*English Heritage/Heritage Images/Getty Images*)
5. Necropolis station, Westminster Bridge Road, c.1900. (*The Print Collector/Getty Images*)
6. Victory Arch, Waterloo station, 21 March 1922. (*SSPL/Getty Images*)
7. Crowds in Waterloo station heading off to Ascot. (*William Gordon Davis/Mansell/The LIFE Picture Collection/via Getty Images*)
8. London & North Eastern Railway (LNER) poster showing the dining room of the Great Eastern Hotel at Liverpool Street station. Artwork by Gordon Nicoll. (*SSPL/Getty Images*)
9. 'The Gate of Goodbye', F.J. Mortimer, 1917. (*Hulton Archive/Getty Images*)
10. Victoria station, c.1950. (*Central Press/Archive Photos/Getty Images*)
11. Marylebone station, c.1950. (*Allan Cash Picture Library/Alamy Stock Photo*)
12. Euston station main concourse, 2019. (*Willy Barton/Shutterstock.com*)
13. Interior of London Bridge station, 2019. (*TK Kurikawa/Shutterstock.com*)
14. View across Regent's Canal towards Granary Square, 2019. (*Sam Mellish/In Pictures via Getty Images Images*)
15. Interior of King's Cross station, 2018. (*Jeff Whyte/Shutterstock.com*)
16. Statue of Sir John Betjeman at St Pancras station. (*cowardlion/Shutterstock.com*)

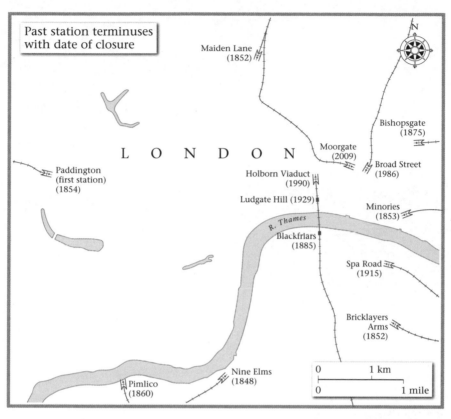

Past station terminuses with date of closure

Maiden Lane (1852)

Bishopsgate (1875)

Moorgate (2009)

Broad Street (1986)

L O N D O N

Paddington (first station) (1854)

Holborn Viaduct (1990)

Ludgate Hill (1929)

Minories (1853)

R. Thames

Blackfriars (1885)

Spa Road (1915)

Bricklayers Arms (1852)

Nine Elms (1848)

Pimlico (1860)

0   1 km

0   1 mile

N

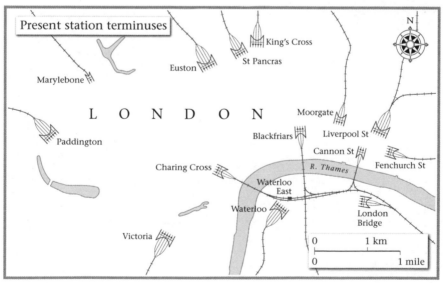

Present station terminuses

King's Cross

St Pancras

Euston

Marylebone

L O N D O N

Moorgate

Paddington

Blackfriars

Liverpool St

Cannon St

Fenchurch St

Charing Cross

R. Thames

Waterloo East

Waterloo

London Bridge

Victoria

0   1 km

0   1 mile

N

ACKNOWLEDGEMENTS

I AM GRATEFUL to my fellow cricketer Martin Matthews who suggested the idea for this book while we were chatting between overs a couple of years ago. Thanks are due to Simon Carne and Bernard Gambrill who both read the manuscript and made useful suggestions, Michael Holden for supplying a jigsaw of Waterloo station to help me through the lockdown, Joe Brown for providing figures on London's rail mileage, Liam Browne for helping me on the station tour, and Rupert Brennan Brown as ever. Special mention must be made of Chris Randall, who went through the manuscript with a sub editor's eye for detail as well as making numerous structural suggestions. Toby Mundy is my supportive agent and James Nightingale my patient editor at Atlantic Books for whom this is my eighth book. The errors, of course, are all mine.

I decided on using 'terminuses' rather than 'termini'. There seems no good reason to use Latin plurals for a technology that the Romans, despite their fantastic ingenuity, did not develop.

INTRODUCTION

S TATIONS WERE AN afterthought when the first railways were
built. The Stockton & Darlington, a pioneering but technologically primitive railway, had no stations at all when its first trains
ran in 1825. The Liverpool & Manchester, which opened five years
later as the first intercity modern railway, did a little better, with
huts at either end. Initially, stations on the early railways were crude
affairs, little more than a path between tracks to enable passengers
to clamber aboard and possibly a ticket office that might be located
in the local pub.

By the time the railways reached London in 1836, six years after
the completion of the Liverpool & Manchester Railway, providing
facilities for passengers was still seen by the railway companies as
an irritating necessity rather than as a way of encouraging greater
use.

The first terminus, London Bridge, opened in December 1836,
provided little for its early passengers and had no architectural
merit, but Euston, completed the following year, was a far grander
affair as befitted the capital's first main-line station. It was not
so much that the passengers were offered any facilities to help
them on their way but, rather, the railway company, the London
& Birmingham, decided to erect a huge Doric arch in front of

the station that served no purpose other than to demonstrate the importance of the company and of this new technology.

Things did begin to improve. The railway companies started to realize that passengers wanted a bit more than a 'platform' to access the trains, such as waiting rooms, toilets, newsagents, porters, ticket offices and easy connections to onward transport. The opening of these two stations triggered a quite remarkable period of station construction, which over the space of a mere four decades provided London with more than a dozen terminuses, nearly all of which, as this book describes, survive today. Only one, Marylebone, was built after 1874, and that was one of the most modest. It is a bigger collection of major terminus stations than has been built in any other city of the world and the process of the development and construction of these stations created the London of today. Vast swathes of housing and other older buildings, even churches and schools, were swept away in the railway companies' rush to create this new form of transport that, in turn, caused further upheaval.

The companies were rapacious land grabbers whose rivalry was responsible for the establishment of such a large number of stations, but they had one aim in common: they wanted to get as near the centre of the capital as possible. Several companies started with stations that were further out and found that this severely constrained their ability to attract passengers. The reason why the stations ended up as a ring around the centre, nearly all connected by the Underground's Circle Line, is a key part of this story. There are other Londons that can be imagined – one, for example, with a huge central station somewhere in the heart of the city, or another where there are fewer but better coordinated stations. However, as the book shows, competition rather than cooperation was the zeitgeist and explains London's exceptionalism. Other cities, like

Paris, had numerous terminus stations but there was more order and planning in the process of their development. In London, it was the whim of the railway companies, moderated only by the light touch of Parliament, that resulted in the pattern of the capital's railways.

Each of these stations, even the smaller ones such as Fenchurch Street, required not only, obviously, a set of tracks leading into them, which caused further disruption to the existing built environment above and beyond their construction, but also quickly spawned other development, such as goods depots, warehouses, depositories and road access. All these stations were, as we would call them today, megaprojects, massive disruptive forces whose impact stretched well beyond their boundaries.

London was already on its way to becoming the world's largest city when the railways first arrived in the 1830s and by the end of the nineteenth century was far larger and more affluent than any other in the world. The growth of the railways and of the city was a symbiotic process that academics have been unable to disentangle. All that can be said conclusively is that one would not have happened without the other.

These stations are all buildings in two parts, a fantastic blend of architecture and engineering that at times overlap. The façades, which consist mainly of hotels and offices, are the work of architects, or sometimes just the railway company manager who was blessed with a few design skills. Even though railways were a new technology, indeed a revolutionary one that had an impact on the way of life for everyone in the country, the architecture was mostly backward-looking. The styles harked back to the classical Greek and Roman eras, to medieval Gothic, to the Renaissance, with the Italianate style predominating, but never looked to the future, never celebrated the modern world that the railways themselves were creating. As the introduction to an exhibition of station architecture held in Paris in the late 1970s suggests, 'In order to disguise the upheavals of the introduction of the railway into the town, the quasi-totalities of nineteenth-century station buildings take on the appearances of Greek temples, and Roman baths, Romanesque basilicas and Gothic cathedrals, Renaissance chateaux and Baroque abbeys'.[1] Behind the facades, vast engine sheds were erected, often representing leading-edge technology of the era. It was all great fun for the railway companies, but less so for the passengers as none of these styles particularly suited the functioning of the railways.

We should, though, not complain, especially since, as I set out in the final chapter, nearly all the stations have been improved since the doldrums of the 1960s, when Euston's arch and its Great Hall were demolished and other stations such as St Pancras and Charing Cross might have gone the same way. Instead, by and large – with the odd exception – London's terminuses have been greatly enhanced, even much unloved London Bridge, by refurbishments and additions, most notably the new side entrance to King's Cross.

This has been a happy book to write, a positive story for these hard times and one that John Betjeman, who features strongly in the last chapter, would greatly appreciate. The prospects for the future have only been darkened by the coronavirus pandemic sweeping through the country as I write. The effect on the railways has been devastating, with the government and the railway companies urging people not to use the railways, which until then had enjoyed more than two decades of almost uninterrupted growth, reaching record passenger numbers. The long-term impact remains to be seen as some passengers may not return to train travel, either because they have discovered that they can work from home, or because they are concerned about the risk of viral transmission. The terminus stations, while still functioning, are desolate places, bereft of the lively hustle and bustle that demonstrates their vitality and with their shops and cafés shuttered. Oddly, that made it a good time for me to study their architecture and design, and I am confident that they will regain their *joie de vivre* in the fullness of time.

Christian Wolmar

July 2020

ONE

STARTING SLOWLY

THE RAILWAYS CAME late to London, half a dozen years after the opening of the pioneering Liverpool & Manchester in 1830, but they quickly made up for lost time. Railways soon spread all around the capital and were a vital component of the rapid growth that turned London into the world's first megacity. London not only acquired the world's first underground railway network, beating all other cities across the globe by almost forty years, but also can boast today of having 598 railway stations and 756 route miles of line,[1] and, most notably, more terminus stations than any other city in the world.

Those magnificent 'cathedrals of steam', built between 1836 and the end of the nineteenth century, have shaped London in many ways, creating new districts and destroying old ones, and influencing the type and location of housing and other developments across the capital. They, in turn, were built and located for reasons that can be understood only by considering the history and geography of the Thames basin in which London grew from a small Roman settlement established in the first century AD around where Vauxhall Bridge stands today. The Thames, and in particular its meandering arcs, have caused trouble ever since to London's transport system, and the railways are no exception. Almost uniquely, too, of the British railway system, there was an element of planning and forethought about the location of the terminus stations that explains their location dotted along a ring around the West End and the City.

It is impossible to untangle the symbiotic relationship between the railway and the growth of the capital. In 1831, London's population of 1.7 million was squeezed into an area of just eighteen square miles. It was already on the way to being the world's biggest city and an incredibly cramped one. At the time, Hammersmith was known for its strawberries and orchards, and market gardens flourished on the gravel terraces west of Chelsea and up the Lea Valley. On the clay lands, large fields provided grain for people and hay for horses, while well laid out parks extended from the numerous country houses. Today, London, with its thirty-two boroughs and City Corporations, is thirty-four times larger at 618 square miles, whereas the population, at 8.8 million, has only grown by a factor of five. While undoubtedly the motor car has fuelled that expansion and allowed a reduction in density to take place, the process was started and developed in earnest by the existence of the railways, including the Underground and, later, trams.

Much of London before the advent of the railways was little changed from its Georgian heyday. It was still a dark place. Gas light was first used in London on Westminster Bridge in 1813 but spread only slowly until the mid-1820s, with most streets still being illuminated by infrequent oil lamps and pedestrians having to be escorted home by 'link-boys' bearing lights. According to Peter Ackroyd, 'the outskirts retained a rural aspect… The great public buildings, with which the seat of empire was soon to be decorated, had not yet arisen. The characteristic entertainments were those of the late eighteenth century, too, with the dogfights, the cockfights, the pillory and the public executions.'[2]

However, changes were afoot. The area now encompassed by central London at the dawn of the railway age was booming, with massive developments on the great estates as some of their aristocratic owners realized that they were sitting on invaluable assets. London had undergone rapid transformation in the previous half century, particularly in the prosperous period in the aftermath of the Napoleonic Wars.

Whereas John Nash had been the principal architect of swathes of London during the late Georgian and Regency periods, such as Regent Street and the various terraces around Regent's Park, the mantle had passed to Thomas Cubitt who was responsible for even more notable developments. After creating much of modern-day Bloomsbury, including Tavistock and Russell squares on land owned by the Duke of Bedford, Cubitt turned his attention to the Grosvenor Estate south of Hyde Park where he established both Belgravia and Pimlico on land that had previously been used as market gardens.

In his book *A Short History of London*, Simon Jenkins applauds these developments, suggesting that they were built to far higher standards than Nash's terraces and that even today 'their creamy cliffs of stucco… symbolize upmarket living to rich expatriates the world over'.[3] There were other equally successful developments during the first three decades of the nineteenth century, including on the fields owned by the Bishop of London in Paddington and Bayswater; but a speculative scheme further west just beyond Notting Hill, supported by the owners, the Ladbroke family, proved a step too far and the rather grand terraces were soon sublet to poor families described by *The Times* as 'a more filthy and disgusting crew we have seldom had the misfortune to encounter'.[4] The pleasant squares built up by the large landowners remained interspersed with areas of slum housing, much of which would be cleared for railway development during the course of the century.

It is important to note that the outward suburban spread, which the railways would do much to stimulate, had already begun. To the north, St John's Wood, Camden Town and Islington had grown up with sizeable housing suitable for the burgeoning middle classes. Further north, there was ribbon development of housing through Tottenham to Upper Edmonton, although away from the main road there were only fields and marshland. On the south bank of the Thames, there was continuous building between Rotherhithe and Lambeth, most of which were festering slums. Further south, however, there were more salubrious areas up to the New Kent Road and stretching out to Kennington and Walworth but nothing much beyond apart from villages.

In the west, beyond the elegant new squares, Chelsea remained a discrete village and along the Thames the Millbank slums were a terrible eyesore. The villages of Kensington, Hammersmith and Turnham Green, although linked to London by ribbon development, were not yet really part of the capital. Park Lane and the first section of the Edgware Road marked the north-west limit of London as Kilburn and Edgware were distant villages separated from the capital by large strips of agricultural land; the old Roman road itself was little more than a lane among the farms and fields.

In the east, thanks to intense activity in the Docklands, houses were replacing the fields in Bethnal Green. A few affluent master mariners and boat owners lived in the neat villas of Wapping and Shadwell but again there was considerable open space.

While for the most part the environs of London were sparsely populated and the various villages still small, with all this building activity London was well on the way to overtaking Peking (now Beijing) to become the largest city in the world. Its growth coincided perfectly with the advent of the railways.

Despite this growth, London's social infrastructure lagged behind. Sanitation was non-existent, with periodic outbreaks of deadly diseases such as cholera and typhus; there was no welfare system apart from the very basic Poor Law and most children didn't attend school. Furthermore, although most building development in this period was on greenfield sites, the poorer people whose housing happened to be in the way were unceremoniously evicted without compensation or regard for their prospects. Consequently, they were forced to find alternative accommodation further away from the centre but still within walking distance as otherwise there was little prospect of finding employment. The concentration of people in the centre of what was then a relatively small city was mainly due to a lack of affordable transport for the masses; outer expansion to areas that millions of commuters now know as Zone 2 was the catalyst for all this to change. Around a tenth of London's population still lived in the City of London itself but the wealthier merchants, bankers and lawyers had moved out to the West End or the villas of Sydenham, Clapham or Stoke Newington. The phenomenon of separation of work and home that the railways would both enable and encourage had begun.

The early stages of a transport system were emerging, thanks to the ingenuity of a number of pioneering entrepreneurs. The first horse-drawn omnibuses were introduced on London's streets in 1829 by a coachbuilder, George Shillibeer, who had seen them being successfully used during a trip to Paris. While promoting the idea, he was commissioned to construct and operate an omnibus for Newington Academy for Girls, which became the world's first school bus. His company then went on to provide a regular service using twenty-seater coaches running between Paddington and the Bank of England in the City, anticipating almost precisely the route the Metropolitan Railway, the world's first underground line, would take three and a half decades later.

Passengers on these early omnibuses paid sixpence or a shilling (2.5p–5p, or around £3–£5 in today's money), which was still unaffordable for all but a small minority of the best-paid workers. The reporter in the *Morning Post* was impressed: 'Saturday the new vehicle, called the Omnibus, commenced running from Paddington to the City, and excited considerable notice, both from the novel form of the carriage, and the elegance with which it is fitted out. It is capable of accommodating 16 or 18 persons, all inside, and we apprehend it would be almost impossible to make it overturn, owing to the great width of the carriage. It was drawn by three beautiful bays abreast, after the French fashion.'[5] But the writer went on to warn rather presciently that there were concerns that the vehicle might find the narrow streets of the capital rather difficult to manoeuvre.

The other early form of public transport was the hansom cab. Introduced in 1834, the two-wheeled cab was pulled by one horse, making it cheaper than its predecessors. However, the drivers were infamous for their insolence and dishonesty, as well as, more worryingly, their dangerous driving, which was often made worse by their penchant for drink. Their fares, even before the customary overcharging, were out of reach of working-class Londoners but they were well patronized by the growing middle classes. Consequently, both forms of transport thrived with 3,000 omnibuses operating by 1854, a number that was surpassed by the number of cabs of various kinds plying their trade in the capital.

Given the cost of these new methods of transport, it was not surprising that it was the railways that were to become the real agents of change, particularly in respect of travel to and from work, because they could be both profitable and affordable. Their impact would be profound and long lasting. The success of the world's first modern railway, the Liverpool & Manchester, which opened in September 1830, had not gone unnoticed in the capital. While it was by no means the first railway, a concept that had its origins in the wagonways that had sprung up in the seventeenth century, the Liverpool & Manchester was groundbreaking in a number of respects – it was the first railway to connect two major cities carrying passengers as well as freight in both directions on a double-tracked line with trains that were hauled by steam locomotives throughout the route.[6] The railway was, therefore, revolutionary, changing the very nature of transport in Britain and then, rapidly, across the world as the widespread benefits of deploying this new invention were so patently obvious.

It was, though, no accident that the railways had first been developed in the North of England, rather than in the capital. The North was the cradle of the Industrial Revolution, where the various inventions that were beginning to harness the power of steam ever more efficiently had been developed. Putting the source of this power, a steam engine, on wheels that ran on rails had slowly emerged as the best way to make use of the energy that had become available as the equipment became ever more efficient. It had taken years, decades even, for the idea of wheels on rails to emerge, after many false starts. Attempts to run wheeled steam engines on roads had floundered because the surface of early nineteenth-century highways simply wasn't up to the task and steering for these behemoths had yet to be developed. So, iron wheels on iron rails was the answer as demonstrated by the successful opening of the Liverpool & Manchester.

After that, the railways never looked back. There were bumps on the way and a few half-hearted and abortive attempts to use horses rather than steam locomotives but essentially the development of railways across the world was unstoppable. By the start of the First World War, less than a century later, Britain would have 18,000 miles of railway, while the United States, which also opened its first railway in 1830, would have a quarter of a million miles, meaning that a staggering eight miles of track was built every day in the US for the whole eighty-four-year period.

Various extensions were soon added to the Liverpool & Manchester and a few other isolated lines popped up elsewhere in Britain, as far afield as Cornwall and Kent but not, at that stage, in the capital. London had, though, been the site of several early precursors of modern railways. The most significant was the Surrey Iron Railway, the city's first line. Originally, the intention had been to build a railway or a canal between the Thames and Portsmouth, doing away with the need for goods to be carried by sea through the straits of Dover where the ships might come up against a hostile French navy. The purpose of the line was to serve factories that had sprung up along the Wandle, a tributary of the Thames that gave its name to Wandsworth; although navigable, it was a very slow way to transport goods. A canal was considered but proved impractical because of water shortages and the difficulty of improving the meandering Wandle.

Therefore, the promoters pushed through a Bill in Parliament in 1801 to build a line from a wharf on the Thames at Wandsworth to Croydon, with the option of later adding a number of short branch lines. The first sections opened in 1802 and the line was completed the following year. However, the idea of eventually reaching Portsmouth never got off the drawing board, although an extension to Merstham, further into Surrey, was completed.

The railway, which, impressively, was double tracked throughout, was operated by horses pulling wagons on rails that were just over 4ft apart, considerably narrower than the 4ft 8½in that later became the standard gauge on railways in Britain, most European countries and the USA. Unlike the railways that, within a few decades, sprung up throughout the capital, the owners of the line did not operate it themselves but, rather, allowed all-comers to use it in exchange for payment of a toll.

Unfortunately, the Surrey Iron Railway struggled throughout its life, with the owners unable to pay any dividends most years and only stretching to modest ones even when the business was profitable. Despite this, the line somehow survived the advent of the railways in London but its eventual demise was caused by the London & Brighton taking over part of the extension to Merstham in 1837, which damaged the Surrey Iron Railway's profitability and resulted in traffic ceasing entirely in 1846. The authors of a book on London's railways conclude that the Surrey Iron Railway and its extension, the Croydon, Merstham & Godstone, was never really viable once the ambitious aim to reach Portsmouth was abandoned: 'The two railways were promoted as part of a trunk line and once that plan failed, the local traffic that they could attract was very limited. Under those circumstances, closure was inevitable.'[7]

London was also the site of one of the most significant demonstrations of the potential of steam locomotives, although it was a trial of the technology rather than a showcase for the concept of railways. Richard Trevithick is one of the lesser-known pioneers of the development of the railways, but he is deserving of wider recognition. Born in 1771 in Cornwall, where steam pumps to keep mines clear of water were commonplace, Trevithick first developed a more efficient version of James Watt's groundbreaking steam engine, and then came up with the idea of putting one on wheels. After a successful first test at Camborne in Cornwall on Christmas Eve 1801 of his *Puffing Devil*, the subsequent trial three days later has gone down in history for all the wrong reasons. When the locomotive, which had no steering mechanism, got stuck in a gully, Trevithick and his team adjourned to the pub for a meal that history notes was of roast goose watered down with considerable amounts of ale. Unfortunately, Trevithick and his team left the fire burning in the engine, the water boiled off and the machine was destroyed.

Undeterred, his next invention proved far more significant. He realized he had to put his wheeled engine on rails. After producing a couple of locomotives for mines with mixed results, he visited London in the summer of 1808 to show off his invention on a circular track, ironically near the site of the present-day Euston station. His engine, developed as part of a wager, was playfully called *Catch Me Who Can* as Trevithick wanted to show that it would outpace and outlast a horse. Cannily, he built his track behind walls so that he could charge entry to those who wanted to see it and levy an extra fee on anyone who wanted to ride on a carriage hauled by his locomotive. Initially, the show was a success but interest soon tailed off and it closed down within a few months.

The fact that these two early experiments took place in the South-East was anomalous. It was in the North, and particularly the North-West, often in mines, where virtually all tests and trials of the new technology were carried out. London would, however, see the inauguration of a new type of railway, one that was ahead of its time and would result in the creation of a piece of infrastructure that, despite being little noticed by Londoners today, would have a profound influence on south-east London.

TWO

THE RAILWAY IN
THE SKY

L ONDON'S FIRST RAILWAY, the London & Greenwich Railway,
had its origins in a previous project, the Kentish Railway,
which emerged during the mid-1820s. This was a period of
widespread enthusiasm for railways despite the fact that steam
locomotives were very much still in the development stage and
not yet a realistic proposition as the power source. The successful
opening in 1825 of the Stockton & Darlington Railway, a primitive
line mainly operated by horses but using some steam locomotives,
demonstrated the potential of the technology and helped stimulate
the first period of 'railway mania' as it became known. Proposals for
lines were submitted to Parliament by more than fifty companies
that together envisaged the construction of some 3,000 miles of
railway lines. Most of these schemes never got past the design
stage, but several were the genesis of what became some of the
nation's first railway lines.

In December 1824, the Kentish Railway published a prospectus
for a line that would extend across the whole of Kent from London
to Dover, serving towns and villages including Greenwich,

Woolwich, Gravesend, Chatham and Canterbury. The idea was to use mainly 'locomotive machines' as the prospectus called them, although horses were expected to supplement them. Unlike many other schemes of this period, which tended to rely on back-of-the-envelope calculations, the Kentish Railway provided an impressively detailed forecast of passenger numbers and potential profit. In fact, it was far better set out than the equivalent prospectuses for many subsequent plans for more successful schemes.

The promoters estimated that, in the Kent countryside, the line would cost £5,000 per mile but recognized that closer to London, where potential for income was greater, expenditure would probably be double that amount. They calculated that there were around 150 horse-drawn coaches a day carrying passengers between Woolwich and London and generating £26,000 per year: 'As locomotive machinery, moving at *twice the speed* and with greater safety, must in a very great degree supersede the coaches, the Company will probably obtain from passengers alone, independently of the baggage, an income of £20,000 or 20 per cent of the capital of £100,000 requisite to carry the railway to Woolwich.'[1]

Somewhat surprisingly, their chosen engineer was no less a figure than Thomas Telford, who had established his reputation as a road, bridge and canal builder, and an adviser to canal companies in bitter planning battles against their great rivals, the railways. Nevertheless, the promoters hoped that his name would attract the investment they needed to get the scheme started. They believed that once the section from London to Woolwich was completed and shown to be profitable, it would be easier to fund the rest of the line.

However, like so many other railway schemes of this era, their optimism was sadly misplaced. The company had sought to raise

£1m (around £100m in today's values) but investors were simply unwilling to risk parting with their money on such a radical idea as a lengthy railway running through London, particularly as the technology was in its infancy.

The only line that did emerge in this initial period of railway mania in the South-East was the Canterbury & Whitstable, a six-mile largely cable-hauled line that eventually opened in 1830 after numerous early travails and that has rather unfairly mostly been forgotten. Despite being technologically advanced, it proved to be a somewhat unsuccessful little railway. Built primarily to carry freight that had previously been transported on the winding River Stour as well as passengers, particularly those heading for the beaches at Whitstable, it was never financially viable. The railway was more expensive to build than anticipated and always struggled to pay dividends to its investors before finally being subsumed into the South Eastern Railway in 1844.

Nevertheless, the seeds had been sown for a railway running between south-east London and Kent, although, as was often the case in this entrepreneurial era, it needed the efforts and persistence of one man to champion the scheme and see it through to completion. George Thomas Landmann was a former colonel in the Royal Engineers and a civil engineer who had built forts to protect against potential American invaders when serving in the British army in Canada. His plan was for a railway of three and a half miles starting near the foot of the new London Bridge, whose recent opening in 1831 greatly improved links from Southwark to the City. Landmann envisaged a route that ran in a straight line to Deptford and then in a curve north-eastwards to Greenwich. Realizing that the first mile of the line would go through an already congested part of south-east London and would have to cross at least a dozen streets, he planned to run the railway on a series of viaducts that would limit disruption at ground level but prove exceedingly expensive to build.

The proximity of London Bridge station to the new improved crossing over the Thames was seen as attractive for workers in the City and the East End. Yet, in a way, this was premature as commuting long distances between work and home was not yet commonplace. Most of London's workforce still lived within walking distance of their workplace and the capital's economy had only just started to take off. However, Deptford and Greenwich, with a combined population of 45,000, both offered large potential markets for the railway. Deptford had a thriving dockyard with a huge workforce where many notable ships had been built; the surrounding area of market gardens and meadows was ripe for development that could attract more people onto the railway. Greenwich, with its long association with the Royal Navy, employed significant numbers of people in ship chandlery and other marine occupations. The little town was dominated by the famous Royal Naval College, but apart from the various maritime connections, it was the neighbouring park that offered the most likely source of income for the nascent railway as it was a favourite haunt for Londoners eager to escape the fetid air of the capital. The park could be reached easily, if somewhat slowly, by boat along the Thames, though, unsurprisingly, the ferry owners were quick to oppose the new railway scheme.

They weren't alone. Objections came from the vast array of coach and horse omnibus operators on the busy road linking London and Greenwich where there was even a series of trials of 'steam road carriages' along the route. The most notable of these was *The Era*, a double-deck vehicle that accommodated six passengers inside and fourteen on top, and was said to travel at 10 mph. There were, too, a couple of smaller 'steam road carriages' running to Deptford, but while their portrayal in various surviving watercolours makes them appear well built and successful in attracting passengers, in reality they were simply too heavy to be a viable long-term proposition on the crude roads of the time, which all but disintegrated in wet weather.

George Shillibeer, who, as we saw in Chapter 1, had introduced the horse omnibus to London in 1829, was another vehement opponent of the railway. Having decided to shift his twenty vehicles to what he considered to be the lucrative route between London and Greenwich, he now faced the prospect of his business being overwhelmed by the putative railway.

Despite this fierce opposition from rivals and doubts over the ability of the London & Greenwich to raise sufficient funds for its ambitious plans, Landmann obtained Parliamentary approval for the line in May 1833. However, the level of scepticism that prevailed at the time can be seen in this dismissive quote in the *Quarterly Review*, a literary and political periodical: 'Can anything be more palpably ridiculous than the prospect held out of locomotives travelling twice as fast as stage coaches... we will back Old Father Thames against the Greenwich railway for any sum.'[2]

The railway's promoters secured Parliamentary backing by highlighting a number of advantages, some significantly less convincing than others. The line, they said, could be used to convey fire engines (a dubious suggestion); it would provide quick access for troops to Dover when completed (the Napoleonic Wars were fresh in the nation's memory); and it could prove useful for transporting troops in the event of civil disorder (something that did, indeed, become commonplace on many railways across the world and had already occurred on the Liverpool & Manchester). There would, too, be fewer accidents on the overcrowded river and, rather fancifully, they suggested, less congestion on London Bridge from crowds watching the constant stream of boats sailing on the Thames. Safety overall was a big concern at the time and the promoters were keen to assure the public that many precautions had been taken to prevent not only derailments but also trains falling off the viaducts.

However, despite Parliamentary approval for the Bill, there was no certainty that money would be available to build the line. The prospectus, launched in November 1831, had sought to raise £1m, but investors were reluctant to come forward. With more than 19,000 of the 20,000 shares still to be sold, George Walter, one of the directors of the nascent company, went on a sales trip across Britain visiting brokers in Birmingham, Manchester and Liverpool who were paid a commission to sell the shares. He also wrote various letters to newspapers, sometimes under pseudonyms, countering the arguments of opponents and stressing the value of the line. At the same time, pamphlets appeared, either directly or indirectly from the company, vigorously promoting the line. One, with the less than subtle title of *The Advantages of Railways with Locomotive Engines, Especially the London & Greenwich Railway*, stressed how the market gardeners of Deptford would be able to use the railway to transport their manure cheaply at night, something which, thankfully for passengers, never happened.

The most enticing inducement was the promise of annual profits of up to 30 per cent, based on highly optimistic predictions of passenger numbers and low estimates of costs, a not uncommon feature of these early railway schemes. Two further potential revenue streams were highlighted by the promoters. The area under the 878 arches on which the railway was planned to be built could, it was hoped, be rented out, and fees from the walkers on the roadway and gravel footpath that was planned to be built on each side of the base of the viaducts would be another potential source of income. In fact, in the early days of the line, when it only operated between London and Deptford, passengers from Greenwich were encouraged to walk along that footpath to catch the train at Deptford.

A cottage served as a temporary station and ticket office, with the back door of the dwelling leading on to the footpath towards Deptford. As the author of the book on the history of the line reports, this afforded a pleasant walk on a sunny day but, as it was unlit, 'it was not the best means of reaching Deptford Station on a wet winter's night for on the path from the cottage to the bridge… [was] a pond fifty feet long and 3 ½ feet wide in a direct line between the lantern [at the station] and the footbridge into which more than a dozen people had been lured by February 1837';[3] this was a mere three months after the opening of the line. Clearly, getting to the train was, initially at least, more dangerous than travelling on it. The path on the arches alongside the tracks was popular for a while, being used by around 350 people a day in 1839, a useful source of revenue for the railway.

Walter's campaign to raise money was successful and ensured the London & Greenwich sealed its place in history as the capital's first railway. With Parliamentary permission obtained, which always required the financing to be in place, it was time to start the lengthy and difficult process of buying out the landowners over whose property the viaducts would be built. Negotiations were undertaken with 500 separate owners and disputes had to be resolved by juries in more than thirty cases. Demolition work

came next and its extent would be remarkable, setting an example
that would be followed in the construction of several other terminuses and their lines out of London. Most house demolition
was justified on the grounds that the dwellings were insanitary,
cholera-ridden slums and therefore it was in the public interest to
clear them. As much of the clearance work for the line was carried
out in Southwark, an area of mostly poor housing, the London &
Greenwich had a strong case. Nevertheless, some residents of the
most insalubrious slums in Bermondsey were reluctant to move,
and threatened violence against the navvies constructing the line.
Further towards Greenwich, however, there were fewer houses and
it was around Corbett's Lane, Bermondsey, the halfway point, that
work started in April 1834 on the viaducts towards London.

The scale of the enterprise was unprecedented and the initial
work of building the viaducts was an object of great curiosity
for Londoners. In fact, the huge number of bricks used in their
construction resulted in a shortage for housebuilding elsewhere in
the capital. At the peak of the work, a remarkable 100,000 bricks
were being laid every day. More than 600 men were employed,
and by the autumn of 1835, a temporary single-track railway to
transport material had been installed on 540 completed arches. A
section of the path had also been completed and earned the first
income for the railway company.

With vast quantities of bricks set aside for the section towards
Greenwich, the company hoped to open the whole line by the
original scheduled date of Christmas 1835. In truth, however,
despite a further 150 men being drafted in, the deadline was
unachievable. Further delays occurred when two unfinished arches
in Bermondsey collapsed one night in January 1836, fortunately not
resulting in any injuries or fatalities, which would have been the

case had the incident occurred during the day. The most serious setback was caused by the need to comply with a section of the Act which specified that the bridge over the River Ravensbourne had to be moveable to allow boats through, even though the Ravensbourne was little more than a wide stream (this could have been avoided with permission from all the occupiers of the local quays and wharves but that proved impossible to obtain). After much procrastination, a drawbridge was built but it is doubtful that it was ever raised to allow any boats through.

The men building the line were not averse to an occasional fight and at weekends pitched battles took place between the English and the more numerous Irish. Most of the navvies lodged around Tooley Street, adjoining today's London Bridge station, and the company decided to segregate the two groups in areas called 'Irish Grounds' and 'English Grounds', the latter of which still survives as a small street running parallel to the Thames.

The various trials of technology attracted huge interest from Londoners who had not, apart from Trevithick's brief efforts two decades earlier, seen working steam locomotives. Extensive press coverage of every aspect of the railway's progress further fuelled interest. Despite an occasional mishap, such as the collapse of the two arches in Bermondsey, there was sufficient confidence in the technology to enable the first section of the railway to be opened in February 1836. This ran between Deptford and Spa Road, about a mile short of London Bridge, owing to the westernmost arches being the most difficult to build in a densely populated area. This meant that the wholly inadequate 'station' at Spa Road could claim to be London's first railway terminus. However, only the most obsessive trainspotter would accord it that title since it was a makeshift affair with virtually no amenities to serve the travelling

public. According to the author of the history of the London &
Greenwich Railway, 'Spa Road station in 1836 consisted of the
wooden staircase on the south side of the viaduct and a small
wooden booking office at ground level [and] a narrow platform to
accommodate about six passengers was provided on the viaduct'.[4]

It seems from contemporary accounts that the platform was
barely a yard wide and was situated between the tracks, meaning
that people had to climb up carriage steps to reach the compartments. Apart from the steps up to the top of the viaduct, there was
no building or protection against the elements at Spa Road, which
the railway treated as a 'stopping place', rather than a station. The
reason for this parsimony was that the railway had been reluctant
to provide any services to Spa Road as Landmann and his fellow
directors wanted to make sure that London Bridge became the key
station serving the western end of the line. It was the Commissioner
of Pavements, a Crown agency, that insisted on the railway serving
Spa Road as it reckoned this was the most convenient point for
passengers to reach Westminster Bridge.

Oddly, at this time trains actually ran through on a small section
beyond Spa Road to Bermondsey Street, although there was no
station there. It was not until 14 December 1836 that the line finally
reached London Bridge. Several thousand guests, including the
Lord Mayor, attended the opening and they were entertained by a
group of musicians dressed as Beefeaters rather unwisely travelling
on the roof of one of the carriages.

Initially, trains only ran eastwards as far as Deptford with
Spa Road being the only intermediate stop and it took a further
two years for the line to be completed to Greenwich. From the
outset, services were impressively frequent, with trains every
fifteen minutes on weekdays between 8 a.m. and 10 p.m., with a

reduced service at weekends. However, despite promises made in the prospectus, no goods were carried, although the General Post Office did use the trains for the carriage of mail from 1837. In an effort to recoup the high capital cost of building the railway and to provide a return for investors, fares were steep; in December 1838, when the line to Greenwich was completed, a first-class ticket from London Bridge cost one shilling (5p) and second class was eightpence (3.3p). Nevertheless, despite the expense, travellers were attracted away from uncomfortable coaches and omnibuses, which ran on inadequate roads. River steamers, however, remained popular as they were relatively cheap and provided a comfortable and fast service.

It was now time for the company to design a terminus station worthy of the name. Early stations across the country's rail network were mostly built in the Italianate or Gothic styles to offer reassurance to travellers who might be nervous of using a technology that was still novel and perceived as dangerous. London was no exception. In the early stages of railway development, station design largely harked back to a comforting past, and it wasn't until the late twentieth century and early twenty-first century that, in London, architects dared to create stations in a genuine modern style, such as Waterloo International, the new parts of St Pancras and the courageous west entrance of King's Cross. The early incarnations of London Bridge were all based on Italianate themes and Londoners had to wait until the opening of St Pancras in 1868 for their first taste of station Gothic.

The original London Bridge terminus was, it has to be said, a pretty modest affair. In fact, throughout its history as a key part of London's railway network, the station has failed to achieve the iconic status of other terminuses such as King's Cross and Paddington. As

Alan Jackson, the author of a book on London's terminus stations, puts it, the first building, which was on the north side of the present station, 'was a very spartan affair'.[5] There were, at the beginning, just three tracks and two platforms at the stub end of the viaduct, reached by a sixty-yard ramp given the unprepossessing name of Dottin Street (after Abel Dottin, one of the London & Greenwich directors and later its chairman) and a series of steps. There was no protection from the elements until after a few weeks a tarred canvas, bought for just £27 10 shillings (it was so makeshift that contemporary reports spoke of 'an old sail'), was hung up to provide a modicum of shelter after the top of Dottin Street had become almost impassable due to the mud and slush that accumulated there.

The booking office and the company's headquarters were in a three-storey block at the top of the ramp. Drawings for an arch with four Corinthian columns topped by a clock had been drafted by the railway company the previous year, which might have been as grand as the one eventually erected in front of Euston station. But, as was often the case in these pioneering days of railway construction, the company's ambitions outpaced its financial resources and there was no money to build it. The platforms extended about 400 feet from the end of the viaduct but that was pretty much it. This is not untypical of contemporary stations across Britain and indeed the world. The early railway companies devoted so much energy to raising funds and constructing lines that they had little left over to provide facilities such as station buildings, shelter, permanent raised platforms and easy access.

The London Bridge site was a constant source of difficulty for the London & Greenwich and the other railway companies that were soon seeking to use it. Expansion plans risked confrontation with landowners who, unsurprisingly, baulked at the prospect of their property being demolished or of their land values being reduced by the noise and dirt created by the railway. Acquiring many small properties around London Bridge had already delayed the completion of the line but it was the presence of St Thomas's Hospital adjoining the site of the planned terminus that would prove to be an enduring source of trouble. The hospital had only recently been expanded in 1830 and its governors obtained Parliamentary approval to ensure that a small garden at the front of the building, which they felt was a good source of fresh air for patients, was retained and not acquired by the railway. Another public establishment, St Olave's Free Grammar School, on the north side of the station, clearly did not have the same political clout as St Thomas's because its centuries-old building had already been demolished in 1830 to make way for the improved London Bridge Approach. While the first stone was laid for a new school building in November 1834, expansion plans of the railway prevented it from ever being built.

Although the station may have been a disappointment, the magnificent viaduct remains the most remarkable architectural legacy of London's railway pioneers, although most passengers travelling on trains out of London Bridge today will have little idea of the impact this astonishing addition to London's built environment had in the mid-1800s. The assortment of garages, repair shops, retail outlets and workshops that are now housed under the arches rather detracts from the sheer scale of London & Greenwich's enterprise nearly two centuries ago, which remains pretty much intact and still supports the key railway route from the centre of the capital to south-east London and Kent. Partly hidden, the arches are taken for granted by passengers and passers-by, mainly because there are few places where it's possible to get a proper perspective of their majesty in such a built-up area. When first constructed, however, the viaducts inspired a sense of awe in Londoners, and contemporary writers were wont to liken them, with some accuracy, to a Roman aqueduct.

The railway had various plans to make use of the arches. One idea was to create housing and two demonstration houses were built under the viaduct near Deptford station. These could, according to the railway company, accommodate some of the many people who were displaced by the construction even though, under legislation of the time, the company was under no obligation to do so. They were to be pioneering users of gas for lighting and cooking – some forty years before this became commonplace – because it was felt that smoke from coal would be unpleasant for passengers on the trains above. However, despite such innovation the concept was, unsurprisingly, not a success. A plastered frontage was erected onto the south footpath to disguise the fact that residents were being asked to live in what was essentially a big cave with little natural lighting. But, aside from one house let at £20 per year, there were few takers, especially after it was discovered that rain seeped into the houses as soon as there was a heavy shower. Moreover, there were structural problems with several arches that had been shoddily constructed and needed rebuilding. The whole plan was soon abandoned and the gas, which was expensive to provide, cut off. Instead, the company tried numerous other ways of monetizing the eventual total of 878 arches, none of which were successful, with the result that five years after the opening of the railway only fifty-two had been let out to commercial enterprises.

Above the arches, there were technical issues with the train tracks as a result of granite sleepers being laid along most of the line. This was still a period of technical experimentation for railway technology, and granite, clearly more durable than wood, was thought to be a cheaper solution. However, the inflexible nature of granite, particularly when compared with wood sleepers, resulted in rail breaks and, far more frequently, cracks in the chairs, the iron clamps on which the rails rest. The problem was that other railways using granite sleepers laid the sleepers on the earth, which had some 'give', while on the London & Greenwich they rested on rigid brickwork with the result that all the vibration transmitted to the rails and chairs. Inevitably, the London & Greenwich eventually replaced them with wooden ones, at great cost.

London Bridge station was at the outset a rather drab environment for passengers. The London & Greenwich had not yet realized the money-making possibility of providing shops or catering facilities to serve its passengers, something that would soon become commonplace at other London terminuses. Despite the lack of ambition and available finance, the station would not remain such a modest affair for very long. Several other railway companies were keen to make use of the lengthy viaduct created by the London & Greenwich's gargantuan efforts. Four other railways had obtained Parliamentary authorization to connect with the London & Greenwich; of these, the London & Croydon had the most developed proposals. It wanted to use the first few miles of the viaduct for its trains to Corbett's Lane in Bermondsey, where they would fork south towards Croydon. Therefore, the railway, which had managed to obtain capital as well as Parliamentary approval, needed its own station at London Bridge and acquired a parcel of land from the London & Greenwich to erect a rather more substantial terminus than the original.

However, in one of those strange compromises that resulted from the fact that the early railways were developed by undercapitalized private companies with the short-term necessity of making a profit, the London & Croydon Railway's station was developed to the north of the London & Greenwich, even though ultimately its trains were destined to head south of the series of viaducts. This meant that its tracks would have to cross those of the London & Greenwich Railway, creating potential delays. In a typical bit of Victorian dog-eat-dog rivalry, Landmann felt that pushing the Croydon lines over to the north side meant that the railway would be forever dependent on his company's lines on the viaduct as there would be no alternative route, even though this meant that their trains would have to cross over the London & Greenwich's lines, causing great inconvenience.

The Croydon company's station was intended to be far grander than the original, not least because this new 'tenant' wanted to show that it was a more substantial undertaking than its landlord, despite being dependent on the London & Greenwich's lines to operate. Work on the new terminus started in 1838 and it opened on 5 June 1839 when the London & Croydon started running services, and, at last, there was a proper station at London Bridge. The contemporary descriptions suggest this long-demolished building was impressive and, as intended, completely overshadowed its neighbour. At around 300 feet long and 100 feet wide, it boasted a train shed supported by a series of pillars on one side and a brick wall on the other, with a shelter over all three tracks protecting passengers from the elements. The platforms were reached by separate steps for first- and second-class passengers from Joiner Street below, where there was a booking office. This clearly impressed the author of an 1839 book on the London & Croydon, who, with a typical Victorian eye for detail, wrote: 'We reach the west front which is an elegant façade of stone in the Roman style of architecture.

This leads immediately into a vestibule 60 feet in length, 30 feet in breadth and 22 feet high, the roof of which rests on a double range of Roman Doric columns, coated, as are the walls of the interior and of the staircases, with a new kind of white cement, capable of a polish equal to that of marble. This is the booking office of the Croydon Railway.'[6]

At the opening, the London & Croydon ran twelve trains a day on the nine-mile route to Croydon. While the company itself is long forgotten, having soon merged with the London & Brighton to form the far bigger London, Brighton & South Coast Railway, it was highly innovative and supported a technological experiment that, had it been successful, could have led to the creation of a very different type of railway system across the UK. In place of the established steam locomotive technology, the London & Croydon attempted to build an 'atmospheric' railway. This was powered by static steam engines that created a vacuum in a continuous pipe between the tracks into which a piston, attached to the train, would be pulled along by the creation of a vacuum. The potential advantage was that the locomotive did not have to haul its own considerable weight, which saved on fuel. However, there was a major problem maintaining the vacuum between the tracks. The tubes that once whisked money to cashiers and quickly returned the change in department stores operated on the same principle. While such a system worked efficiently for small loads, upscaling the technology for use by railways proved too difficult. The London & Croydon Railway built several miles of line and gained permission from the London & Greenwich to build an atmospheric track on the side of the existing one. There were several successful trial runs, with a claimed maximum speed of 70 mph, but after the amalgamation of the railway with the Brighton company, the directors ditched the idea, viewing the technology as unproven and unreliable. This was just one of several failed attempts to build an atmospheric railway in the capital but it proved to be a technology that could not overcome the fundamental difficulties of creating and maintaining a vacuum efficiently. Isambard Kingdom Brunel had, too, been very interested in the concept and built a similar railway as an extension of the Great Western in Devon but it also proved to be a failure for the same reason.

Soon after the London & Croydon started operating, it became apparent that two tracks on the viaduct were not enough. With other companies also seeking to use this 'path in the sky' through south-east London, more tracks were soon added onto a widened viaduct. In 1842, two extra tracks were laid for what were by then three companies using the viaduct as far as Corbett's Lane. In the following decades, further additions were made so that by 1901, when the final widening was made, there were eleven tracks laid piecemeal between London Bridge and Spa Road. The station, which had once been 'London's first terminus station', was at the start of the twentieth century little used; it closed in 1915 as a First World War economy measure and never reopened.

The cash-strapped London & Greenwich soon gave up running its own trains and instead leased the viaduct to the South Eastern Railway from 1 January 1845. The company's sole role thereafter, until its dissolution in 1923 when the railway companies were amalgamated into just four big concerns, was to collect the rent and distribute the profits to shareholders. It had never been a very large concern, employing just over 150 people when it opened in 1836. Drivers were recruited from the Liverpool & Manchester because they had relevant experience that could be passed on to new local recruits. By contemporary standards, the company was a good employer, rewarding workers when they did well. Indeed, today's passengers might look enviously at their predecessors who over the winter of 1841–2 enjoyed six months without any train delays whatsoever, a period in which some 20,000 services were operated. The owners of the London & Greenwich were so pleased by this, they paid their drivers and firemen a bonus, a just reward given that the exceptional punctuality was achieved while work was being carried out to widen the viaduct to accommodate extra tracks and services of the London & Croydon.

It wasn't always this good, though. A letter in *The Times* has a very familiar ring for today's passengers: 'I went by the Greenwich Railway and as they profess to go every quarter of an hour, I was at their London entrance at about 35 minutes after four, hoping to leave at the quarter to 5. A train eventually arrived at 5 p.m. but despite taking on passengers, it did not move.' The letter continues: 'on asking the cause for not going, no satisfactory reason was given. Passengers were still arriving; sixpences were taken; continued application was made for seats in the overloaded carriages, and at half past five we moved.' Even then the train only proceeded a couple of hundred yards, merely to reverse to hook up with another one. The hapless author of the letter only arrived in Deptford 'after a very slow passage, at a few minutes before six'. The cause was a minor accident to 'an uptown train' but what angered our early complainant would be very much in line with the feelings of today's passengers: 'What I complain of is, that knowing that assistance was sent off, no intimation was given to those who might be in a hurry, no explanations, no apology for the delay except on arrival an assistant accounted for the delay by the train being overloaded.' He concluded: 'the concern has got your money then they laugh at you'.[7]

Another outraged member of the public, trying to catch a train in Deptford, complained that the various clocks on the station were not accurate. He saw it was 'four minutes slower than your watch. It *must* be right you think because it belongs to a railway company.'[8] Not so, as in the station another clock was five minutes faster than the one downstairs and the train left as he was getting to the platform. Another source of complaint was prurience on the part of railway staff as a result of the low platforms. These apparently, according to a contemporary newspaper report, 'caused lady passengers some distress because the conductors were rather lax in letting down the carriage steps to the fullest extent, thus exacting a display of the beauty of their legs and ankles'. This neglect of duty was thought to be deliberate because 'when helping the weaker sex into carriages, these officials were apt to press the ladies' fingers and stare them full in the face'.[9]

London Bridge station soon had to be rebuilt again. The arrival of the London & Croydon was followed quickly afterwards by services of two other companies that had been authorized to use the viaduct, the London & Brighton and the South Eastern. This resulted in plans for an even larger joint station that would be squeezed into the area between St Thomas's Hospital and Tooley Street, the street shielded from the Thames by what used to be a series of wharves that have now been 'repurposed'.

The need for this expanded station was all too clear. By 1839, there were more than 4,000 passengers daily; with the new railways attracting considerable custom right from the start as they offered many new destinations, the original terminus was soon overstretched. Initially, the London & Brighton had to squeeze into the existing station when its first trains began operating to the south coast in July 1841. The following year new tracks were laid on the viaduct to cope with the South Eastern's services to Tonbridge in Kent, which were extended to Dover two years later.

The design of the new joint station was something of a practice run for King's Cross, built a decade later, as it was based on a similar Italian palazzo design with a typical bell tower housing a clock and a weather vane at the southern end. The contractor was William Cubitt, whose brother Lewis would take on the same role at King's Cross. There was an elegant two-storey frontage reached by a wide approach road from Borough High Street that skirted around the protected St Thomas's Hospital grounds. The impressive structure housed a booking hall, parcels offices and waiting rooms. There was another little block adjoining the main frontage for offices, and behind these two buildings Cubitt had created a new train shed covering the old London & Greenwich station providing, belatedly, protection from the elements for passengers.

Oddly, though, this rather pleasant building lasted barely five years, which was quite often the fate of commercial premises at the time as the Victorians were not sentimental about their creations and were always ready to make changes in the name of progress. Indeed, parts of these buildings, described by the author of the history of the London & Greenwich as 'the best to have occupied the site',[10] had not even been completed before the whole lot was pulled down for further extensions in order to cope with the ever rising number of passengers.

Inevitably, the various railway companies fell out and that was to lead to the demolition of the new station. The South Eastern Railway, reluctant to pay the tolls demanded by the London & Greenwich, conspired with the London & Croydon to build a short spur to Bricklayers Arms, a separate terminus named after a well-known coaching inn, on the Old Kent Road. It was a compact little terminus, another model for the yet to be built King's Cross, as Alan Jackson explains:

> Architectural gloss in the fashionable Italian-villa style, with some Baroque details, was provided by Lewis Cubitt. His main contribution was a screen across the end, penetrated by 22-ft archways with exaggerated keystones and by doorways protected by panelled hoods on heavy stone brackets… At one side of the station was a tiled colonnade where passengers alighted from their vehicles, passing through to the first and second class booking offices and waiting rooms alongside the departure platform.[11]

The design was typical of early stations, with separate tracks and different passageways for arriving and departing passengers. There was a special carriageway onto the platforms and a loading dock for the use of travellers wishing to attach their own private coaches onto trains, a common practice for the aristocracy at the time.

When Bricklayers Arms opened in May 1844, there was an hourly Croydon service that was priced below the London Bridge trains in an effort to attract more passengers. The South Eastern soon started running about half its main-line trains to Folkestone and Dover to and from Bricklayers Arms, and arranged for omnibuses to the West End to meet every incoming service, an early example of integrated transport. The public, however, were not fooled by claims that it was a 'West End terminus' on the basis that the routes to Waterloo and Westminster bridges were slightly shorter, and shunned the inconveniently sited station, preferring to keep using London Bridge. Within a year the Bricklayers Arms services were scaled back because of the lack of patronage.

According to Jackson, however, there was one mysterious group of travellers who used a first-class carriage attached to the last goods train of the day, leaving Bricklayers Arms at 11 p.m., to connect with the first steamer of the morning at Folkestone or Dover. He asks: 'Who were these "travellers"? Probably diplomatic couriers and the occasional newspaperman but what a convenient and inconspicuous means this must have offered of leaving the country in those days of no passports.' He muses that 'the facility was sometimes used by young bloods escaping from gaming debts or respectable merchants decamping with trembling mistresses'.[12]

Despite a brief effort to increase services in 1849, passenger traffic ceased three years later after an accident resulted in the partial collapse of the station when a train derailed, smashing into a column supporting the roof. Instead, Bricklayers Arms was turned into a heavily used goods depot for livestock and freight that could not be handled in the increasingly crowded London Bridge station. The only passengers still using it were Queen Victoria and her retinue who found it convenient to get to from Buckingham Palace for trips to Brighton. When it became too crowded with sheep and cows, however, a special station was built for her at Wandsworth Road that she used until her death in 1901. Bricklayers Arms survived as a goods depot until 1981 when most of it was demolished to make way for a trading estate, though some former stables and other railway buildings survive.

Realizing Bricklayers Arms was a failure, the ever-ambitious South Eastern decided to build its own terminus at London Bridge. The unfinished joint station was demolished and in order to separate itself off from its neighbours and rivals, the South Eastern erected a high wall as a screen. A new three-storey frontage was designed by its own architect, Samuel Beazley. The new station had a flat roof and a curved canopy supported by iron pillars, but it did not impress the *Illustrated London News*, which thought it was 'of less merit than its predecessor' with nothing of note apart from the chimney clock that projected above the cornice, decorated in birthday cake fashion 'in a manner by no means advantageous to Mr Beazley'.[13]

Completed in 1851, one key innovation was that space had been created in a 'London Bridge Arcade' for shops to cater for passengers whose numbers were growing almost exponentially. On the other side of the screen, the London, Brighton & South Coast created from the merger of the Croydon and Brighton companies expanded its services rapidly with passenger numbers doubling to 30,000 a day between 1850 and 1854. It is difficult to argue with Oliver Green, the author of a short book on London stations, who concludes: 'The machinations and fallouts between a number of competing Victorian railway companies were the cause of more than a century's chaos at London Bridge. Decisions taken in the 1850s and 1860s have blighted its layout to this day, and London Bridge remains the most difficult station in the capital to use.'[14]

The attempt to create a rival to London Bridge, stimulated – as would be the creation of so many of London's future stations – by antagonism between the numerous rail companies reaching the capital, was doomed to failure because of the location of the alternative. Getting nearer to the centre, to where people wanted to go for work and, later, leisure, was the essential ingredient for any new terminus and most of those subsequently built met that requirement. Despite the wholly predictable failure of Bricklayers Arms, in the 1840s the railway mania was in full swing and other terminuses around London soon began to alter the very shape of the capital. Surprisingly, an element of planning ensured there was some order to the chaotic process characterized by the London Bridge saga.

THREE

THE FIRST
CATHEDRALS

Lᴏɴᴅᴏɴ Bʀɪᴅɢᴇ ᴍᴀʏ have been the capital's first railway terminus, *pace* Spa Road, but it was atypical in two respects. It has never qualified as a 'cathedral of steam' and has always lacked a 'wow' factor. As Alan Jackson, author of *London's Termini*, puts it, albeit rather harshly: 'Thanks to its hybrid origins, subsequent neglect and German bombs, it is indisputably the most hideous of all the termini in external appearance.'[1]

He was, though, writing in 1969 before the recent refurbishment and redesign that, as described in the final chapter, undoubtedly represent a vast improvement with a stunning new concourse. But for all that, London Bridge remains a rather messy amalgam of two stations, with trains on different levels. Ironically, today, London Bridge is quite literally overshadowed by its new neighbour, the Shard – the twenty-first-century version of the cathedral, the megaoffice *cum* hotel *cum* luxury restaurant *cum* potential repository of laundered money.

Furthermore, as we have already seen, London Bridge was essentially serving a local market, mostly of people travelling to and from what is now suburban London and the Kent commuter belt. Even today, the furthest destinations served by trains from London Bridge are towns on the east Kent coast, around seventy-five miles from the capital.

In contrast, over the next quarter of a century three stations would emerge in a ring around the north and western outer reaches of the built-up area of London that would serve main lines stretching far into the regions; all can lay claim to being impressive additions to London's cultural and architectural heritage. None of them would at first provide much of a service to suburban London as their focus would be on longer distance travel. Instead, their initial function was to bring goods, raw materials and manufactures, as well as food, to the city from the industrial areas of the Midlands and the North. However, railway companies were quick to learn from the success of the Liverpool & Manchester Railway that passengers, too, could represent a healthy source of revenue.

The first main-line railway to reach London was the London & Birmingham. Indeed, it was the world's first trunk railway and, like many of its successors, it failed to get as near to the centre of the capital as it had originally intended. Euston was a groundbreaker, but sadly it has suffered ever since for being both inconveniently sited and badly laid out.

The idea for a railway linking London and Birmingham was first mooted in 1823, seven years prior to the opening of the Liverpool & Manchester and well before the notion of using steam locomotives rather than horses was established as the best traction for railways. The project was first promoted by Sir John Rennie, the engineer who had built London Bridge and who envisaged a route westwards from London via Oxford and Banbury, an idea later taken up by the Great Western Railway. Rennie's plan, as with so many schemes of the initial railway mania of the 1820s, came to nothing. It did, though, lead to another in 1829, this time with a line through Coventry with George Stephenson and his son Robert as the joint engineers.

The project stagnated for a couple of years but was revitalized when the London & Birmingham became connected with the plan to build the Grand Junction Railway from Birmingham to a junction with the Liverpool & Manchester Railway near Warrington. Optimism grew with the passing of the 1832 Reform Act, which widened the male franchise and created an expectation of change, not least because of the perceived benefits of railway expansion. Although the two projects were developed separately, effectively the idea was to create a single 190-mile railway that connected the capital with the nation's two other key industrial areas, the Midlands and the North-West.

A typically optimistic prospectus published by the promoters of the London & Birmingham Railway promised high returns, but opposition was even more vociferous than anything faced by the London & Greenwich. Since most of the £5.5m raised to build the line came from Lancashire cotton manufacturers, who realized the combined railways would open up vast markets for their products, there was a perception in London and on the southern stretches of the route that this was a northern incursion. Add to that the usual attempts by local landowners to cash in on their good fortune of the railway having to cross their land, and consequently the Parliamentary process dragged on for several years. In 1832, a well-organized group of aristocrats, including the Earl of Essex who was keen to protect his Cassiobury Estate near Watford and the Earl of Clarendon who owned the Grove Estate, also in Hertfordshire, killed off the first attempt to obtain Parliamentary approval. A second attempt with a different route through Hertfordshire was successfully manoeuvred through Parliament the following year and work started in November 1833. In fairness to the local landowners, they were to some extent correct in thinking that the railway offered them few advantages. Many Londoners, too, were sceptical, noting that the first station north of Euston was to be Harrow, eleven miles away, which meant the line was of no use to the growing numbers moving to the expanding suburbs.

Although George Stephenson was nominally the chief engineer of both the London & Birmingham and the Grand Junction, his son Robert had the task of overseeing construction of the former. Given that the combined lines were six times the length of the Liverpool & Manchester, Robert Stephenson was keen to ensure that there were no steep gradients and made the expensive, but far-sighted, decision to limit the gradient to a mere 1 in 330, effectively creating a level railway. The construction of several lengthy tunnels and numerous embankments greatly increased the cost of the railway but future generations of railway operators and passengers would have cause to be extremely grateful for the creation of such a smooth and straight railway. Stephenson's achievement was all the greater since the London & Birmingham was, at the time, by far the longest railway built in the UK, and required a host of new construction and management skills.

However, at the London end it proved impossible to maintain such a slight gradient. Initially, the Bill specified a terminus at Camden Town, which could be reached without a sharper gradient, although the intention of the London & Birmingham promoters had always been to go further south towards central London. Islington was considered, as it would have given easy access to the Regent's Canal, for transhipments to and from London's docks.

Sites near the Strand and Marble Arch were other options, but eventually land at Euston Square was bought and legislation was obtained to locate the terminus there.

Within a mile or so of the proposed station at Euston the railway would have to go either over or under the Regent's Canal; conscious of the enormous expense of tunnelling, Stephenson chose the former, thereby creating a difficult section of line with a gradient of 1 in 70. While that may not appear significant, early locomotives lacked power and Robert Stephenson was not confident that his engines could cope, a rare moment of doubt from a man who at the time was designing the best locomotives in the world. Therefore, he decided that the initial mile or so from Euston up to Camden Town (confusingly sometimes inter-changeably called Primrose Hill, which is slightly to the west) would be operated by static engines that hauled trains up by cable. It was a cumbersome operating method. When leaving Euston station, which initially had just two platforms, one each for arrivals and departures, a group of strong men called 'bankriders' would push the loaded carriages to the 'Messenger', the name given to the winding cable, and fasten it to the train. Then, a blast of air was sent along a pneumatic tube which sounded a trumpet inside the engine house (the noise was described as a 'melancholic mysterious moaning'). It soon became familiar to the residents of Camden near the Regent's Canal as it was amplified by two tall chimneys that sat above the engine house that straddled the tracks. That was the signal to start hauling the 'endless' cable – in reality a tarred rope – which was just over two miles long. It was strong enough to haul up trains of a dozen coaches, weighing some sixty tons, at a maximum speed of 20 mph, though for safety reasons this was normally kept to 10 mph. It was easier on the way down to the station, when the locomotive was disconnected and the train simply rolled back to Euston, with a brakeman ensuring that it did not exceed the maximum of 10 mph.

More powerful locomotives were introduced in 1844 to replace the static engines, though Stephenson was reluctant to let them go, arguing that they were still needed. Indeed, right up to the end of steam in the middle of the last century, locomotives continued to struggle to get up the incline and for much of that time pilot or banking engines had to be used. (As a trainspotter in the early 1960s, I remember watching powerful Coronation class engines stuttering and slipping badly as they tried to pull away from Euston's platforms on a wet day.)

Robert Stephenson's decision to construct a mostly flat railway with a terminus at Euston meant there was a limited need to demolish existing housing, unlike at London Bridge or, indeed, at almost every other London railway terminus that followed. Nevertheless, there was considerable upheaval at Camden during the construction of a depot and other railway buildings, an early demonstration of the disruptive nature of the iron road. Charles Dickens, who had an instinctive mistrust of the railways, was appalled by the digging of a cutting leading to Primrose Hill tunnel and described the work in great detail in *Dombey and Son* (1848):

The first shock of a great earthquake had... rent the whole neighbourhood to its centre. Traces of its course were visible on every side. Houses were knocked down; streets broken through and stopped; deep pits and trenches dug into the ground; enormous heaps of earth and clay thrown up; buildings that were undermined and shaking, propped up by great beams of wood. Here, a chaos of carts,

overthrown and jumbled together, lay topsy-turvy at the
bottom of a steep unnatural hill; there confused treasures
of iron soaked and rusted in something that had acciden-
tally become a pond.

He concluded, with heavy irony, that 'the yet unfinished and
unopened Railroad was in progress; and, from the very core of all
this dire disorder, trailed smoothly away, upon its mighty course of
civilisation and improvement'.[2]

Other members of the artistic community were more supportive.
John Bourne, an engraver and lithographer, produced a sympathetic series of drawings in 1836 illustrating the excavations and
construction being carried out by the railway in London. He
described his series of fifty illustrations as depicting a chronicle
of 'order growing out of disorder'. Bourne was 'enthralled by the
masterpieces of engineering and architecture that were hoisting
themselves out of the sticky London clay'.[3]

Unlike in the countryside where several landowners forced the
railway to change its route, at the London end there was only one
troublesome opponent, but it was a particularly large and powerful
one. Eton College, which owned the massive 243-acre Chalcots
Estate to the north and west of Camden Town, did everything
possible to obstruct progress and, crucially, extract maximum
compensation for any potential disruption. The College resisted
the railway on the grounds that it would cut through potentially
lucrative building land and cause disturbance to its leaseholders on
the recently constructed Adelaide Road, the first street to be laid
out in the area. Also, it realized that South Hampstead would be
one of the next areas marked for urban expansion and wanted to
ensure that the railway did not damage potential development.

However, there was no other way through north London as heading directly north from Camden Town would have forced the railway towards the heights of Hampstead Heath and Highgate, a daunting obstacle. Instead, turning westwards, there was only the lower northern reaches of Primrose Hill to overcome. In the event, protracted negotiations between the London & Birmingham and Eton College resulted in the railway agreeing, reluctantly, to the construction of an expensive 330-foot-long tunnel under Eton's land, cut out of the London clay rather than constructed using the far cheaper method of 'cut and cover' that was later used for the early London Underground lines. Moreover, the College made three further demands. It insisted that the tunnel should be strong enough to allow building on top of it; that the railway should be enclosed with 'ornamental' fencing; and that the eastern tunnel entrance should have a portal enclosed with a classically designed bulwark so as to fit with Eton's proposed housing developments. The agreement forced on the railway was unequivocal: 'The mouth of the Tunnel at the eastern end shall be made good and finished with a substantial and ornamental facing of brickwork or masonry to the satisfaction of the Provost and College'.[4]

Primrose Hill is one of the few tunnels to receive a mention in Gordon Biddle's seminal work *Britain's Historic Railway Buildings*, which describes 'its 22ft high semi-circular double recessed arch radically rusticated in cream coloured ashlar [squared, finely cut stone] between huge Italianate towers topped by heavily modillioned [bracketed] caps'.[5] The Camden Railway Heritage Trust, too, waxes lyrical about the design and possibly gets a little overexcited by mentioning that 'flanking the piers, the curved wing walls of Suffolk bricks have vermiculated stone podiums broken by channelled stone pillars and crowned by segmental pediments'.[6]

Nevertheless, this conveys why Eton College was satisfied with the resulting structure, which, unfortunately, is difficult to see today in what is a built-up area where summer vegetation tends to cover up most of its features. However, there is a partial viewing point right next to the portal in King Henry's Road just off Primrose Hill Road. In fact, had it not been for the College's obduracy, the need for the tunnel could have been avoided as the tracks are never more than fifty feet below the surface and the line could easily have been run in a cutting, which would have saved the railway company thousands of pounds. However, not only would that have deprived Eton and today's Londoners of a swathe of prime real estate now occupied by a mix of luxury detached houses and a line of council-owned tower blocks, it would also have caused the type of disruption and dirt so deplored by Dickens.

At the opening of the London & Birmingham in July 1837, Euston was a rather unexciting lopsided station with the tracks on the eastern side of a rather large space. This was the result of an attempt to share Euston with the Great Western Railway, which was being built at the same time as the London & Birmingham; as we shall see later, however, the plan fell through. The asymmetrical aspect was made even worse when one of Britain's most iconic railway structures was added a year after services first started. This was the seventy-two-foot-high Euston Arch, more accurately known as a *propylæum*, as it had four Doric columns supporting a huge triangular cornice decorated with lions' heads. It was built on the western side of the initial platforms as it was intended to mark the separation between the two railways, but the decision of the Great Western to build its station at Paddington left the arch on one side of the London & Birmingham's terminus and served to emphasize the whole asymmetrical nature of the original Euston station. The arch was completed in March 1838 and represented, in truth, the only remarkable aspect of the station during these early years. It served no practical purpose, although passengers approaching the station from what is now Euston Road were able to glimpse between the columns the green pastures of Primrose Hill and Hampstead.

The arch, designed by Philip Hardwick, was the first example in the world of a railway company showing off. The London & Birmingham wanted to demonstrate its importance to a public that had yet to be completely won over by the concept of fast travel. The arch was, in fact, Victorian public relations at its most extreme. The directors of the London & Birmingham Railway felt it was their duty to provide this completely redundant addition that served no purpose, but which cost the substantial sum of £35,000. Justifying the expenditure in a report to the shareholders in February 1837, the directors wrote rather pompously:

> The entrance to the London passenger station opening immediately upon what will necessarily become the Grand Avenue for travelling between the Metropolis and the midland and northern parts of the Kingdom, the Directors thought that it should receive some architectural embellishment. They adopted accordingly a design of Mr. Hardwick's for a grand but simple portico, which they considered well adapted to the national character of the undertaking.

It wasn't just about PR, however. The northerners who financed the railway were demonstrating their superiority over the effete southerners for whom commerce and industry was seen as a rather

lowly concern, as the historian of the line explains: 'In its architecture and function, [the arch] stood like a gauntlet thrown down
into the hitherto largely unsullied South by "Industry", here represented by the mechanical artefacts of the mostly Northern-based
Industrial Revolution… Industry was here to stay, said Euston, and
London might as well get used to the idea.[7]

There were four lodges, two on either side of the arch, naturally in
matching classical style, with an imposing set of bronze gates between
each pair. One of the lodges housed an office for outgoing parcels
while on the other the gates were used as the entrance for heavy
goods going by train and personal carriages. Wealthier passengers
could load their carriages onto flat wagons while their horses were
transported in a separate box. It was the Victorian equivalent of
Motorail, the car carrier service that would briefly operate out of the
station more than a century later, although Victorian-era passengers
could remain in their carriages for the duration of the journey while
motorists were not allowed to sit out the journey in their cars.

In truth, the gesture of creating this grandiose entrance was
rather premature. At the time the station was completed, annual
passenger numbers across the country on the few disconnected lines
were in the tens of thousands and therefore the railways, in truth,
did not have much to boast about except expectation. The arch,
though, was an important portent for the future just as its demise
in the 1960s (see Chapter 13) would have enormous symbolism.

In fact, neither the station nor the arch were universally appreciated. A Victorian author, Samuel Sidney, wrote in 1851: 'the tall
columns of the portico entrance look down on you so grimly…
The gateway leads to a square court-yard and a building the
exterior of which may be described, in the language of guide books
when referring to something which cannot be praised, as "a plain,

unpretending, stucco structure" with a convenient wooden shed in front, barely to save passengers from getting wet in rainy weather'.[8]

Not surprisingly, Augustus Pugin, the main protagonist of the Victorian Gothic Revival, was highly critical of the arch, which he dismissed as Hardwick showing off: 'This piece of Brobdingnagian absurdity must have cost the company a sum which would have built a first-rate station, replete with convenience, and which would have been really grand from its simplicity.'[9] However, John Betjeman, the twentieth-century poet and a doughty fighter for railway heritage, loved the arch, calling it 'simple and huge' and 'a monument to railway achievement',[10] and fought gamely but unsuccessfully for its retention when Euston was redeveloped in the 1960s.

Sidney was also annoyed that the station was sited a couple of hundred yards back from New Road – now called Euston Road – an inconvenience that remains to this day, 'compelling the passenger to perspire under his carpet-bag, railway-wrapper, umbrella, and hat-box, all the way from the platform to the edge of Euston Square'. The entire experience of entering the station was unwelcoming: 'the front of the booking-offices, in their garment of clean stucco, look so primly respectable that you cannot help feeling ashamed of yourself – feeling as uncomfortable as when you have called too early on an economically genteel couple, and been shown into a handsome drawing-room, on a frosty day, without a fire.'[11]

For travellers heading north, the station was indeed a rather modest, inconvenient affair. There was little protection from the elements for passengers who regularly faced lengthy waits given the infrequency of the service and the palaver of attaching the carriages to the rope at the beginning of every journey. The train shed over the platforms was draughty and there was no waiting room. As John Kellett in his book on the impact of the railways on cities put it, 'Euston's splendid arch led only to the ramshackle collection of one-storey brick ticket offices which so much engaged Pugin's scorn."[12]

In the first couple of years, the lack of facilities did not matter much as there were few trains. When services started on 20 July 1837, there were just three trains a day in each direction taking around an hour to reach Boxmoor, near Hemel Hempstead, twenty-five miles from Euston. Oddly, initially the cable did not work and steam engines, at both front and back, were used to push and pull trains up the incline, a process called banking, but after October 1837 the trains were hauled up using the 'Messenger', an arrangement that lasted until 1844.

Services soon increased in frequency, as well as running further down the line. From 9 April 1838, passengers could take the train as far as Denbigh Hall, just beyond Bletchley. They then had the option of travelling by stagecoach to Rugby – surely the first-ever example of a rail replacement service? – before rejoining the railway to reach Birmingham. Even this cumbersome journey was well used. Francis Coghlan, who wrote a series of travel guides for rail passengers and tourists in the mid-nineteenth century, noted that there were 135 people making use of the fifteen-seater stagecoaches operating over the unfinished section when he travelled to Birmingham a couple of weeks after the service began. When the line finally opened all the way to Birmingham on 17 September 1838, the 113-mile journey took just five and a quarter hours at an average speed of 21 mph. That compared very favourably with the alternative of a stagecoach, which, despite improvements to the roads in the early 1800s, still took a full day's uncomfortable travel.

The trains definitely provided more comfort but the offering was still fairly basic. In a book published in 1838, Coghlan offered rather useful advice to the novice passengers on where to sit in what were called the second-class 'waggons' since they were open to the elements: 'In the first place, get as far from the engine as possible – for three reasons… *First*, should an explosion take place, you may happily get off with the loss of an arm or a leg… [whereas those sitting nearer] would very probably be *"smashed to smithereens"*. After this cheerful injunction about a danger that, fortunately, was very rare even in the early days of locomotive development, he continued, '*Secondly* – the vibration is very much diminished the further you are away from the engine. *Thirdly* – always sit (if you can get a seat) with your back towards the engine, against the boarded part of the wagon; by this plan, you will avoid being chilled by a cold current of air which passes through these open wagons, and also save you from being nearly blinded by the small cinders which escape through the funnel.'[13] At least by then services had become more frequent, with nine return workings daily.

The London & Birmingham rather belatedly began to realize that the lack of facilities, which, as Pugin suggested, contrasted rather too obviously with the magnificence of the arch, was likely to put off some travellers. Moreover, the directors began to understand that there was money to be made by providing extra facilities. Two four-storey buildings, officially known as the 'London and Birmingham Railway Hotel and Dormitory', the first railway hotels in the world, were quickly erected on either side of the station in order to accommodate passengers taking early trains or arriving late from afar. Both were opened by early 1840 but offered contrasting accommodation. The eastern-side hotel, managed by the aptly named Mr Bacon, was aimed at first-class passengers and provided suitable comforts, while the other offered only basic dormitory accommodation for those unable or unwilling to pay to have their own room. The hotels were eventually joined together by a new united building in 1880 that rather unfortunately obliterated the view of the arch from Euston Road.

However, the lack of capacity on the rails had begun to cause delays to services, which needed addressing. With various connections available in Birmingham, which was already becoming a hub of the rail network, the number of daily trains was increasing rapidly. The London & Birmingham amalgamated with the Manchester & Birmingham Railway and the Grand Junction Railway in 1846 to form the London & North Western Railway, which would soon become the world's biggest company. Consequently, two new platforms were built on the vacant land to the west of Euston station that had previously been reserved for the Great Western Railway.

Euston – the ambitious company's headquarters and showcase – needed improvement. The station was for its first fifteen years of existence, until the opening of King's Cross, the only gateway to the North and, indeed, a point of access for the whole railway network west and north of London through interchanges with the Great Western Railway (via Bletchley, albeit with a change of gauge at Oxford), the various companies operating in the North and, by 1848, Scotland. It was, in effect, London's main railway station as only the routes to the Kent and Sussex coasts and Southampton could not be reached from the terminus. However, over time, as the lines that had been promoted in the railway mania of the early 1840s were completed, it was clear that Euston was unequal to the task.

Moreover, it was not only passenger numbers that were soaring, as goods and parcels traffic was increasing exponentially at a rate that showed no sign of abating. The size of the market for goods in London ensured that Euston quickly became the main entry point for all kinds of products and foodstuffs as well as much trade in the opposite direction. As Samuel Sidney recounted:

Sheep have been sent from Perth to London, and Covent Garden has supplied tons of the finer description of vegetables to the citizens of Glasgow; every Saturday five tons of the best fish in season are despatched from Billingsgate to Birmingham, and milk is conveyed in padlocked tins, from and beyond Harrow, at the rate of about one penny per gallon... All graziers within a day of the rail are able to compete in the London market... and these animals can be brought from the furthest grazing grounds in the kingdom without any loss of weight, and in much better condition than the fat oxen were formerly driven to Smithfield from the rich pastures round Aylesbury, or the Valley of the Thames.[14]

Thus, while Sidney might not have been enamoured with Euston's architecture, he was impressed with its role as the hub of Britain's rail network:

Euston, including its dependency, Camden Station [the site of the main goods depot], is the greatest railway port in England, or indeed in the world. It is the principal gate through which flows and reflows the traffic of a line which has cost more than twenty-two millions sterling; which annually earns more than two millions and a half for the conveyance of passengers, and merchandise, and live stock; and which directly employs more than ten thousand servants, beside the tens of thousands to whom, in mills or mines, in ironworks, in steam-boats and coasters, it gives indirect employment. What London is to the world, Euston is to Great Britain.[15]

In order to cater for this growth, the company decided to invest heavily in the station, creating both its greatest architectural achievement and making the worst mistake in its seventy-seven-year history. Therefore, soon after taking over the station, the London & North Western Railway, eager to emphasize its ambitions, decided to spend £150,000 building a massive new central administrative block at the heart of the station, which would also accommodate the expected increase in passenger numbers. However, tragically, the building was erected between the new and old platforms, taking up virtually all the available space and severely restricting the potential to accommodate more train movements. This design effectively split the station in two, which made it impossible to add anything but short platforms behind the new block. The historian of the London & Birmingham declared, 'It was in every respect the right sort of building and in almost every other respect it was entirely in the wrong place.'[16] This mistake would lead to the demise of this architectural gem in the 1960s and in retrospect, given the way this layout stymied growth at the station, it is surprising that the new section survived that long. That was largely down to the fact that it contained two masterpieces, the Great Hall and the Shareholders' Meeting Room, as few of their visitors would dissent from the fact that these were the greatest internal architectural feature of any of the London stations.

The Great Hall, designed by the younger Philip Hardwick, the son of the architect of the original station, became its most famous feature. Completed in 1849, it was the largest and by far the most impressive railway waiting room in Britain and was described by Betjeman as 'one of London's finest rooms'.[17] It was a combined concourse and waiting room that set the pattern for many similar halls in major stations across Europe and North America. After passing through the arch and the yard behind it, passengers entered the Great Hall through one of five doorways and into a grand space designed in what was described at the time as 'a Roman Ionic' style, lit by high windows that cast a strong shadow on what was the largest flat-panelled ceiling in the world. The centrepiece was a double staircase leading to the platforms, guarded by an oversize statue of George Stephenson. Passengers waited on the ground floor of the Hall, often having to stand as there were not enough seats, until a railway official rang a bell and announced the departure time of their train. After being summoned, passengers would ascend by the imposing double staircase to reach the platforms.

Alan Jackson is correct in his assessment: 'Few other English buildings could offer anything to match the deeply-coffered ceiling of the Great Hall, embellished with massive curved consoles and plaster bas-reliefs in each corner, the whole beautifully lit by attic windows.'[18] The bas-reliefs designed by John Thomas, who was also the sculptor of the statues in Parliament, which was being rebuilt at the time, featured muscular Adonis-like men and Amazonian women who were rather strange allegorical representations of eight destinations served by the railway: London, Birmingham, Northampton, Chester, Manchester, Carlisle, Lancaster and Liverpool.

Adjoining the Great Hall were two booking halls, one for long distance, the other, a smaller one, for the Midlands and branch lines. Beside the Great Hall, another new long and narrow building housed a parcels office and next to that were the Queen's Apartments, in effect what would be known now as a first-class lounge, which was 'intended to afford privacy and comfort to royalty and other notables using the railway. There were two rooms, one an antechamber, both decorated in the "Greek" style, with white and buff walls "painted in

large panels with the most fairy-like scroll ornaments and flowers".[19]
It was an elegant way to start a journey as the windows of the main
room stretched from floor to ceiling and at the appropriate time they
were opened to allow the VIP passengers to walk straight onto the
departure platform.

Rather less well known as there was no regular public access, but
arguably even more notable, was the meeting room upstairs, which
had space for 400 people and was an elegant Baroque apartment
at the top of the double staircase. In the words of Betjeman it was
'of an elegance never equalled in English railway architecture'.[20]
The entrance door was surmounted by a bold bas-relief statue
of Britannia and her lion supporters, a homage to the heraldic
emblem of the London & North Western Railway that featured
on all its carriages and locomotives.

While the architectural splendour was rightly lauded both at
the time and subsequently, the significance of this big investment
by the railway company went well beyond Euston. The message
being sent to the public was rather different from the arch that
preceded these additions by a decade. Now the railway seemed to
be saying that travel was a positive and pleasant experience that
everyone, rather than a privileged few, could enjoy. It was the first
grand gesture made to ordinary people by a railway. The Great Hall
seemed to be designed deliberately to attract the casual passenger
by making them feel important and welcome, rather like the lavish
lobbies in a luxury hotel. David Jenkinson, the author of the history
of the London & Birmingham, remembered using it: 'The Great
Hall was a welcoming sort of place for all its hugeness and one
could actually enjoy sitting there.'[21]

The fares in the early days did not really reflect this 'welcome to
all-comers' philosophy as they were set high, initially because the

company had a monopoly on travel between London and a vast swathe of Britain. This remained the case until two other gateways to the North and the Midlands, respectively King's Cross in 1852 and St Pancras in 1868, emerged, providing strong competition. The initial one-way first-class fare between London and Birmingham was £1 10 shillings (£1.50, or about £125 today adjusted for inflation); in second class it was £1 (£83). Oddly, it was only 27 shillings to put a two-wheeled carriage on the flat wagon, although horses were extra, as were dogs, which cost an exorbitant ten shillings (50p).

Tickets were sold at 'booking offices', a name that has survived to the present day, and were pink or yellow for first class, white or blue for second. Getting people to understand the process was not easy given the novelty of railway travel and there was the perpetual problem of ticket collectors allowing people through for a few pence that they then pocketed. Given that working-class people earned a few pence per day, and had little to spare after paying for basics, the service was not really intended for them. However, the burgeoning middle classes would have appreciated the pleasant spaciousness of the Great Hall, as would the shareholders, who were earning a good rate of return from their investment, in their well-appointed meeting room upstairs.

In fact, as Jenkinson points out, 'no other British railway quite copied this famous room, even though the message it proclaimed was taken up enthusiastically by many of them'.[22] Certainly, the other railway companies wanted more passengers and realized that they were crucial to financial success, but as we shall see, when they established their own massive London terminuses, they opted for imposing grand façades and palatial luxurious hotels. While their 'cathedrals' looked grand from the outside, they were often rather messy and draughty once passengers crossed the threshold.

There was a logic in the plan for Euston to be shared with the Great Western as the latter's lines in Kensal Green, just four miles north of the terminus, were adjacent to those of the London & Birmingham, which meant the trains of both companies could have run alongside each other into London. However, the rivalry between rail companies and the inevitable issues over matters such as timetables and priorities meant such cooperation was the exception rather than the norm.

The Great Western was, arguably, even grander in conception than the London & Birmingham. That was very much down to one man, Isambard Brunel, who was plucked from obscurity at the tender age of just twenty-seven to be the railway's chief engineer.

The initiative for the Great Western Railway, as with the London & Birmingham, came not from the capital but from four Bristol-based businessmen who saw it as a way of reviving the flagging economy of what was still Britain's second city, despite being hit hard by the abolition of one of its key businesses, the slave trade. Brunel's ambitious plan was for a flat level railway that was almost entirely straight for the whole of its near 120-mile route between London and Bristol.

Moreover, not for Brunel the constraints of the 'narrow gauge' of 4ft 8½in, which had been used by George Stephenson for the Liverpool & Manchester Railway and most subsequent lines. A wider gauge, he contended, would give greater stability and comfort and was worth the extra cost required by the bigger land take and the extra engineering required to carve a wider path for the railway. After various assessments, he opted for 7ft 0¼in, precisely 50 per cent wider than the standard gauge.

The Bill to enable the line struggled through Parliament because of widespread opposition, not least from canal owners and other railway companies that both had vested interests. It was considered for no fewer than fifty-seven days in the Commons Committee, only for the Lords to initially reject it, necessitating a rewrite and a resubmission. When the Bill was finally passed after more than two years of effort, it contained provision for the terminus at Euston that was never to be. Interestingly, it was between the failure of the first Bill and the introduction of the second one that Brunel changed the gauge of the proposed railway from standard to broad.

Many historians suggest it was the fact that the Great Western was being built to the broad gauge that was the cause of the rift with the London & Birmingham, but this would have been easily solvable by the insertion of a third rail in order to accommodate both companies' trains. In fact, the row was a traditional bust-up between two large railway companies, an all too frequent occurrence at a time when no one was giving any thought to the creation of a unified rail network; much effort was, however, put into ways of ensuring shareholders received a good return on their investment. Lengthy negotiations between the two railway companies, led respectively by Robert Stephenson and Brunel, broke down.

A statement by the Great Western Railway issued in 1836 made clear that it was a failure to agree the terms of the lease that prevented a deal. Brunel had wanted either to buy the land on which its part of the station would stand or at least to be offered a lease of a minimum of twenty-one years. Stephenson, on the other hand, perhaps realizing that the London & Birmingham Railway would want to expand substantially in the near future, only sought to grant land on a lease that could be terminated at five years' notice, an offer that the directors of the Great Western rightly considered unacceptable given their long-term perspective on the business. Brunel was, in any case, far happier to plan a completely new and separate terminus for his spectacular railway, although he had to wait rather a long time before finance was made available for him to fulfil his ambition.

Consequently, Brunel scoured west London for an alternative to Euston, considering sites in Brentford, Acton, Hammersmith, Brompton and even Vauxhall Bridge, but Paddington's proximity to the Grand Union Canal, with its key connection to the London docks, was a deciding factor. Paddington had, in fact, always been Brunel's favoured option and as early as 1836 he had sketched out a masterplan for his planned terminus. That drawing, which survives, revealed his intentions. It was a pioneering effort since, at the time, no other terminus had been built, apart from the modest efforts at either end of the Liverpool & Manchester. No such timidity for Brunel, whose design for a large station with around a dozen tracks shows that, as the historian of the station explains, 'a broad central roadway marked "private carriages" ran down the middle of the station with... a turning space with rounded corners; beyond this the big plan shows several tracks running up to the platform edge'.[23] Brunel was using the fact that the station was in a hollow, below street level, to create a roadway for the private carriages that would be loaded onto the trains. It is interesting that at the time this was seen by the likes of Brunel as a significant part of the passenger market. While the carriage owners would have had a grand entrance to themselves, Brunel envisaged everyone else would have to enter by the side. In fact, by the time Paddington was completed, nearly two decades later, the practice of people adding their own carriages to trains was being phased out.

However, the dispute over the terminus and the subsequent requirement of a further Act to enable land acquisition in

Paddington left no time to develop a grand terminus that could be ready for the start of services between London and Bristol. Instead, a modest station was hastily built on a site a few hundred yards to the west, just north of Bishops Walk (now called Bishop's Bridge Road), that had originally been earmarked to become a goods depot.

Trains started running between the temporary terminus at Bishop's Bridge and Maidenhead, twenty-two miles away, in June 1838 with fares of five shillings and sixpence (27.5p) in first class, three shillings and sixpence (17.5p) in second. Despite an irregular and sparse service in the first week, more than 10,000 people used the trains, which also served stops at West Drayton and Slough, bringing receipts of more than £1,550, much to the satisfaction of the directors. The Great Western started carrying freight the following year and in 1840 a third class, using uncovered trucks hitched to these goods trains, was provided. This dangerous practice was stopped after a tragic accident the following year when a goods train derailed at Sonning in Berkshire killing nine people, most of them workers building the Houses of Parliament who were returning home for the weekend.

It was not until 30 June 1841 that the whole route to Bristol was opened, although in the interim various coach services to take passengers around unfinished sections enabled regular travel between the nation's two biggest cities. The temporary Bishop's Bridge terminus may not have made the sort of statement that Brunel would have wished for, but it was adequate for the fourteen daily departures that were operating by 1839. The station was largely of timber construction but the various facilities for passengers and the offices were in the arches of the bridge under Bishop's Bridge Road and they were fronted by a façade designed, inevitably, in a classical style. Strangely, the present site of the station was used as a temporary goods depot.

The most notable visitor to Bishop's Bridge was Queen Victoria who took her first train trip from Slough, at the time the nearest station to Windsor, on 13 June 1842. The Prince Consort, Albert, had in fact used the railway several times since early 1840 but this was the first journey by the reigning monarch. It was a hairy ride, with Daniel Gooch, who designed the Great Western's famously fast locomotives, rather showing off by driving the train at an average speed of 44 mph. If he was trying to impress the Queen, he had made a big mistake. She was apparently 'not amused' and thereafter asked for any train she travelled on to proceed more cautiously. As a result of Victoria's request, the Great Western subsequently fitted a special signal onto the roof of the royal saloon so that the driver could be notified if she felt that the train was going too fast.

Bishop's Bridge was used as the terminus until 1854 with extra facilities gradually added as traffic grew, thanks both to expansion by the Great Western and the addition of connections with other railways. Most of these were under the control of the Great Western, which by the end of the 1840s was serving Oxford, Birmingham and Wolverhampton, breaking the monopoly enjoyed by the London & North Western. This led to a series of expansions at Bishop's Bridge, including a new carriage shop and shed, a large engine house and a replacement roof. However, it was clear that a new terminus was undoubtedly needed.

Indeed, it was surprising that the temporary station with its four platforms and leaky wooden roof survived for so long. The reason was Brunel's desire for a grand terminus, which had been stymied by the constant shortage of available finance. Even though funds were still in short supply when work started on the new Paddington station in 1851, the company having recently cut its dividend from 4 per cent to just 2 per cent, the pressure on the little Bishop's Bridge terminus had become so intense that there was no alternative. Brunel had personally designed many of the stations on the Great Western, including Bristol Temple Meads, and, as we have seen, in 1836 had sketched out his conception for the terminus. Although he decided that Paddington needed another architect to help him create the design, Brunel was never one to take a back seat and he was full of ideas, setting out the broad outline of what was conceived as a grand terminus. Typically, when he appointed as architect the very eminent Matthew Digby Wyatt, who had been secretary to the Royal Commission for the 1851 Great Exhibition, Brunel made it clear that he personally would act as his assistant, an unlikely arrangement that must have been terrifying for poor Wyatt.

The site was in a cutting, which meant that, uniquely of London's cathedrals of steam, Paddington has no magnificent façade; instead the grandeur was in the interior and particularly above, with the extraordinary roof that was in the style of the Crystal Palace, the centrepiece of the Great Exhibition. Brunel sketched out the design for an enormous iron and glass roof but left the decorative detail to Wyatt who used patterns derived from traditional Moorish motifs to adorn the supporting columns and walls. Brunel had been so impressed by the Joseph Paxton-designed Crystal Palace, which had been installed initially on nearby Hyde Park, that he instructed Wyatt to use it as the basis for his design. The key, for Brunel, was that Paddington should be impressive as a gateway to the West but also remain functional. The *Illustrated London News* summed up its conception perfectly: 'The principle adopted by them [Brunel and Wyatt] was to avoid any recurrence to existing style and to make the experiment of designing everything in accordance with the structural purpose, or nature of the materials employed – iron and cement.'[24] The station made admirable use of the topography as, according to Betjeman, it was 'an aisled cathedral in a cutting' which was 'admirably planned and copes with traffic greater than even [Brunel] could have envisaged'.[25] It is not surprising that Paddington was subsequently chosen as the subject of one of the best-known Victorian paintings, *The Railway Station* by William Powell Frith; a bustling scene of men in Brunel-style stovepipe hats, women in bright summer dresses and overdressed children made to pose stiffly for the artist, all set against a background of porters removing cases from the top of a train dwarfed by the airy roof of the station.

Betjeman's comparison with a cathedral was apt, as Brunel clearly set out to create one. The main glass and iron roof was supported by wrought-iron arches, also known as ribs, that divided the vast train shed into three, separated by wide transepts. Throughout the station, the detailing was wonderfully intricate and the much-praised colour scheme of brown and cream was retained by the Great Western throughout its existence and is still used today by the train company that has adopted the same name. The aisles, the widest of which was more than 100 feet across, were intended to be used by 'traversers', huge cranes that would be able to lift carriages and even locomotives from one line to another, but these never materialized, quite possibly because they may well have been technically too demanding to install in such a restricted space. Nevertheless, whether it was by accident or design, the generous width of these platforms added to the feeling of airiness, giving passengers the space and opportunity to admire the fabulous roof. There was considerable space at the buffer stops, too, where the concourse was a garden known as The Lawn, a name that long survived the disappearance of the grass.

There were three departure and two arrival platforms when the station opened early in 1854. Two inner platforms were used for overspill and could be reached by an ingenious method. To avoid passengers having to trudge up and down stairs to use them, a hydraulically powered drawbridge was laid across two of the departure platforms when they were clear. Turntables were available for loading private carriages but these were soon phased out as the practice was abandoned.

The Royal Family, who had homes easily linked by a trip on the Great Western, had to be catered for in the well-founded expectation that they would travel regularly between Windsor and London by rail, despite the Queen's misgivings about speed. A private entrance to the departure platform – even in 1854, it was normal to separate arrivals from departures – was provided for the sole use of royalty and included an exclusive royal waiting room, 'discreetly lit by a barred, ground floor window and filled with stuffy French furniture'.[26] The walls were enamelled in a salmon tint, inlaid with gilt moulding and interspersed by grey silk panels, all suitably staid and solemn for the Queen and her entourage.

The architectural historian Oliver Green sums up the success of Paddington, which has been expanded but whose shape remains largely unchanged since it was completed, as 'a light and elegant design, but also an extremely sound and functional piece of engineering, which has served its purpose for more than 150 years'.[27] By the time the new Paddington station was fully functioning, another major railway station on the northern periphery of the city, King's Cross, had already been completed and rules governing the location of future stations had been established.

FOUR

A MODICUM
OF ORDER

URING THE SIXTEEN-YEAR gap between the completion of
Euston and the opening of Paddington, a number of railway
companies were eagerly eyeing London, ready to pounce on the
right piece of land, whether occupied or not, to build their own
terminus. Most were serving longer distance routes as, despite
the relative success of the London & Greenwich, suburban traffic
was not seen as a likely source of major income. Indeed, it was
only in the second half of the nineteenth century that stations
serving suburban destinations started to be built, with no fewer
than seven opening between 1860 and 1875, all mainly focused on
local traffic.

The railway mania of the 1840s was the most chaotic period in
railway history. After the initial burst of interest in railways, stimulated by the profitability of early schemes such as the Liverpool
& Manchester, there was a period in the 1830s when potential
promoters took stock of a network that consisted of a series of
disparate lines. The economic situation in the late 1830s was
uncertain and across the country only fifty miles of new line were

authorized by Parliament in the five years ending in 1843, bringing
the total miles of railway to around 1,400.

Then it went crazy. Suddenly, with interest rates low and the early
railway companies boasting strong profits and paying out generous
dividends, there was a rush to invest in railways. Hundreds of Bills
started being deposited in Parliament backed by investors looking
for higher earnings than they could receive from government
bonds. In 1846 alone, 550 Bills were put forward for consideration
and between 1844 and 1847 a total of 9,500 miles of new railway
were authorized, of which ultimately around two-thirds were
built. It was a classic boom, which saw railway share prices soar
to unprecedented levels and which at its height in 1847 resulted
in railway construction absorbing a staggering 6.7 per cent of the
nation's economic activity.

While many genuine promoters made good money for their
investors and built lasting railways, numerous others were crooks
who were only seeking to defraud them or fools who put forward
unworkable projects. There was a brief attempt to bring some
order to the chaos through the creation in 1844 of a Parliamentary
board chaired by Lord Dalhousie, who later as Governor General
of India would design the subcontinent's railway network. Within
a couple of years, the committee foundered on the hard rocks of
the Victorian dogma of fostering competition and reluctance to
intervene in markets and was disbanded.

This process of building railways was totally unplanned in that
MPs and peers simply made a judgement on whether the Bill for
a particular project represented a viable and adequately funded
scheme. There was no consideration of whether the line would
contribute to the nation's economy or serve the needs of local
people. The inevitable outcome was duplication of lines in some

parts of the country, while others, where no promoters had come forward or where their plans had been rejected, were left without any railway connection at all. The reason was simple. The fate of the capital could not simply be left in the hands of Parliamentarians making random and uncoordinated decisions when faced by an avalanche of Bills for railway projects in London. In this brief period of railway mania, nineteen Bills seeking to build lines in London were put forward, and inevitably each one cited the need for a terminus or a major through station in the centre of the capital. There were, too, plans for a huge central station with lines radiating out to all four points of the compass, notably one put forward by Charles Pearson, who would later be the originator of the Metropolitan Railway, the world's first underground railway.

Faced with the potential wholesale destruction of large parts of London, involving demolition of more than 10,000 houses and the clearance of 200 acres of land, the government decided that a Royal Commission was urgently needed. The area of London under consideration by the Commission was bounded by Park Lane in the west, Marylebone and Euston roads in the north, Lambeth Road and the Thames in the south, and the Square Mile of the City. Five commissioners were appointed, proving to be crucial as they were relatively independent, which was not always the case with inquiries set up by Parliament. Rather than bowing to the powerful lobbying of the railway promoters, they interviewed a range of witnesses, including representatives of local parishes and the City of London, who were not necessarily minded to support unfettered railway development. Although in their report published in 1846 the commissioners accepted that railways running into the centre of London would benefit local people, they felt that these advantages were overstated in the face of what would be widespread destruction of existing buildings. Having to travel slightly further to catch a train, they argued, was not an insuperable difficulty for rail passengers venturing to distant parts of the kingdom. They also, rather oddly, took into account Admiralty concerns that more bridges over the Thames would pose a risk to shipping and only recommended one extra bridge over the river.

The Commission's key finding was that no railways would be allowed into the area of what it called the 'quadrilateral' covered by its remit. As a result, it effectively barred railways from the West End and the City of London, a decision that would have an enormous impact on the siting of future terminals. Although the Commission had no legislative power and its recommendations were only advisory, by and large they were adhered to, with a few notable exceptions as several stations did eventually encroach slightly into the forbidden territory and four railway bridges were built over the Thames – at Battersea, Charing Cross, Blackfriars and Cannon Street. The Commission also suggested a Waterloo–London Bridge line, which, in fact, was built in the 1860s, and a connection to Docklands from the north, which eventually became the North London Railway with a terminus at Broad Street.

Despite this, railway planning in London was still light touch. Decisions on the siting, construction, size and reach of stations were left to private companies, albeit tempered by having to navigate a Parliamentary process run by politicians who frequently had a vested interest, either as a landowner or railway company shareholder (not for them today's encumbrance of having to complete a register of interests).

Beyond the Commission's remit was the need to make life better for passengers. Terminuses, which are essentially railway dead ends, are both inconvenient for passengers and operationally difficult. At journey's end a locomotive is up against the buffers, hemmed in by carriages. Hooking up another locomotive to the other end of the train and getting the driver to walk the length of the platform to start the next journey is time consuming when compared with the ease with which a train's journey continues in a through station. London, as mentioned earlier, has more terminuses than any other city in the world and no major through station, which means its rail passengers have had to cope with the inconvenience of being dumped en masse at a place likely to be well short of their destination, relieved somewhat by the creation of the London Underground Circle Line. By and large, though, London became a place where changing trains was the norm.

However, the influence of this small group of commissioners, rather randomly selected, was largely positive. Their decisions would have a wider impact on the pattern and extent of London's economic growth in the second half of the nineteenth century. This was a turning point in Britain's railway history as it was the first time that Parliamentarians had considered the wider social costs and benefits of a railway, rather than merely assessing its immediate financial viability.

It could also be argued that the Commission did the railway companies two favours. Firstly, it saved them vast amounts of money because, as John Moxon, the chairman of the London & Croydon Railway, identified, 'every railway we apprehend in the first mile costs more than in any other part of the line'.[1] That last mile into Euston from Camden Town, for example, cost the London & Birmingham £380,000, by far the most expensive section of the route (the company's underestimate of the cost forced it to return to Parliament in 1839 for permission to raise more capital). This was true of every subsequent terminus built in the capital and, with the construction of HS2, remains the case even today – the projected route out of Euston of this new high-speed line between London and Birmingham, and later Leeds and Manchester, runs parallel with that of the London & Birmingham and the most expensive section is the first few miles out of the terminus.

Secondly, a by-product of the creation of a ring of terminus stations around London was that some form of connection between them became inevitable and, as the roads were so crowded, a railway was the only feasible answer. Although the commissioners rejected Pearson's idea of a central terminal, their decision effectively gave him the opening he needed to push for an underground railway linking the terminals. At a subsequent Commission in 1854–5, Pearson's idea for this new type of railway received a sympathetic hearing and the Commission's recommendations paved the way for the development of the world's first underground line between Paddington and Farringdon, and eventually for the Circle Line that would link seven of London's major terminuses[2] as well as the Tube lines built later that would offer numerous other connections between them.

Therefore, when it came to building King's Cross, the third of these early main-line stations in the ring around New Road, there was no possibility of stretching any further south than the boundary set by the Commission – and even getting that far proved rather difficult because of the obstacle of the Regent's Canal and the need for extensive demolition.

King's Cross, like Euston, was created by an ambitious and aggressive company whose roots were in the North. Had local investors and landowners been involved, it is likely that they could have influenced Parliament and been allowed to build further towards the centre of London.

Although late on the scene – it did not run its first service, between the Lincolnshire towns of Grimsby and Louth, until March 1848 – the Great Northern Railway was intent on making up for lost time with a programme of rapid expansion. Through a series of mergers and the purchase of running rights, the Great Northern was soon knocking on the door of the capital. Its great rival was the Midland Railway whose creator, George Hudson, tried every trick in the book to block its drive towards the capital. Once the Great Northern had defeated its opponents, including Hudson, whose fraudulent dealings in railway shares led to his exile in disgrace, its proposal for a line between London and York received Parliamentary assent.

Great Northern services began operating to and from London in August 1850. The company realized that the following year's Great Exhibition could be a huge money-spinner for the railway and hastily cobbled together a temporary terminus at Maiden Lane. The timing of the Great Exhibition was propitious as the pre-railway transport system would never have coped with the enormous number of people that attended the Exhibition, which attracted six million visitors during the six months it was open. Most visitors from outside the capital travelled by rail, many on special trains from towns and even villages across the country.

Maiden Lane was even more constrained and modest than Great Western's temporary terminus at Bishop's Bridge, consisting of little more than a couple of timber platforms between Copenhagen tunnel and the yet-to-be completed Gas Works tunnel in what is now York Way. The station, which had a curved frontage, was designed by Lewis Cubitt, and had two low shed roofs of slates, with large louvres to let out smoke, held up by wrought-iron trusses and columns. The design proved unsatisfactory and the original intention to construct a building in a similar style at King's Cross was hastily abandoned.

Because many of the towns and cities served by the Great Northern were in what had previously been London & North Western Railway territory, there was for the first time genuine competition for passengers between rival railways in large parts of England north of London and this was heightened when they all tried to induce the visitors to the Great Exhibition to use their route to London. The Great Western, too, entered the fray, deliberately attacking the London & North Western by expanding into places such as the West Midlands and Cheshire. And, by cutting fares for exhibition-goers, the ferry companies operating from Hull down to the Thames triggered a price war with the railways.

The Great Northern was at the heart of this battle, ultimately offering a John Lewis style 'Never knowingly undersold' deal, promising fares that were sixpence cheaper than any offered by its rivals. The Great Northern's aggressive marketing resulted in thousands of people arriving at the inadequate Maiden Lane station on heavily loaded trains. Getting home was even worse, as hapless passengers jostled to board the limited number of trains that could be accommodated there. Since there was no telegraph, which was only introduced a few years later, staff at Maiden Lane had no idea what special trains were scheduled. On one occasion 3,000 Yorkshire-bound passengers descended upon the station from the Exhibition only to find that there was room on the train for only 1,000 people. A riot ensued as the irate passengers commandeered a Lincoln-bound service and demanded that it took them back to Yorkshire. Eventually, after much indecision from the company, cattle trucks were found to accommodate them on the journey north.

This off-hand treatment of Exhibition passengers damaged Great Northern's reputation and highlighted the urgent need to find a replacement for Maiden Lane. Disgruntled passengers pointed out that, half a mile down the road, the London & North Western's Euston station offered far better facilities and as a consequence it attracted many more visitors to the Exhibition than the Great Northern. Royalty, too, joined the clamour for improvements. Queen Victoria and Prince Albert were forced to make do with Maiden Lane's sparse facilities when travelling to Scotland in 1851 to oversee work on their newly acquired Balmoral Castle. The all too obvious inadequacy of the tiny Maiden Lane convinced Great Northern that a new station at King's Cross was urgently needed, even though, as ever, the company struggled to find the cash.

King's Cross was an excellent location given its proximity both to the Regent's Canal and to a junction linking four major roads – Caledonian, New, Gray's Inn and Pentonville. A statue of George IV, erected to overlook the junction soon after his death in 1830, gave the area its name. These roads ensured King's Cross was already an important transport hub and it is no coincidence that today it has Underground connections with more lines than any other station.

The canal, however, was a problem and dithering over how to get across it delayed completion of the new terminus by two years. After much deliberation, the Great Northern did not follow London & Birmingham's example at Euston of crossing over the canal, a decision that later the Midland Railway would imitate. Instead, the engineers of the Great Northern thought it was better to construct a tunnel under the canal, rather than a viaduct over it, even though this was a more expensive option.

The station itself was built on a ten-acre site that had previously housed the London Smallpox and Fever Hospitals. The Great Northern Railway was something of a Cubitt family enterprise, as the route had been planned by Sir William Cubitt and his son Joseph who appointed Lewis, William's nephew, as station architect. His first decision was to have an arched roof, rather than a flat one. This allowed for longer spans between columns, which reduced the risk of a derailed locomotive hitting a column and bringing down the roof. While previous arched roofs, like the 156-foot-wide structure at Liverpool Lime Street, had used iron and glass, Lewis Cubitt, under budgetary and time restraints, chose wood, which had only ever been used on small stations. It proved an expensive mistake; the wood only lasted fifteen years in the damp London weather and had to be replaced by iron. Cubitt's roof had two spans, each 105 feet wide supported by iron shoes attached to brick walls on each side and one in the middle. As with Paddington, the design was greatly influenced by Paxton's Crystal Palace and the arches, at 800 feet long, were extremely impressive.

Having spent up to half a million pounds in Parliamentary, legal and survey costs in order to defeat objections stimulated by Hudson, the Great Northern was, by necessity, a no-frills railway devoid of architectural extravagance. Cubitt was told to keep costs to a minimum and consequently inside the station there were no decorative additions. The frontage, too, was simple in the extreme with the two huge arches or 'lunettes' joined by a tower that would not have looked out of place in an Italian piazza. Its clock, made by Dent of London, the company that also made the timepiece for Big Ben, was second-hand as it had already been displayed at the Great Exhibition where, apparently, it had not lost a single second in six weeks of being on show. This massive yet elegant timepiece, purchased for £200, had only three nine-feet faces – the fourth was never installed since it would not have been visible to passengers. Unlike the clock later made by Dent's rival, Walker, for St Pancras whose hands moved with a jerk every thirty seconds, the movement was invisible to all but the most discerning eye as it was set for every half second. However, that fails to explain why, throughout the history of the two rival companies, their station clocks were out of sync, with one invariably a minute or two faster than the other.

The arches at each end of the frontage were flanked by plain square buttress piers, topped by flat brick fascias. The series of six arches, stretching up around thirty feet, also had no embellishments or statues, which provided a clean and simple look that would be in great contrast to its future Gothic neighbour. The whole building cost just £123,000, far less than either Euston or Paddington. The simplicity may have been born of parsimony but it has stood the test of time, particularly since a clutch of ugly 1960s additions were removed in the refurbishment completed in 2012. All of the walls consisted of standard yellow stock brick and the station is best described in Lewis Cubitt's own words: 'The building will depend for its effect on the largeness of some of the features, its fitness for its purpose and its characteristic expression of that purpose.'[3]

When the station opened in October 1852, it was the largest in Britain but only had two platforms: arrivals on the eastern side, and departures on the west. The large fourteen-track central section was for parked carriages, a fairly standard arrangement at the time. There was originally no concourse, merely a narrow cross pathway between the buffers and the six arches at the front to allow people to go from one platform to another.

Initially, this proved adequate since there were only a dozen trains a day in each direction. But as the number of services quickly increased, two further platforms were added. With the rail network expanding rapidly in the aftermath of the 1840s mania, services reached Scotland and new destinations in the North and Midlands. Additionally, branch lines increased local traffic, which had originally been neglected by the Great Northern. This put a great strain on the rather poorly designed interior of King's Cross, and the situation became almost intolerable when the Midland Railway started sharing the station with the Great Northern. The Midland had finally reached London, after many years of trying, thanks to a track-sharing arrangement with the Great Northern. It was a situation that was inherently unsatisfactory given the escalation in traffic, particularly freight, and led to the construction of St Pancras, the Midland's own terminus next door (see Chapter 6).

Operating conditions at King's Cross were never easy because of the decision to go under the Regent's Canal. Building what became known as the Gas Works tunnel was technically demanding and has been a constraint on the working of the station ever since, causing operating difficulties that have yet to be fully resolved despite many subsequent improvements. The tunnel lies 656 feet from the outer ends of the platforms and the tracks are about thirty feet higher, creating a relatively steep gradient of 1 in 107, which, according to Gordon Biddle, the eminent railway historian, 'created a fiercesome start for trains throughout the days of steam'.[4] There was at least one occasion when a driver, unaware his engine was slipping, allowed it to slide back, colliding with a train behind. Eventually, three parallel tunnels were built to ease congestion in the station's throat but only two remain in railway use, and both feed into Copenhagen tunnel, the second set of parallel tunnels north of King's Cross. The third, redundant for many years, is being brought back into use to relieve congestion.

For all its simplicity, King's Cross was not a very practical station. It was, like Euston, too short, constrained by the tunnels taking trains under the Regent's Canal. When suburban traffic grew, two extra platforms had to be built on the eastern side to run trains to the villas and avenues springing up across north London, from Hornsey and Crouch End, and out as far as Finchley and Barnet. (What is now the Barnet branch of the Northern Line was initially operated by the Great Northern and carried large numbers of commuters.)

The three stations in a ring around the Regent's Canal – Euston, Paddington and King's Cross – soon to be joined by St Pancras and much later by Marylebone, were not the discrete, relatively contained spaces we see today. They formed what could be termed a 'railway mile', a continuous ribbon of development that transformed the area between the canal and New Road – built in the previous century as one of the world's first bypasses – into a bustling industrial belt. Cumberland Basin, behind Euston and Battlebridge near King's Cross, quickly became a key transfer point between water and track. Depending on one's point of view, the frenetic nature of the area could be seen as a tribute to human enterprise and ingenuity or, perhaps, a nightmarish testimony to the hell created by the Industrial Revolution. It was unarguably a hive of activity with thousands of railwaymen, canal boat sailors, porters, farriers, and drivers loading, unloading and moving wagons, and transferring, mostly by hand, goods between the canals, railways and roads. As a result, cheap housing developments sprung up to the north of New Road to accommodate an army of low-paid workers.

According to the architect Terry Farrell, 'Paddington soon became the world's first modern transport interchange, with the railway, the canal and London's first horse-bus service all located there',[5] but the activity behind Euston and, particularly, King's Cross was on a much bigger scale. Soon massive goods yards emerged behind both of them, creating a long line of warehouses and sheds adjoining the canal. The Regent's Canal linking the Grand Union at Paddington with the docks in east London via the Limehouse Cut had only been completed in 1820 and had proved very successful. By the mid-1820s it had become a major freight waterway carrying half a million tons annually of inbound and outbound traffic, as freight from many ships in the docks was disgorged at Limehouse straight onto barges. While the canals and the railways are often perceived as having emerged in very separate eras, in fact their development was not far apart in time and the choice of location of the railways was influenced by their proximity to the existing canal network. Integrating these two relatively new forms of transport was an obvious and efficient move by the railway companies and many of the ancillary industries that became dependent on them.

Goods began arriving at King's Cross as soon as the Great Northern's tracks reached London. The Great Northern was much more bullish than either the Great Western or the London & Birmingham about the importance of freight in its business model, and ensured that from the outset it had the infrastructure to handle vast amounts of freight. To the back of the stations that were dotted along New Road, a swathe of warehouses and storage depots developed along the couple of miles of canal between Camden Town and the Islington tunnel. Robert Stephenson had insisted on the purchase of the land to the north of the Regent's Canal from Lord Southampton, but the directors of the London & Birmingham initially felt this was an unwarranted expense. They were soon proved wrong as more land was purchased on the south side of the canal, creating an extensive yard that covered thirty-three acres.

The London & Birmingham quickly erected a large warehouse on the north bank of the canal, adding a short branch to the waterway that ran right into the building to allow the transfer of goods between barges and wagons to take place under cover. By 1839, a thriving but smoky and malodorous area employing hundreds of people had developed; another goods shed had been built, along with no fewer than eighteen coke ovens to make smokeless fuel for locomotives. There was a huge hole lined with timber piles in Wharf Road where Baltic Sea ice brought into the UK was stored until the summer when it was used by several local ice cream businesses that sprung up in the Italian community just to the east of King's Cross station. There were stalls for fifty horses and any number of offices. Sidings branched out from a central stem at around sixty degrees, which has been described as a pinnate pattern (like an ash tree or a feather).

Various private companies soon built warehouses for the same purpose of transhipment. Pickfords, which was seeking to diversify into rail transport having started as a canal agent, opened theirs in December 1841. The company was one of three agents to obtain the right of carriage and distribution of goods on the line to Birmingham, although its relationship with the railway company was not always harmonious owing to continuous petty disputes over access, charges and licences. The ever-expanding yard was redesigned twice in the middle of the century with a new goods shed and offices, and in 1866 a locomotive shed that could accommodate 100 locomotives was completed. By then Camden had become a major transport hub that despatched thirty goods trains northwards daily.

The most famous of the early buildings was the Roundhouse, completed in 1847 as a shed for locomotives with a thirty-six-foot turntable in the middle. It could house twenty-three locomotives but survived less than a decade in its original function owing to a major remodelling of the Camden goods yard that left it without easy access from the tracks. It was turned into a grain and potato store in the 1860s and then for almost a century became a bonded warehouse for Scottish whisky brought from the Highlands by W. & A. Gilbey. Its transformation into an iconic concert venue lasted between 1966 and 1983, but happily, after nearly two decades of virtual abandonment, it was renovated in 2004 and is now a theatre and entertainment venue with a capacity of 3,300, a demonstration of its scale. The yard in Camden was built with a series of vaults and catacombs underneath, used for stables and general stores, and later as coal and wine storage. It is now home to parts of Camden Market, a tourist hotspot.

The goods station directly to the back of King's Cross was on an even grander scale. The fifty-nine-acre site rapidly developed into an area of warehouses, sheds, stables, offices and eventually more than 100 sidings. The railway carried three main types of goods: minerals such as coal, ore and aggregates like stone; livestock, which had traditionally been driven south along the roads around King's Cross down to Smithfield; and general merchandise, which included anything from small parcels and packages to raw cotton and bicycles. Of these, in terms of weight and value, coal was the dominant product. Carrying coal had been key to the establishment of railways in the North, and as soon as the lines reached the capital, there was a need for a range of facilities to support them. The Great Northern already had a thriving coal business in the North and quickly became the first railway to transport large quantities of the black gold to London. It did this by exploiting new sources of coal in south Yorkshire and by ensuring that the necessary infrastructure was in place to make the process more efficient. To make unloading quicker, coal drops – where wagons dropped their coal between the rails as a rapid method of unloading – were built, with two series facing each other at right angles to the canal. The eastern set, completed in 1851, consisted of twenty-four brick sections, each containing a huge hopper into which the coal was dropped. It could then be bagged or dropped into carts for further transport. This was such a successful innovation that a second set, with thirty sections, was built opposite, and although the London & North Western was not such a major coal carrier as the Great Northern, it nevertheless began to use the vaults at Camden as coal drops in the same way. The Great Northern fought a price war with coastal freight shippers, which had traditionally brought sea coal to the capital, and consequently Londoners benefited enormously, with the cost almost halving, from thirty shillings a ton to seventeen shillings.

The whole area behind the stations became a hive of activity that matched anything in the industrial North. Farrell describes it as 'a kind of industrial linear belt between the canal and New Road. Within this belt was a smoking industrial complex that anyone from Manchester, Huddersfield and the Black Country might well have recognised as familiar. The goods were offloaded here, gas works were built to manufacture, store and distribute coal gas and great stables were built, with granaries to feed the horses.'[6] The sheer scale of activity and the efficient organization of the whole process were unprecedented. The volume of goods being transported in and out of the capital through this area of depots, sidings and stations grew every year, as did London's population and its importance in relation to the rest of the country: 'The great goods depots of London possess an importance superior even to that of the passenger termini themselves and furnish to the keen observer fields of study every whit as interesting as those afforded by the heterogeneous masses of humanity which daily pack themselves into express and local trains.'[7]

The most imposing early building in the King's Cross goods station was Lewis Cubitt's towering six-storey granary warehouse, completed in 1852. On either side of the front of the granary there were goods sheds, one for arrivals, and one for departures, each 600 feet long and enclosing twelve tracks covered by an iron roof. The wagons were moved by horses, rather than shunting engines, into and out of the sheds with the help of turnplates. Carts came in through an elevated roadway under which there was stabling for 120 horses, giving an idea of the scale of operations. The granary was a technological innovation as a system of hydraulic-powered lifts and hoists was used to move the goods up and down the six storeys, a relatively new technology that was later replaced by electricity.

Horses were not just used locally but were the main form of transport for cargo arriving and leaving the goods station, both on the roads and along the canals that reached the Thames at Brentford in the west and Limehouse in the east where docks had been established for the transhipment of freight.

Another early building, opened in 1850, was a three-storey office block on the east side, where working conditions were grim, according to an early account of its operation: its clerks had to work for many years in 'rather dark, stuffy offices with smoke-grimed ceilings and an atmosphere compounded of overnight gas-burning and the indefinable mouldiness of adjacent "book rooms"'.[8]

Alongside the granary, there was a carriage shed that from 1857 was used by the Midland Railway when its services started running into King's Cross.

Not all the construction behind the stations was railway related. In 1865, the elegant and, inevitably, Italianate, German Gymnasium was built just to the west of King's Cross, close to where the suburban extension would be added a decade later. The triangular-roofed building, which cost £6,000 to construct, belonged to the German Gymnastics Society, a sporting association set up in 1861. Its main claim to fame is that it hosted a precursor to the Olympic Games from 1866 to 1908 organized by the National Olympian Association.

In the 1860s, an even larger set of structures was built that would dominate the skyline for the next 150 years. These were the nine gasholders erected between 1861 and 1867 that would supply much of London's gas to meet demand for what was becoming an important power source for lighting, cooking and, later, heating. The gas was produced by the nearby gas works until production in the area ceased at the end of the century and was transferred to more remote locations, away from city centres, thus easing the discomfort of the clerks working in the offices nearby.

Numerous other buildings including a potato warehouse – testimony to another example of the entrepreneurial skill of the Great Northern, as it was the first railway company to bring enormous quantities of potatoes to the capital – coal and fish offices and several goods sheds, most of which were used by companies such as freight forwarders and storage companies, were constructed over the next decades, further increasing the hustle and bustle of what was a huge tract of land along the canal. The canals largely lost their freight traffic by the end of the nineteenth century but the area continued to be a major railway centre right until after the Second World War when the decline of railfreight and other changes in the railways led to the abandonment of what became known as the Railway Lands and was subject to a massive redevelopment in the early twenty-first century (covered in Chapter 12).

The railways in the North and West had the advantage of serving large parts of the country, and consequently could base their business models on attracting long-distance passengers and considerable quantities of freight. Those in the South (see Chapter 7) had less fertile territory with little prospect for freight and a much smaller area to cover. The railways in the East struggled, too, as Eastern England was sparsely populated and the East End traditionally housed London's poor. Nevertheless, two companies managed to reach London from the East in the early years of the railway age, but it would be another quarter of a century before an eastern railway managed to create a cathedral of steam.

FIVE

BREACHING THE CITY WALLS

THE CITY OF LONDON was the Holy Grail for the early railways. They realized that every extra yard closer to the City would increase their chances of tapping into huge markets for train travel, as at the time it was not only a financial centre but also the site of small factories and workshops that were the main source of the capital's employment. In short, the potential passenger and freight market was immense.

Early on, two railway companies running services from the East established a terminus to serve the City. The first, the Eastern Counties Railway, created a temporary terminus at Mile End in 1839 and Shoreditch – later to be renamed Bishopsgate – the following year. Despite the move nearer to the City, this was another example of a temporary terminus that was too far away from the centre to be convenient and rapidly became inadequate for its purpose. Temporary, in this case, however, turned out to be nearly three and a half decades, regardless of a proposal from the railway company as early as 1845 to construct an alternative terminus.

This long gap was caused by the Eastern Counties Railway's financial struggles throughout its history. Despite territorial expansion and mergers with several rivals, the company never managed to establish a solid financial base because the East of England was sparsely populated and impoverished, and it made the mistake of failing to exploit the potentially more lucrative market of London's East End, which was on its doorstep.

The railway reached the edge of the capital on the Braithwaite viaduct, a series of arches named after John Braithwaite, a steam locomotive designer and engineer for the Eastern Counties Railway. The company's prospectus envisaged a line from London all the way to Norwich and Yarmouth, but these destinations weren't reached until 1845 and 1848 respectively. Braithwaite spent considerable time working out how to get through east London before finally deciding on a route that terminated at High Street, Shoreditch. Compared to later railways, the demolition of existing homes was relatively limited though still considerable. Braithwaite's survey provides a fascinating insight into the kind of housing that was common at the time. He explained that construction of the viaduct, which stretched for a mile and a quarter on 160 arches, would involve the demolition of 'no more than 373 houses of which 140 were very old and consisted of two rooms and let to weekly tenants at sums varying from 2/6d [12.5p] to 3/6d [37.5p] each. 130 are four and five roomed houses in a most ruinous state. 50 are larger but equally ruinous and not more than 30 are in a good state of repair or of much value.'[1]

The emphasis on the 'ruinous' state of the houses suggests an element of self-justification in arguing that the railway was doing London a favour by ridding it of insalubrious housing. But the poor tenants, who were evicted with, at best, a week's notice, must have felt otherwise. Much of the assessment of the housing on the route was, in truth, probably accurate given the poverty-stricken nature of the area around the terminus at Shoreditch. The station may only have been a few hundred yards from the centre of the City of London but the contrast could hardly have been greater. Its location was, in Alan Jackson's words, 'unfortunate', as it was within 'a stone's throw of Old Jago, one of London's foulest slums, inhabited almost entirely by criminals'.[2] Such was the reputation of the area that when it opened, the railway's expenditure included the sum of £15 14 shillings for firearms and ammunition for its policemen. The terminus was built on the site of Webb Square, which, according to vivid evidence given by the Reverend Timothy Gibson to the Royal Commission on Metropolitan Railway Termini, was 'a sort of receptacle for pickpockets, housebreakers and prostitutes, great numbers of whom were removed'.[3] Despite their 'removal', the area was still desperately poor and the location of the station 'inconvenient' as George Hudson, the railway king, who was later briefly chairman of the Eastern Counties, later remarked. As ever, those 'removed' tended to settle in nearby hovels, merely increasing the level of overcrowding in the surviving buildings.

Like other early London terminus stations, it had separate departure and arrival platforms, between which were three other sets of tracks for stabling unused carriages. Initially, the viaduct itself only had two tracks, though more were soon added. All the tracks in the station had turntables, to ensure engines could be used more flexibly, but otherwise there were few facilities, and none for passengers. When the station was completed – after the inevitable delay caused by lack of funds – its frontage was impressive at around 130 feet long. It was designed, of course, in a classical 'Italian style', with two elegant balustrade-lined staircases at the front leading to the booking hall and trains, which were above street level due to the tracks being on a viaduct. Despite the completion of this three-storey building that was intended to impress and reassure passengers, the station was inconveniently distant from the City and marred by the poor condition of the narrow local streets. Such was its reputation, many people refused to travel through the station at night, which did little to help the financial situation of the ever-struggling Eastern Counties Railway.

Being cash-strapped didn't prevent the Eastern Counties from organizing a traditional opening ceremony, which was held on 22 June 1839. However, it may have explained why the fare on offer was not up to the standard of other station openings. A reporter from the *Railway Times* complained that 'the banquet was not nearly so splendid as that which recently honoured the opening of the Croydon line, or of the Southampton last summer – especially as regards the variety and abundance of the wines'. He bemoaned the fact that whereas at previous events champagne flowed freely, this time 'an order from one of the stewards was requisite to secure to any particular section of a table the presence of a single bottle'.[4]

Right from its opening, Bishopsgate station, the name adopted in 1846, was shared with another impecunious railway, the Northern & Eastern, which could not afford the expense of its own London terminus. The company had ambitious plans to run a line all the way to York but only reached Hertford and Bishop's Stortford, and had to share the tracks between Stratford and Bishopsgate, as well as station offices, with the Eastern Counties. Curiously, both companies initially used 5ft gauge[5] for their tracks because Braithwaite believed the railway would be 'permanently insulated' from other lines and argued that uniformity was not in itself advantageous. In fact, Braithwaite was wrong, and the lines were converted to standard 4ft 8½in five years after opening. What he and many of his contemporaries failed to understand was that creating a network of railway lines was critical to maximizing the benefits of this new technology.

For all its drawbacks, Bishopsgate station soon became busier. The Eastern Counties, which merged its services with those of Northern & Eastern, reached Cambridge in 1844 and Peterborough three years later; further expansions to destinations in the East of England continued throughout the next couple of decades. The company, however, was permanently on the lookout for a new terminus but although a number of alternatives were considered, including one in the West End, it was not until 1864 that a decision was made over where it should be sited. By then the Eastern Counties had merged with four other smaller railways to form the much larger Great Eastern and it was this new company that received permission to build Liverpool Street station (see Chapter 9).

The other early arrival from the East, the London & Blackwall Railway, managed to squeeze just over the boundary into the City before the 1846 Commission on Metropolitan Railway Termini prevented any further incursions. The impetus for the railway, which was authorized by Parliament in 1836, was to take business from the well-established shipping services along the Thames. There were frequent steamer services between London and destinations such as Woolwich; the pleasure gardens of Rosherville near Gravesend; Southend; and Thanet. All were well used, despite being slow, and most of them docked at Brunswick Wharf, which was in Blackwall by the entrance to the East India Dock. The six-and-a-half-mile boat trip from there to London Bridge took about an hour, whereas the land route was less than four miles. Even in the early years of the railway, trains were much faster than water transport, so there was potential to cut travelling time on this route by about forty-five minutes. There was, too, a good potential market among the large number of people, estimated by the London & Blackwall directors to be 4,300, who travelled daily by coach or horse omnibus to work at the docks. The company's full name was the London & Blackwall Railway and Steam Navigation Depot Company, which suggested that it had wider ambitions than just operating a railway. Indeed, once the railway line was functioning, the company did start operating steamers from Blackwall pier, taking travellers along the Thames and across the English Channel to places as far afield as Rotterdam and Antwerp.

Because the line ran through a built-up area, the London & Blackwall was, like the London & Greenwich and the Eastern Counties, constructed on a brick viaduct for much of its route. This was a short railway targeting dock passengers and as a result there were no fewer than six intermediate stations, one every half mile, to serve passengers living in the East End. The London & Blackwall was a unique railway as it was powered mostly by stationary engines with the extra twist of needing gravity and human muscle at both ends for the final few hundred yards. The directors of the company had felt that running steam locomotives on such a stop-start route would be difficult. They were also concerned that the engines would be a fire hazard given the proximity of many flimsy houses adjoining the tracks and the number of highly flammable sailing ships that were a constant presence in the Limehouse Basin.

Consequently, they adopted a cable system, devised largely by Robert Stephenson.[6] Despite his predilection for locomotives, which he had introduced on the pioneering Liverpool & Manchester Railway, Stephenson argued that steam engines would be more expensive to operate and would require four, rather than two, lines of track to enable them to be turned and shunted. The cable system had stationary engines at both ends of the line that drove huge drums, rather like outsize cotton reels, to pull cables made of hemp rope. The drums wound in the rope for the length of one complete journey and then let it out again for the return trip. These engines pulled a continuous cable to which grippers underneath the middle of the coaches were attached. It was not terribly efficient, however, as the cable would often become twisted or stretched, and tended to break. A mystified Stephenson replaced the hemp with metal, with little effect. In fact, the extra weight of the new cable put a strain on the stationary engines.

While such a short railway might seem rather unexciting, its opening on 6 July 1840 was a major event. Fifteen hundred VIPs attended a lavish dinner of turtle and grouse, washed down with claret, supplied by a Mr Lovegrove, who was the proprietor of the Brunswick Hotel conveniently sited near the eastern terminus of the line. There was none of the parsimony of the Eastern Counties, though sadly the opinion of the *Railway Times* reporter is not available. The Brunswick had a reputation for fine dining whose particular speciality was, according to a contemporary journalist, 'whitebait with the luxurious accompaniment of cold punch' and, according to the writer, 'this, by aid of the Blackwall Railway, may be wafted in ten minutes'[7] after leaving the City.

The terminus – temporary, of course – was at Minories (the site of the first Docklands Light Railway terminus at Tower Gateway, which opened in 1987 and is today still part of a greatly expanded network) and consisted of little more than two platforms protected by a wooden roof. When the line was extended to Fenchurch Street, the cable was not lengthened. Instead, trains arriving at

Minories were disconnected from the cable while the train was still in motion and allowed to roll gently up the slight 1 in 150 incline to reach the new station less than a quarter of a mile away. A similar arrangement was also used at the Blackwall end with coaches being allowed to coast the last couple of hundred yards into the small terminus.

This operating system was extremely cumbersome and required careful operation by the guards, one of whom would sit in each carriage. Every carriage had a specific destination and was worked by a guard who would release the grippers as it approached the correct intermediate station where it would coast to a halt at the platform. On the return journey, the carriages would be reattached to the cable and taken to the end of the line. At both terminuses, the initial thrust to start the trains came from railwaymen who would push the carriages for the first few yards, after which gravity took over until the cable section was reached.

Initially, trains ran every fifteen minutes with a fare of sixpence (2.5p) for first class and fourpence (1.7p) for third – oddly, there was no second class. Passenger numbers failed to meet expectations at first, although freight traffic exceeded them. When Minories was no longer needed as a terminus, a siding and a platform were built there for unloading goods. Since it was elevated, unloading was particularly easy as bagged and bailed goods were able to slide down into storage rooms, with the result that by 1854 the station was handling 100 tons per day. Passenger traffic received a boost when the troublesome cable traction was abandoned in 1849, and it was at this point that the 5ft gauge was replaced by standard gauge. A planned connection with the Eastern Counties had to wait until both railways were operating on standard gauge and Fenchurch Street station was expanded in 1854.

When Fenchurch Street first opened in July 1841 it was little more than a slightly larger version of Minories, with the same kind of wooden roof and nothing of any architectural note. While the area around the station was not as impoverished as at the Eastern Counties' terminus at Shoreditch, it was no Mayfair. A local surgeon wrote to the General Board of Health in 1849 explaining that the pavements in the area had long been 'in a most disgraceful condition' with large holes receiving not only rainwater but 'offensive matter of other descriptions'. To ensure we know what he meant he went on to describe how a passageway from Crutched Friars to Fenchurch Street was 'a great thoroughfare for pedestrians – but no decent person can pass through it without being annoyed by urinary and excrementitious [*sic*] deposits'.[8]

Fenchurch Street did, however, have one innovation – the world's first station bookstall, run by William Marshall whose newspaper distribution company would later come to rival W.H. Smith. The station was greatly expanded and improved when the London & Blackwall started sharing it with the much larger London, Tilbury & Southend Railway. The latter was a joint venture with the Eastern Counties that began operating when the completely rebuilt station opened on 13 April 1854.

The station was designed by George Berkeley, the chief engineer of the London, Tilbury & Southend, rather than by an architect. It is praised by Betjeman as a good example of the engineer-architect tradition that, as he points out, a couple of decades later produced the Royal Albert Hall. The façade, which survives virtually unchanged to this day, is of grey bricks with stone adornments but the most pleasant section was at the first-floor level where there are eleven arched windows topped by a crescent-shaped pediment with the ubiquitous clock in the middle. There was originally a flat canopy at the front, but it soon collapsed and was replaced by a zig-zag shaped awning, which Betjeman felt, 'besides being efficient, has fairground charm'.[9]

The train shed had a crescent-shaped roof made of iron but which let in some light in glazed sections. The booking hall at street level was divided into two, one for each of the two railways. From there, passengers climbed an ornate staircase to a first-floor concourse with arched windows and a roof that allowed in light during the day but was very gloomy at night. Tucked away in a rather hidden part of the City, Fenchurch Street has always been the least known of London's terminuses and uniquely, even today, it has no connection with the Underground, the nearest station being Tower Hill, a few minutes' walk away. Equally oddly, the station is actually located in London Street and Fenchurch Place, a small road specifically constructed to serve the station, whereas Fenchurch Street itself runs about 165 feet north-west of the station.

The London, Tilbury & Southend Railway soon became the dominant operator from the station but the London & Blackwall survived until 1862 when it was taken over by the newly merged Great Eastern. The directors, however, were well rewarded for their initiative in creating the railway. The entire line was rented to the Great Eastern at the generous sum of 4.5 per cent of the company's capital, but since all operations and maintenance were the responsibility of the new railway, the directors were left with nothing to do other than dine on the proceeds. As Alan Jackson recounts rather amusingly, 'it was shortly after this that the sinecurist Blackwall directors felt able to give up their board room to the first-class ladies. They did, however, continue to meet elsewhere twice a year until the 1923 grouping [when more than 120 railways were merged into four big companies], to receive their guaranteed rent and declare a dividend, and then, weakened by their exertions, to dine and wine together.'[10]

Due to its direct link to the docks, vast quantities of freight were transported to and from Fenchurch Street. No fewer than six depots, together with huge swathes of sidings, opened within half a mile of the terminus in the years immediately after its opening. They were located in the eastern part of the City, which, to this day, remains less prosperous than much of the rest, in streets such as Commercial Road and Royal Mint Street, and left a legacy of warehouses and store buildings, a few of which still survive. A consequence of this widespread development was the demolition of buildings in many penurious areas of the City, part of the process by which the railways in London were a principal driver of slum clearance programmes.

These thriving yards, operated by different railways such as the London & North Western and the Midland as well as the Eastern Counties, meant that tracks on the approach to Fenchurch Street could not, at times, keep up with the sheer volume of traffic. Fenchurch Street rapidly built up passenger numbers with 7 million annually – approximately 25,000 daily since there was very little traffic on Sundays – and a peak of 33 million by the end of the nineteenth century, after which numbers started tailing off as the development of the telephone greatly reduced the need for messengers to travel between the docks and the City.

Given that Fenchurch Street had initially only four platforms until a fifth was added around the turn of the century, overcrowding on trains was commonplace and at times unbearable. A witness to the 1904 Royal Commission on London Traffic talked of 'a great rush of people before [the train] stops to get seats in the carriages and I have seen people knocked over, and it is not altogether decent, in fact, to see sixteen or seventeen people inside one compartment'.[11] Another witness noted that he had seen as many as twenty-six people in a first-class compartment 'among whom were two females'.[12] Both contributions may not have been entirely reliable, however, since they were made by representatives of West Ham Tramways, very much a rival concern.

Despite its modest size, Fenchurch Street's location in the City and its popularity with passengers made it commercially attractive for other railway companies. Many of them ran trains from there to destinations that were not limited to the coastal and Thames-side towns in Essex that make up the current timetable. Some of these services migrated to Broad Street when it opened in 1865 and to the new Liverpool Street nine years later. Today, Fenchurch Street's tucked-away location and its limited services mean that it is something of a hidden little gem, the terminus that few Londoners and even fewer tourists know about, let alone use.

There are advantages to being in a rather unfashionable part of London, secreted down a City side street. Fenchurch Street is the one terminus that, as Betjeman put it, 'has been less messed about than any London terminus',[13] with only the London & Blackwall offices to the east of the station façade having disappeared. However, the opposite is the case with poor Broad Street, the biggest casualty among the terminuses that have not survived the constant changes made to London's railways in their near two centuries of existence.

Broad Street was the terminus built for the North London Railway that had originally operated out of Fenchurch Street and was the second to be built inside the City boundary. The North London was unusual in that it was radial and suburban, rather than attempting to serve central London, and as Wayne Asher, the author of the history of the line, says, it 'had precious little to do with north London or the needs of its citizens at all'.[14] Indeed, the North London's history is complex even by the standards of Victorian railways with their mergers, battles with rivals, failures and aggressive expansions. The story of how the line morphed over a long period into a vital and very busy part of today's London Overground, seeing off an attempt by Richard Beeching to shut it down, is far too convoluted to detail here. Its origins, as the East and West India Docks & Birmingham Junction Railway, a title that explains its original purpose, lay in the desire of the London & North Western, which promoted and financed the North London, to access the docks in east London directly without passing through the centre of the City.

The first section of the line from Islington to Bow Junction opened in 1850; a year later it was connected to the London & North Western at Camden and ran through to Poplar, which became the first railway-owned dock in the capital. The connection at Bow, however, enabled its services to run between Fenchurch Street and Camden, and later, through to Primrose Hill. A four-mile detour round east London meant it was a slow route, but unexpectedly popular, thanks to the North London's cheap fares and frequent trains.

However, recognizing this was an unsatisfactory route, and conscious of the fact that Fenchurch Street was increasingly becoming overcrowded, the North London began to search for its own terminus. Backed by the might of the London & North Western Railway, which was on its way to becoming Britain's largest company, a site at the junction of Broad Street and Liverpool Street was chosen. This required two miles of new line running south from the existing tracks of the North London at

Kingsland, near Hackney, into the new station, which would be
next to the proposed site of the Liverpool Street terminus of the
Great Eastern (this did not open until nearly a decade later due to
delays). It would have made far more sense for the North London
and the Great Eastern to have designed a joint station and coordinated services to the various destinations rather than, as happened,
constantly trying to outdo each other, but, as ever, rivalry ruled.

Betjeman described how Broad Street, 'with its splendid roofs
and chimney stacks, and brickwork and ironwork, looks more
important than its larger neighbour, Liverpool Street, which is sunk
in the valley beside it'.[15] This is explained by the fact that the latter's
platforms were below street level while the tracks into Broad Street
entered the terminus on yet another viaduct. As was now becoming
usual with railway building in the capital, the construction of the
viaduct required the demolition of 4,000 homes in the Shoreditch
and Haggerston areas, a rather astonishing number for a mere two
miles of track and a relatively small terminus, but an illustration of
the cramped nature of the housing on the edge of the City.

While railway companies came increasingly under pressure
from the public during the course of the century to provide at
least some compensation to those displaced by their construction
of new lines, in the 1860s there were few statutory requirements
for them to fulfil except to provide a list of those affected. During
the scrutiny of the Bill, however, the Parliamentarians decided to
place an obligation on the North London to provide one morning
workmen's train from Dalston and a return service in the evening
at a fare of just one penny. In fact, even that was too expensive for
many of the day labourers who were displaced by the railway and
few actually were able to take advantage of the offer, but the intent
to help those displaced by the railway was clear.

The work to build the connection to the existing tracks and open three new stations was considerable. Again, there seems to have been no architect involved with responsibility for construction as the design was left to William Baker, the chief engineer of the London & North Western. The opening of the line was delayed by the discovery of large numbers of human remains, thought to be either a plague pit or the burial plots of the old Bethlehem Hospital (colloquially known as Bedlam), which had been nearby.

Once again, the opening of the station was celebrated, this time by a ceremonial breakfast attended by the Lord Mayor and Sheriffs of the City, as befitted its status as a commuter railway for City folk. The railway had three tracks on the viaduct that provided a service for many expanding suburban areas, with four trains per hour to both Chalk Farm in the north and Bow in the east, which for a while continued as an almost circular trip to Fenchurch Street. Soon services to Richmond, Kingston, Kensington, Willesden Junction and Watford were added. There were a few main-line trains, too, principally to Cambridge, but for the most part throughout its history Broad Street provided suburban services.

The importance of goods traffic was emphasized by the fact that, despite its location within the City, Broad Street had an adjoining goods depot for the London & North Western. It was at street level below the passenger station and wagons were raised and lowered from the yard above by hydraulic lifts. This ensured that a minimum amount of the very valuable land was taken up and demonstrates that the North London, despite operating in a small area, was very much a mixed use railway, with freight trains being an important component of its services. Broad Street was a great success, with traffic more than doubling within a decade, which led to the station eventually having eight platforms.

Betjeman liked Broad Street, describing it as 'a large and handsome terminus built in the Lombardic style' consisting of 'two two-storey blocks with round-arched first floor windows and tall mansard roofs'.[16] Inevitably, given the Italianate style, between the blocks there was a seventy-five-foot clock tower, decorated with open ironwork and the usual clock, which looked rather misplaced as it was too small for the size of the tower. At street level there were two booking halls and elegant arcaded staircases on either side of the station to reach the platforms, which were protected by a rather plain and undistinguished train shed. Curiously, so taken was the North London with this style of architecture that mini-Broad Streets were built along its line, and various branches, each of which invariably included a vast booking hall, an arcade of shops and, incongruously, a billiard hall.

In its heyday at the turn of the century, the terminus of the North London Railway had more daily train services than Euston and Paddington combined, and was third in passenger numbers of London stations behind its neighbour Liverpool Street and Victoria. That did not, however, save Broad Street, whose use declined rapidly after the Second World War and which, by 1972, was described by Betjeman as 'the saddest of all London stations'[17] and by Jackson as a station where 'occasional trains creep in with an apologetic air'.[18] Part of the train shed was removed in 1968 to save costs and the malevolent intention of British Rail was all too obvious. Aware of the development value of the land, BR deliberately wound down services further, paving the way for closure. In fact, the proposed closure was part of a wider plan by the state-owned operator to shut the whole of the North London line, a decision that was fortunately prevented by campaigners and the efforts of the Greater London Council.

Broad Street, unprotected by any listing and with many of its platforms unused, was not so fortunate and, soon after services stopped in 1986, was demolished to make way for the Broadgate development, which, until the creation of Canary Wharf in London's Docklands, was the capital's largest ever redevelopment scheme. Broad Street's best memorial was the successful soundtrack by Paul McCartney to his terrible film *Give My Regards to Broad Street*, which included a sequence shot in the near-deserted station.

SIX

UPSTAGING KING'S CROSS – OR NOT?

S T PANCRAS IS one of Britain's best-known buildings, certainly its most famous station, with several books dedicated to it. In the words of Professor Jack Simmons, the great railway historian, 'no other building in London, or anywhere else... embodies more precisely the achievement of mid-Victorian Britain'.[1]

It is, in fact, two buildings of contrasting styles, seamlessly blended together. There is the neo-Gothic frontage, including the George Gilbert Scott-designed hotel and clock tower, and the train shed, an engineering *tour de force*, which is the work of William Barlow, the Midland Railway's chief engineer, supported by Rowland Mason Ordish, the structural engineer. Either would feature prominently in any listing of Britain's most-loved buildings; but put together, these two masterpieces ensure that St Pancras is the most famous railway station in the nation and quite possibly the world.

We owe both the existence of St Pancras and its extraordinary monumental scale to the Victorian obsession with competition and the persistent rivalry between railway companies. The Midland, as befits its name, was a provincial railway based in Derby, which had expanded to become the fourth largest in the land. It was a dominant provider of trains between Birmingham and York, served cities such as Leeds, Sheffield and Nottingham, and by 1867 it had reached Manchester. Getting to London, however, was crucial to its ambitions. The Midland spent some time running freight and passenger trains to the city, sharing London & North Western's line into Euston and then, from 1857, Great Northern's tracks into King's Cross from Hitchin. The latter arrangement relieved some of the pressure on the North Western's route from Rugby to London, but it was still totally unsatisfactory. The Great Northern's line between Hitchin and London soon reached capacity, due in part to the Midland Railway increasing its carriage of coal from collieries in the Midlands.

The Midland Railway resented sharing King's Cross with the Great Northern, and the feeling was mutual. Not surprisingly, the Great Northern made sure its trains had priority over the Midland's, whose passengers suffered as a result – even though the Midland was paying £20,000 per year for access to Great Northern tracks and platforms. Matters came to a head in 1862, the year in which the International Exhibition was held in the capital, attracting thousands of visitors. Chaotic scenes were a regular occurrence at King's Cross during the Exhibition, with the Midland's coal-carrying freight trains frequently backed-up, waiting to be unloaded. The company, which had been quietly buying land in the St Pancras area, obtained Parliamentary permission for a fifty-mile line from Bedford through to the site of its planned new terminus next to King's Cross.

It is easy to see why St Pancras had to be bigger and better than earlier terminuses and, in particular, neighbouring King's

Cross. The Midland directors had had enough of being messed about by their rivals and having their own terminus was the only feasible solution. But they would not be satisfied with just another banal station that would soon meld, forgotten and unnoticed, into the hurly-burly of the rapidly developing city. It would have to be very special, a statement of the Midland's importance and a reflection of its status as the most prosperous of the nation's railway companies. The company's share price in 1862, when the decision to build the line into London was made, stood at around 130 old pence. This was higher than any of its rivals, including the Great Northern, which was the second most prosperous with a share value of around 120 old pence.

James Allport, the Midland's general manager, had worked on and off for the company since it was formed as the Birmingham & Derby Railway in 1839. He wanted to see the Midland assume a far greater role in the panoply of railway companies. He had the vision to see through the massive construction programme, which ultimately would take thirteen years to complete and cost £5m, twice the estimate presented in the Parliamentary process. Allport was one of the great railway managers of the era, a true Victorian polymath who later would take the radical step of abolishing second class in Midland's trains and, shockingly, put upholstery in third-class coaches. Simmons described him as 'abounding with energy and ideas, [he was] enterprising, cool-headed, and courageous'.[2]

There were, therefore, three main reasons for the creation of this vast new station, with a bigger frontage and larger train shed than any other at the time: the desire for the Midland to become a national, rather than a regional, railway company; the ability to reach the capital on its own tracks; and, most important, not just to keep up with the Joneses next door but to outdo them.

The route of the line through virgin railway territory between the Great Northern and the London & North Western was pretty much pre-determined. It left the existing line at Bedford, ran through Luton and St Albans to Mill Hill in north London and on to St Pancras. Inevitably, the most difficult and costly part of the line was the last few miles into London.

St Pancras was an obvious choice as the terminus. It was next to Euston Road (still called New Road at the time), which, as we have seen, was the boundary for terminuses decided by the 1846 Royal Commission. It was close to the Regent's Canal and it stood between King's Cross and Euston. However, that didn't make it an easy place to build a huge station. For a start, the area was busy and cluttered. There was a gas works, an ancient church (which gave its name to the station; Saint Pancras was a little-known fourteen-year-old martyr beheaded in 304 AD for converting to Christianity and refusing to perform a sacrifice to the Roman gods) with a large and full graveyard and a series of decrepit slums. Then there was the River Fleet, which had been buried underground in a sewer earlier in the century, but still required very stringent precautions to avoid its noisome contents from spewing out (this did happen during the construction of the Metropolitan Railway in June 1862 and caused a delay to the opening of the line). The Midland had to ensure the river was now completely enclosed, a task made all the more urgent when a cholera epidemic broke out during the construction of the tunnel under the station. Given a lack of alternative sites, Simmons was rather harsh when he wrote: 'If the directors and officers of the Midland Company had pooled their collective experience with a view to securing a site for their London station that would combine the greatest possible number of difficulties, they could hardly have fixed on anything better than the one they chose at St Pancras.'[3]

The first big decision for Allport and his committee was whether to go under or over the canal. At King's Cross, Cubitt had made the mistake of tunnelling under the waterway rather than bridging over it, which, as mentioned in Chapter 3, caused operational difficulties throughout the age of steam. Allport opted for bridging, although that was not ideal either since the platforms at St Pancras are around twenty feet above the level of Euston Road, despite a slight descent south of the canal that later caused a few buffer-stop accidents. However, it was the right decision. The tracks still had to be routed beneath the North London Railway just north of the canal, but if the railway had passed underneath the canal then the tracks would have had to have been at a far lower level, requiring a much steeper gradient than the eventual 1 in 182 to reach the surface at Camden, where soon afterwards they enter the mile-long Belsize tunnel.

The second problem was the Midland's need for a connection with the newly built Metropolitan Railway, which opened in 1863. King's Cross already had one, and it was helping to increase capacity, as suburban services continued through to Farringdon, which meant they did not take up valuable platform space in the station. When a connection between the Metropolitan and the London, Chatham & Dover Railway was made via a bridge at Blackfriars, it opened up various cross-river possibilities and the Midland wanted to ensure it could take advantage of these connections for both passenger and, crucially, coal traffic. Because of the height of the station, the line would have to pass underneath it in order to connect with the Metropolitan. Its construction proved controversial as it involved digging up a corner of the graveyard of

St Pancras Church. The contractors initially paid little heed to the human remains, some dating back to the Early Middle Ages, with discarded bones taken away by feral cats, who soon found a new home in the vaults of St Pancras. According to the eminent railway historian C. Hamilton Ellis, writing in 1953, 'their descendants live in the precincts and catacombs of St Pancras quite wild, slayers of rats, eaters of mice and therefore welcome as permanent guests'.[4] Open coffins were seen in the graveyard and the vicar's complaints about skulls being heedlessly scattered about were reported by the press, causing a huge furore.

In response, the Midland employed a well-regarded architect, Arthur Blomfield, to ensure the excavations were carried out more diligently. One of the young men appointed to oversee the work was the novelist and poet Thomas Hardy, whose subsequent writing was undoubtedly influenced by this grisly task. Eight thousand bodies were moved, either to other parts of the cemetery or to new ones at Highgate and Kensal Green; some were even repatriated to France. Simon Bradley, in his monograph on the station, recounts how some of these bones belonged to French Revolutionaries and religious leaders, exiled following the 1789 Revolution and now on their way back to their native land. He notes the irony when this process had to be repeated in the early twenty-first century to enable St Pancras to be repurposed to take on Eurostar trains: 'So the bones of revolutionary and archbishop, with other jumbled skeletons English and French, have been re-exiled to a suburban cemetery in order to speed the journey between Britain and France.'[5]

Once construction of the terminus began in 1866, a great wave of evictions was necessary. Seven streets were demolished, as well as a new church, St Luke's, which had to be rebuilt in Kentish Town at the Midland's expense. St Pancras was responsible for more evictions than any other of the main-line stations, with an estimated 10,000 people displaced from very poor housing with no compensation and barely a few days' notice. They crowded into adjacent slums, such as at Camden Town or Covent Garden, or in workhouses like Cleveland Street, which was notorious for male prostitution, just south of New Road.

Press coverage of both the failure to properly exhume bodies and the misery caused by evictions damaged the Midland's reputation, eliciting much opposition not only among local people but in Parliament. A contemporary historian of the local parish, Frederick Miller, reflected a wider antagonism towards the behemoth: 'The railway is no respecter of persons, living or dead... in disturbing the remains of those who had been interred in the "sure and certain hope of a glorious resurrection", the feelings of survivors have been shocked, and their faith in such institutions almost destroyed.'[6] This was by no means trivial. Railway companies were dependent on societal goodwill and this antagonism could not have happened at a worse time. After a long period of boom following the recovery from the railway mania of the 1840s, a major financial crisis hit the railways in May 1866, triggered by the collapse of the merchant bank Overend, Gurney – an important funder of railway projects. The bank rate soared to 10 per cent, a crippling level for potential promoters of rail projects, and several major companies such as the London & Brighton, the London, Chatham & Dover, the Great Eastern and even the Great Western either went bust or teetered on the edge of collapse. Sir Samuel Peto's successful railway contracting company, responsible for some of the best-built lines in the country, also failed.

Together with the simultaneous spread of the worst cholera outbreak in the capital since 1854, it was not a propitious time to build London's most prestigious and expensive railway station. As Simmons observes, 'it heightens our appreciation of the grandeur of the building... to realize that its serene self-assurance represents an act of unshaken faith, carried through resolutely in conditions of anxiety, and at times of real danger, until it reached its appointed end'.[7] Note, too, that its construction was entirely funded and built by the private sector, in contrast to today's megaprojects, which are invariably funded by the state. This was capitalism at its most raw and daring. Fortunately, the contractors chosen by the Midland directors, Waring Brothers, were reliable, well resourced and able to help the Midland weather the storm. Demolitions continued apace, a financial crisis was averted, and the site was cleared by June 1866.

St Pancras could have been very different but for Burton beer. Barlow's first plans for the station were for a double or even triple span roof for the train shed; he envisaged filling the space underneath, created by the need to run the tracks over the canal, with spoil from the tunnels.

Fortunately, in the figure of James Allport, the Midland had both a commercial genius with great business acumen and someone with a thorough understanding of engineering. It was a combination that proved vital over the next few years. The son of a Birmingham small arms manufacturer, Allport had worked in the railways for thirty years but was still under sixty and had a youthful exuberance for innovation. He realized that there was more money to be made by retaining the vaults rather than dumping spoil in them. In order to best exploit this basement space, a series of 688[8] iron columns, rather than brick piers, were used to support the station with its platforms and tracks. The columns supported a grid of 2,000 wrought-iron girders, which in turn held the iron plates used as the base of the upper deck. The spacing between the columns was carefully calculated to allow the unrestricted passage of the barrels of beer that were the mainstay of the station's freight business. This resulted from Londoners' newly discovered thirst for the fine ales produced in Burton-upon-Trent in Staffordshire, close to the heart of the Midland Railway's network. According to Simon Bradley, the author of a biography of St Pancras, 'the soft water and improved brewing techniques there allowed the production of a clear and stable brew very different from the capital's darker and cloudier stouts and porters'.[9] He adds that this change in taste was largely responsible for the replacement of traditional pewter mugs with glasses, as the Midlands beer was stronger and consequently risked dissolving the pewter, which was partly made of lead. There was a wagon lift at the canal end of the station to carry wagons down to the vaults and railway tracks to allow them to be moved around. This trade, requiring several daily trains, continued to flourish until a decline in the run-up to the Second World War and it ceased entirely in the early 1960s when lorries took over.

The decision to use the vaults had a major impact on the design of the station and led to the creation of one of its notable features, the single span roof. The big advantage was that, unlike at earlier multi-span stations such as Paddington where the columns limit the flexibility of the space, a single span roof avoided the need for columns rising from the undercroft, which would have reduced the amount of usable space at both the platform level and below. Moreover, such columns would have required extra-strong foundations, presenting difficulties in the spaces directly above the tunnel created for the link to the Metropolitan Railway.

Barlow realized that the huge deck being created above street level would effectively act as a horizontal tie holding in place the massive 245-foot span roof and making the concept feasible. Although this would increase the budget and nothing like it had been attempted before, Barlow's brave decision to go ahead with the revolutionary design resulted in the creation of the world's largest single span building (only three subsequent train sheds exceeded the width of the span at St Pancras, all in the United States and none higher than St Pancras's 105 feet). This provided freedom of movement throughout the length of the near 700-foot-long station, which was effectively totally open plan; there was an added advantage, as smoke from the trains dissipated in the shed's airy vastness. The walls were purely decorative as the support came from twenty-five huge arched ribs, each weighing fifty-five tons and just under thirty feet apart. That distance was determined, yet again, by the size of the beer barrels as it was exactly twice the distance between the columns below in the undercroft.

Building the shed was relatively uncomplicated, despite its groundbreaking design and sheer scale. The construction was achieved through the raising of a massive and moveable wooden scaffolding frame, pictures of which survive. Once a section of the roof was completed, the huge frame was moved forward on rails by just a couple of men. To speed up the work, which was progressing too slowly, a second scaffolding was erected in late 1867. Nevertheless, it was not until early 1868 that the first ribs were installed. The whole construction took two years, twice the planned length, but still remarkable given the lack of any machinery. The worst delay, oddly, was caused by a shortage of bricks for the side walls, and although the last ribs were erected in the middle of September, the station still resembled a building site at this stage.

Despite this, the Midland Railway was eager to start running trains into St Pancras to bring in much-needed revenue. One of the scaffolds remained in place, while the other was removed to provide the surface of the platforms, which, as was usual in that period, were wooden. The booking hall and waiting rooms were not complete and temporary ones were hastily put together. Even the side walls were not finished and there were no buffer stops, a rather necessary prerequisite given that the tracks were on a slight downward slope. Throughout the building process, Allport insisted on only the best materials being used, something that has subsequently contributed to the building's resilience. Stone was either Derbyshire gritstone or Bramley Fall stone from Yorkshire, the same quarry that was used for the Euston Arch. Slate was sourced from Wales, and Derbyshire iron was used for the wrought ironwork.

Initially, there were eleven sets of tracks, with those in the middle used, as was usual in those days, to house empty stock. There were initially only five platforms but two more were soon added, a process made far easier by the lack of any supporting columns, showing how the single span roof greatly improved the flexibility of the station.

The metalwork of the roof was painted a dull brown but, under pressure from Allport, who wanted it to reflect the sky, it was repainted light blue, as it was in the twenty-first-century refurbishment. The simplicity of the train shed was in sharp contrast to the Gothic-style station building, with one exception: the pronounced point in the centre of the roof of the shed. However, this may be a coincidence since the station had not been commissioned by the time Barlow designed the shed.

Despite St Pancras's unfinished state, the Midland opted to open it on 1 October 1868. The line to Bedford had long been complete and the company desperately needed income, given the huge cost overrun of its London connection and terminus. It is remarkable that unlike so many other stations and railway lines whose opening was marked with massive banquets and endless celebrations, the first train from St Pancras sped out with no ceremony and very little publicity. That was partly because of the urgency but mainly because the Midland's reputation had been tarnished by delays and, in particular, the issues around moving the bodies in the cemetery. That first train did, though, create a record as its run between Kentish Town in north London and Leicester, ninety-seven miles away, was the longest non-stop scheduled rail journey in the world.

The Midland's focus had been very much on building the line and the train shed, as this was the revenue earner, and little attention had been paid to the rest of the station. Consequently, it was not until 1865 that a competition was held for the design of the station and hotel, and here the company's emphasis on producing a memorable building, to outdo the Great Northern and all the Midland's other rivals, was clear to see.

A dozen architects took part in the contest in the autumn of that year and George Gilbert Scott was chosen as the winner even though his design, at £316,000, was the most expensive and had ignored all the rules. It was bigger and grander than the directors had stipulated – but actually that was precisely what they wanted. Scott was the most famous architect of his age and it was a coup for the provincial railway to employ such an illustrious man. Only two years earlier, he had won the competition to design the Albert Memorial, which was under construction in Kensington Gardens.

For Scott, there was a personal issue, too. He had also previously designed the new government offices that now house the Foreign Office and had chosen a Gothic-style building for the purpose. It was rejected by the Prime Minister, Lord Palmerston, who instead insisted on a more conservative Italianate style. That rankled with Scott, who was a passionate advocate of the Gothic style, and he saw St Pancras as his opportunity to build a huge neo-Gothic building, unconstrained by the demands of government. His masters now were businessmen, intent on upstaging their commercial rivals. More than this, they wanted to establish the Midland as London's most prominent railway and for St Pancras to make the neigh-bouring King's Cross station look 'a very ordinary piece of austere engineer's building'.[10] Scott did not, as has been wrongly suggested, simply recycle his rejected scheme for the Foreign Office, although both were in the Gothic style and asymmetric in conception. Fortunately for him, the decision to choose his design was made a matter of months before the financial crisis caused by the collapse of Overend, Gurney, otherwise a very much more modest St Pancras might be on the site today.

Scott was a remarkable workaholic who produced up to 1,000 buildings – with the help of a team of twenty-five or more staff – in a career spanning nearly half a century. Simon Bradley, in his history of St Pancras, suggests this was made possible because 'Scott seems hardly to have relaxed at all'[11] as his only spare time was spent in prayer and church attendance, a reflection of his lifelong religious devotion which was a key influence in his preference for Gothic. While he had designed many workhouses, prisons, hospitals, colleges, town halls, mansions and even cottages, much of his work focused on churches, both new and restorations. For Scott, Gothic was the only style that was suitable for ecclesias-tical buildings. Gothic was, as it were, God's choice. Scott's initial interest in Gothic stemmed from his early church commissions at a time in the 1830s when, according to Bradley, 'the burning question in church architecture was no longer the choice between classical and Gothic, but how far to reproduce medieval forms convincingly, both in detail and in general outline'.[12]

There were debates among supporters of the Gothic Revival about when the most perfect examples of Gothic architecture were built. The purists decided that the ideal Gothic churches had been built around 1300 and these provided the best blueprint for their work. As the Gothic Revival became increasingly dominant, proselytizers like Scott argued that it was the morally correct form of architecture that went beyond mere reproduction of medieval designs and should incorporate new, post-medieval materials such as structural ironwork. Neo-Gothic, therefore, was even better than Gothic. Not only did it use modern materials to improve building methods, but it adapted them. So, if traditional Gothic was at times small and gloomy, no matter – simply build a large Gothic window. As for the oddity of constructing a public and commercial building in the Gothic style, let it be, Scott wrote in his autobiography, 'on so vast a scale as to rule its neighbourhood, instead of being governed by it'.[13] And in response to critics who thought the style backward-looking, Scott argued he was very much looking to the future: 'Scott's secular Gothic was meant to be flexible and versatile as well as erudite: a go-anywhere style for the modern age.'[14]

In April 1866, Scott's design was accepted by the Midland's directors who only imposed a few modest economy measures, such as reducing the height by two floors of the station offices and one floor from the hotel, which killed off the idea of the Midland moving its headquarters from Derby to the new terminus as there was no longer sufficient space. The clock tower, though slightly lowered, would still be 270 feet high. Even with these reductions, the building would eventually have 500 rooms of which 300 were for guests in the Midland Grand Hotel.

By this time, hotels had become an essential part of any self-respecting terminus. Euston started the trend with its two rather modest hotels, which later merged. Next came the Great Northern Hotel at King's Cross, which was clearly an afterthought. It was an unexciting, spartan building with a curved Regency-style frontage, though it acquired some renown as the setting for the love triangle in Anthony Trollope's *The Belton Estate* (1865). It was designed by Cubitt, with its back to where St Pancras would emerge and separate from the main King's Cross station since there was no way of blending it with the elegant sweeping arches of the main frontage. The Great Northern Hotel cost a mere £30,000 to build, which, as Bradley points out, was a third of the sum splashed out simply to furnish the next-door Midland Grand Hotel nearly twenty years later.

Paddington's hotel, on the other hand, was integrated with the station right from the beginning. When the second – and larger – Paddington station was being designed, the hotel formed the main part of the frontage as the terminus itself was set in a dip. The Great Western Royal Hotel, designed by Philip Hardwick and opened in 1854, had a marked French Renaissance influence and its facilities were very much state of the art. According to Jeffrey Richards and John M. MacKenzie, the authors of a history of railway stations, the hotel's 'external grandeur was matched by an enviable internal efficiency, facilitated by the most up-to-date equipment, including fireproof staircases, electric clocks and an elaborate system of bells'. They go on to point out that the French 'architecture of pleasure' style prevailed in the building of such hotels because 'somehow the puritanical, work-obsessed British associated the idea of "pleasure" with the saucy, sinful Continent'.[15]

The Midland Railway already had experience of hotels since it had built one of the first outside London. The Midland – what else to call it? – at Derby Trijunct station was an elegant red-brick building, modelled on a country house and set in its own grounds with an ornamental fountain in the forecourt. This spacious model was adapted by other companies outside London but was clearly not suitable for the capital where land was at a premium. However, the success of these early railway hotels demonstrated that there was a need to provide a high standard of accommodation to cater for affluent and tired travellers who did not want to go any further than the station after a long train ride. Indeed, as we shall see later, for the remainder of the century, the railways continued to provide quality hotels with excellent restaurants, which helped to drive up the standard of hotel accommodation more generally.

Little work was undertaken on the station buildings before the shed behind St Pancras was completed. Major construction, delayed by the financial crisis of 1866, finally started in April 1867, but progress was fitful. There were a series of disputes between Scott and the Midland when the company wanted to pare back some aspects of the design. Mostly they were minor cuts (it is evident today, for instance, that the niches along the front of the building were designed to take figures that never materialized) and, aside from some furnishings, Scott mostly got his way. Again, as with the shed, there was a lot of attention to the source of materials. The glowing red bricks were from Nottingham and laid with consummate skill while, as described in Gordon Biddle's seminal work on railway architecture, 'the lavish dressings, replete with every kind of adornment, are in different shades of Ancaster and Ketton limestone, red sandstone from Mansfield and grey and red polished granite from Petershead for the shafts and columns'.[16]

With costs mounting, the directors sought further cutbacks and attempted to delay completion of the hotel, leaving the west tower unbuilt. Without it the building would have been lop-sided, according to Biddle, who wrote that it 'forms the dominant feature of the façade, complemented at the east end by the tall, steepled clock tower'.[17]

In the spring of 1872, Scott found an ally in the form of Robert Etzensberger, the newly appointed manager of the Midland Grand Hotel. The experienced Etzensberger, who had previously run Venice's prestigious Victoria Hotel, only took the job on the proviso that the hotel was completed more or less as designed and its upmarket focus retained. The directors relented and the west wing was given the go-ahead. With that hurdle cleared, there was real urgency to complete the hotel by the following spring and consequently it opened its doors on 5 May 1873. The Midland's aim of upstaging King's Cross had been achieved, as Hamilton Ellis described: 'Proudly rose that vast Gothic pile… flamboyant and tremendous beside the Cromwellian dignity of King's Cross next door'.[18] (Not, though, for me, as I much prefer the understated and, as Hamilton Ellis suggests, rather Puritan elegance of its neighbour, which, more than a century and a half after its construction, has much more successfully stood the test of time, retaining a simplicity and modernity that Gothic exuberance could never match. It has the advantage, too, that the arches which prefigure the train shed are not hidden from view by a huge hotel, as at St Pancras, because the Great Northern Hotel was built to the side of the station almost at right angles to it.)

St Pancras's location, set back slightly from Euston Road, allowed Scott to create a ramped approach that today is little used, except by the occasional parked car as no one quite knows what to do with it; taxis use entrances at the side. At the time, however, it provided a wonderful view of Barlow's shed through an arched *porte cochère* fronting the hotel entrance, which was underneath a set of gables and pinnacles apparently inspired by the design of the sixteenth-century Oudenaarde town hall in Belgium. Gothic eclectic might be the best description for it, given there were influences from cathedrals in Bruges, Salisbury, Caernarvon, Amiens, Verona and more. From any angle, according to Gordon Biddle, 'there is a fantasy quality in the pinnacles, turrets, dormers and sheer attention to detail, whether they are stone carvings, brick mouldings or decorative ironwork; the epitome of High Victorian romantic eclecticism'.[19] (In the early 1980s I briefly worked in Camden Council offices opposite St Pancras and wondered how such a wondrous structure could have been allowed to decay almost to the point of collapse. Years earlier, I went to school opposite the almost contemporary and equally extraordinary Natural History Museum, which, in stark contrast, had been lovingly looked after.)

The interior of the hotel was no less opulent. The entrance hall had an ornate carved oak screen, arches, columns and friezes, topped off with a colourful mosaic. A richly decorated grand double staircase led to equally splendid public rooms, which were so spacious, they never seemed crowded even when the hotel was full. The corridors, too, were wide and tall, giving a feeling of relaxed opulence. And there were so many rooms in which guests could spend their spare moments. One innovation was to provide well for 'ladies' who might be travelling on their own. On the first floor, there was a sumptuous and airy 'ladies' coffee room' complete with a billiard table. Its two large windows behind arches were supported by a pair of Corinthian columns decorated playfully in an Arabian style, while at night the gas light chandelier, together with numerous wall lights, made for a cosy but well-lit atmosphere. Adjoining it, there was even a ladies' smoking room, an almost shocking concept given that at the time only ladies of the night were thought to smoke.

C. Hamilton Ellis's description of the inside encapsulates the splendour and the rather pompous air that today might be called bling: 'Glittering lustred gasoliers shed their hot radiance over marble, and heavily gilt plaster, over brocade and buttoned-in velvet. Thousands of feet fell silently in its endless, thickly carpeted corridors, which were suffused by a crimson twilight from half-veiled Gothic windows. The very *necessaria* were splendid in mahogany and decorated Staffordshire ware; the kitchens would have done credit to any royal palace.'[20] As for the exterior, a contemporary edition of *Building News* provides the best description, and attempted to set out Scott's thinking in designing the façade according to a classical hierarchy of decorative features, rather than just providing a mish-mash of random detail: 'We find the simple semi-circular massive ground-floor windows, the ornate, trefoiled, traceried, and cusped first-floor windows, and the two upper tiers of less detail as they are removed from the eye, each designed with reference to their position, instead of, as too often seen, the most elaborate multiplicity placed so far above the eye as to be thrown away.'[21]

Facilities more closely associated with running a railway may have taken second place but had not been entirely forgotten. The spacious booking hall off the main concourse was another example of extravagance with an extremely high, arched roof that could have passed off as a nave in a sizeable church. The wood-panelled ticket office in one corner almost seemed like an afterthought, such was the scale of the room, which received natural light from six pointed arch windows. Passengers waiting to buy tickets could amuse themselves by trying to guess which of the whimsical figures of various key rail workers on the stone brackets was the driver, guard, pointsman or signalbox boy they were supposed to represent. From this hall, several doorways led to the roof-enclosed concourse. Alan Jackson, writing just after British Railways had stopped using steam engines, declares, 'He was a dull man if his imagination was not stirred. For let there be no doubt, St Pancras before the Diesel Age was an experience never to be forgotten. Entering it on a foggy afternoon, the visitor received the full impact of the steam railway, assaulting all his senses at once. Smoke and steam rose slowly to a roof almost out of view, whilst at the far end the atmosphere concentrated to a muddy dark yellow, obscuring the gasometers.'[22] To the ordinary passenger, less enamoured by steam and murk than Jackson, all of this might have seemed a rather mixed blessing, and, as mentioned above, on a good day the scale of the space above the platforms allowed much of the smoke to dissipate.

When fully opened, the Midland Grand Hotel had the distinction of being the most expensive of all the railway hotels, charging fourteen shillings a night for a room, which included dinner and breakfast. Simmons argues that 'for an hotel of this class, the Midland Company's charges were never extortionate'[23] even though little expense had been spared in providing furnishings from Gillow's department store. Following its opening, further luxuries were added to the hotel, such as ten pianos for the drawing and dining rooms from Erard, the renowned Parisian piano maker. The hotel prided itself on maintaining the high standards befitting its architecture as well as catering for all tastes. Memos were sent out regularly to staff to ensure they were up to date with fashions in food and drink. One of these focused on a particular new refreshing drink, Bovril and soda, that was made by putting a teaspoonful of Bovril, which it explained was a 'meat extract paste used as a savoury spread', into a tumbler and then adding the soda.

It is unclear whether anyone actually ordered this strange drink. The hotel was one of the first to install telephones, which, in a novel feature, were specially adapted to allow guests to listen in to London theatre and concert performances.

It was not only beer that was carried by the Midland but a vast amount of other freight, most of which could not be accommodated in the new terminus. A freight station was built on the north side of Agar Town, and although a second building nearby was soon added, the volume of goods arriving in London continued to grow, prompting the search for a much larger depot.

There was an obvious site on the west side of St Pancras and the Midland sought Parliamentary powers to acquire fourteen acres of Somers Town. Unfortunately, the company's unpopularity ensured there was an outcry against the plan, which included forceable movement of a further 10,000 people, albeit from mostly appalling slum housing. This was overcome through an element of quid pro quo; permission was granted in 1876 after the Midland agreed to sell part of the land to build replacement dwellings and an agreement was made with the Metropolitan Artizans' and Labourers' Dwelling Association to erect homes to rehouse some of them, though there is no firm evidence that this actually took place.

Work was slow to start after the land had been cleared, which led to further questioning of the Midland's intentions, but eventually construction on the huge site began. It was screened from public view by a three-quarter-mile-long elegant wall round the whole site, using unusually small Leicestershire bricks set in cement, rather than lime, throughout. According to Simmons, 'the delicacy of the pointing and the evenness of the bricklaying were a much admired achievement',[24] and the two-storey building's long set of arches behind the wall, marked at each corner by bigger ones, was, in the simplicity of its design by the Midland's engineer, John Underwood, more a reference to King's Cross than its immediate neighbour. The trains arrived at the upper floor, which was connected to the lower level by a series of hydraulic lifts, similar to those used in the main station to reach the vaults below. There were special facilities for potato and vegetable merchants, given the proximity of the station to Covent Garden, then the capital's main fruit and vegetable market.

The completion of the Somers Town Goods Depot, which was entirely covered by its roof and was breathtaking in scale, gave the Midland an advantage over the Great Northern whose goods depot at the time was in the open air. At their peak, just after the First World War, before road transport began to eat into the trade, these various depots were handling 2,500 tons of vegetables weekly. Fish was the other main fresh produce, which was sent to London's Billingsgate market (on Sundays, when Billingsgate was closed, it was sold from counters in the depot).

Coal, however, remained the dominant product handled by the depot. When Somers Town was completed, there was a near-continuous ribbon of railway-related structures in a three-quarter-of-a-mile stretch on what in 1857 was renamed Euston Road between Euston and King's Cross. The railway companies, though, were not as dominant and all-powerful in the highly competitive coal business as this might suggest; they were in a constant battle both with each other and, crucially, with coastal shipping, which benefited greatly from the development of more efficient steam engines. In 1867, rail deliveries to London exceeded those shipped to London for the first time, although this was not a conclusive triumph. New steam technology allowed bigger boats to complete the Newcastle–London route in just five days, and hydraulic dockside cranes made loading and unloading more efficient. Sea-borne traders had an added advantage of supplying Thames-side factories and gas works, and consequently they regained their bigger share of the market in the late 1890s.

The railways lost out partly because they were encumbered with old equipment, such as the relatively small coal drops mentioned in Chapter 4, and huge quantities of small wagons. Shorter trains with larger wagons would have increased efficiency but the railway companies' reluctance to invest, resulting from constant competition between them, proved their undoing. As the historians of King's Cross remark, 'the coal trains which rumbled down the main line to London between the wars, and even later, were little different from those which had inaugurated the trade to King's Cross in 1851'.[25] The railways were, as so often in their history, hamstrung by the scale of their sunk investment in a technology that gradually and almost imperceptibly became outdated and in need of replacement. One happy result of this has been the preservation of many buildings in the hinterland to the stations – Coal Drops Yard, for example, was converted in 2019 into ultra-trendy shops and the Coal Office opposite is a high-end restaurant serving Middle Eastern cuisine overlooking the canal and St Pancras station.

Following the completion of Somers Town Goods Depot, no further large-scale changes occurred in the area around the two adjoining stations along Euston Road for almost a century. However, claims by railway companies that slum clearance would lead to an improvement in the surrounding area proved fatuous. While undoubtedly some of the worst housing was eliminated, the overall character of the area was in fact only slightly improved.

The considerable numbers of people displaced by the construction of St Pancras and the adjoining buildings did not simply disappear. Many hung around the area and contributed to the local sense of deprivation. Large railway stations may have been magnets for much economic activity and created thousands of jobs, but their presence also contributed to the deterioration of the area by creating smoke and noise that reduced its desirability. The local supply chain, provided by many small industrial workshops, ensured that those trying to turn the area into a respectable neighbourhood faced an uphill task.

Charles Booth's seminal study *Descriptive Map of London Poverty*, produced in 1889, did categorize a couple of districts to the south of Euston Road around the two stations as 'well to do, middle class' but for the most part the area was characterized, in his words, by 'mixed' and 'poor'. The land clearances had led to the construction of some working-class tenement blocks built by charitable societies, such as Stanley Buildings, which still stands, much refurbished, squeezed between the train sheds of the two stations. There were, though, awful pockets such as Cromer Street, a couple of hundred yards south of the stations, which Booth described as being 'cursed by the street-walking form of prostitution, for which many of the small hotels in the neighbourhood of the railway termini offer facilities'.[26] However, it is only fair to say that these had been red light areas long before the railways were built.

It took a pioneering social reformer to sort out Somers Town, which even in the aftermath of the First World War was still a desperately deprived area. Father Basil Jellicoe, who was the vicar of the local St Mary's Church and the moving force behind the creation of the St Pancras House Improvement Society, wrote at the time of its foundation in 1924: 'Somers Town is really gigantic theft. Overcrowding and poverty are here being used by the Devil to steal from the children of God the health and happiness which are their right.'[27] The construction in the 1920s of the massive Ossulston Estate (built by the London County Council, the forerunner to the Greater London Council) at last created decent housing for local people. However, the prostitutes, the pickpockets and, later, the drug addicts remained in parts of the area until the end of the twentieth century and the subsequent successful redevelopment of both stations and the huge derelict King's Cross Lands behind them.

Somers Town Goods Depot closed in 1973 and was demolished, the result of a decline in freight traffic. Within a decade work started there on the new location for the British Library, another local megaproject whose cost far exceeded its original budget, but which today is also widely celebrated (see Chapter 12).

In most respects, both St Pancras station and the hotel were a success. Despite financial problems during its construction, St Pancras did, as intended, establish the Midland as a major force in the railway industry and its investment soon proved worthwhile. It had been a gamble, though, and one that could easily have resulted in a half-finished building or a major scaling down of the Midland's ambitions for its London terminus.

There were, nevertheless, a few lacunae, particularly with the hotel. There were no en suite bathrooms, just one for each floor, and no heating other than fire grates, which may not have been unusual at the time, but looked out of place by the end of the century and even more so into the twentieth century. Moreover, the hotel proved rather difficult to adapt. Lord Stamp, the president of the London, Midland & Scottish Railway, one of the Big Four that took over the railways in 1923, loathed the station, characterizing it as archaic, and pointed out that 'it is impossible to put in a new piece of heating apparatus or anything of that kind without meeting with the same obstacles that would be encountered in modifying the Rock of Gibraltar'.[28]

Although widely welcomed, St Pancras had its detractors right from the start and their numbers grew over time. It was the ultimate expression of the station cathedral, but did all the Gothic accoutrements really add to its function as a railway terminus? This was a particularly pertinent question since next door there was the most functional and least cluttered station, developed partly out of the need for economy but also because that is what its designer intended. What *ingénue*, when asked, would realize that King's Cross was the older of the two?

Critics of St Pancras, particularly from the Modernist movement that emerged around the start of the twentieth century, bemoaned the fact that so much railway architecture harked back to past styles, rather than developing its own vernacular. Indeed, in relation to the London terminuses, as we have seen, it took time for the railway companies to learn how to provide passengers with facilities needed to improve the 'journey experience', as today's companies would put it.

Having King's Cross as a neighbour was a kind of constant tacit remonstration of the possibility of an alternative, one that was simpler, more elegant and fit for purpose. In April 1872, before the station was completed, the eminent *Quarterly Review* published a scathing critique of St Pancras, as part of a wider attack on the Gothic movement. It highlighted how the fussiness of the design meant 'the eye is constantly troubled and tormented', and suggested that 'the Midland front is inconsistent in style, and meretricious in detail; a piece of common "art manufacture" that makes the Great Northern front appear by contrast positively charming'.[29]

As Bradley explains, for these critics 'King's Cross ticked all the boxes too: form follows function inside and out, materials are honestly and enterprisingly used, and the building was both modern in its day and relevant to contemporary needs.'[30] St Pancras, they argued, was precisely the opposite, and the *Quarterly Review* was in no doubt about who were the culprits – the directors of the Midland who, while they might be good railway administrators, were wholly unqualified to select the design of such an important building in the capital.

Even supporters of Scott question whether the Gothic style was suitable for a railway station. Indeed, one could say the same about the Italianate style that dominated the design of early railway stations but had little relevance for the needs of rail passengers. While great cathedrals like St Pancras demonstrated the confidence of the large Victorian railway companies, they also betrayed an element of timidity. Instead of developing their own vernacular of railway architecture rooted in British culture and better suited to the primary purpose of providing rail travel, the railway companies and, in particular, their architects harked back to the past and to foreign lands. The railways were the very expression of modernity, enabling people to travel further and faster than ever before, yet journeys would begin and end in buildings whose style and structure tended to be rooted in designs that referenced bygone ages. It is difficult to explain this contradiction; it might be that railways simply wanted to reassure their passengers that this modern form of transportation was not quite as revolutionary or unnatural as it seemed. Except, of course, it was.

The failure to build a station whose clear purpose was to make journeys easier for passengers would ultimately threaten the very survival of St Pancras. It may have, consciously, been constructed as one of the nation's great buildings but its design was very much influenced by the prevailing fashion of the age – and fashions inevitably change. As Simon Jenkins, in his book on Britain's best stations, notes, 'As for St Pancras's appearance, just as it had been the child of fashion, so it fell victim to fashion.'[31]

By and large the station thrived until the outbreak of the First World War but thereafter its fortunes were mixed. In the interwar period, the criticisms of St Pancras were reinforced by the deterioration of the station. Just as Scott's favoured style of architecture was falling out of favour, St Pancras itself was beginning to suffer from its inherent design defects. Between the wars, patronage of the hotel fell sharply due to the lack of modern comforts, and in 1935 when it closed, part of it was taken over by the London, Midland & Scottish to use as offices. There was worse news on the horizon. At the same time, the London, Midland & Scottish published a scheme to rebuild Euston and it was suggested that this was part of a wider plan to close St Pancras. This came to naught, as did a plan mooted in the war to cut the number of London terminus stations to just four, with Euston, St Pancras and King's Cross merged as a single station on two levels.

The creation of British Railways in 1948 did nothing to revive St Pancras's fortunes. Much of the main hotel was unused, and even those parts functioning as offices were fitted with awful temporary dividing walls that damaged many of the original fittings. In 1966, British Rail, as befitted its new name, sought to distance itself from the past as so obviously represented by the huge Gothic terminus at St Pancras and planned to pull down the building and merge rail services with King's Cross. However, the preservation movement that had unsuccessfully tried to prevent the demolition of Euston was now far stronger thanks to a shift in public opinion. In the context of a wider move against Modernism and Brutalism, and with the awful example of the soulless new station at Euston dubbed by Betjeman as 'disastrous and inhuman',[32] St Pancras itself was now seen as a great example of Victorian architecture and, once again, considered to be a masterpiece.

In 1968, British Rail retreated and abandoned the closure plans; but for many years St Pancras was a little-used station, running services to only a few Midland destinations. In 1988, most of its suburban services were lost when they were diverted to Moorgate and, later, to Blackfriars with the reopening of the Snow Hill tunnel under the City of London. When I worked opposite the building in the 1980s, watching old curtains fluttering in the wind, and pigeons happily roosting in the former servants' quarters on the fifth and sixth floors, it seemed like it would remain forever as a testimony to the past glories of the railway age that would never be regained. Then came Michael Heseltine and Eurostar (see Chapter 12).

SEVEN

SOUTHERN
INVASION

APART FROM THE London & Greenwich and its associated
railways based at London Bridge, only one other railway
company, the London & South Western Railway, established an
early foothold south of the river. It started life as the London &
Southampton at the beginning of the railway age and, in common
with the other early long-distance railways into London, the initial
impetus came from promoters with interests at the other end of
the line. London was a commercial magnet whose dominance
was growing as capitalism took hold; therefore establishing good
transport links to the Big Smoke was seen as crucial for any provincial
city keen to promote its economic interests. Even so, Southampton,
without a commercial or manufacturing base, was a surprising choice
for such an ambitious early railway; Portsmouth, just to the east,
was a far more substantial and better-developed port. Opponents,
such as the Surrey Canal Company, disdainfully pointed out that
weekly traffic between the capital and Southampton was catered for
by a mere eight stagecoaches, four wagons and one barge on the
Basingstoke Canal. So why, they asked, did it need a railway?

In putting the case for Southampton, the railway's promoters argued that while Southampton Water was difficult for sailing vessels to navigate, it was ideal for the emerging modern steamers. This was prescient because a few decades later Southampton would become the preferred calling point for transatlantic liners.

The railway was first proposed in February 1831 in a meeting at the home of Abel Dottin, one of Southampton's two MPs who went on to become chairman of the London & Greenwich and had the road outside London Bridge station named after him. Investors were initially wary and it was not until 1834 that sufficient funding had been guaranteed to ensure the Bill would be approved by Parliament. The estimated cost of the seventy-mile line was £900,000, which proved to be about a third of the final amount. As well as persuading local businesses and people to invest, the promoters were very successful in raising capital in the North of England. About half of the initial finance came from backers in Lancashire who had been impressed by the success of the pioneering Liverpool & Manchester Railway and saw railways as offering an excellent rate of return.

Progress was slow, however. The finance raised initially was never going to cover the full cost of building and the promoters had to seek permission from Parliament to raise more. The directors' choice of Francis Giles, an excellent engineer but a poor project manager, to oversee the construction process was a major mistake. Many of the small companies he contracted to build the line struggled in the face of the task and ultimately failed. Giles was dismissed in early 1837 and replaced by Joseph Locke, the engineer of the Grand Junction Railway, the line that had linked with the London & Birmingham, and who had learnt his trade under the great George Stephenson. The experienced Locke had the right skills to see the project through, selecting more reliable contractors, including the most famous and successful civil engineer of the age, Thomas Brassey. Together they set out a clear work plan that reassured local landowners who, up to that point, had been infuriated by overrunning construction work and continuing disruption along the line.

Another early mistake, prompted by the usual lack of capital, was the choice of Nine Elms as the initial terminus. It was built on a four-acre site just south of Vauxhall Bridge, which had been purchased cheaply because the swampy marshland occasionally flooded at high tide. As a terminus, Nine Elms was better designed than most of the temporary stations built to accommodate the early incursions into London by railway companies. It was a tall, two-storey structure designed by the experienced William Tite, who, as well as being the London & South Western's architect, had also designed the Royal Exchange in the City. The elegant little building was in the usual classical style fronted by a sizeable porch supported by five large arches between two symmetrical rusticated end blocks. Behind the porch, there was a booking office with an open counter and a waiting room leading to the platforms, which, again as usual for the time, were separated between departures on the west side, and arrivals on the east. The platforms were protected by a low wooden roof with three spans supported by cast-iron columns decorated with a leaf pattern.

Nine Elms also had the advantage of being close to the Thames, which guaranteed easy transfer to and from shipping for both people and freight.

Despite these advantages, the remoteness of Nine Elms from the City of London and the West End was a severe handicap. As soon as services began in the spring of 1838, the railway provided a series of small steamboats to run between Vauxhall and London Bridge, creating what today would be called an integrated transport system. There were scheduled departures from the City precisely an hour before every train was due to leave Nine Elms. Horse omnibuses were also provided by the railway company to connect with the West End and other parts of the City, and, as with other stations at the time, there was a special service for VIPs who were travelling in their own private carriages. Several pack horses were kept at the station for the sole purpose of picking up and returning these carriages; a door-to-door service that, including the driver, cost just half a guinea (52.5p) more. As with all contemporary stations, there was comprehensive provision for goods, with a track on the east side of the station leading to a large goods yard by the river bank where freight could be taken on horse-drawn wagons and transferred to and from lighters by a crane. None of these facilities, however, quite compensated for the station's distance from the key central London locations, with the result that the railway company, right from the outset, started looking at alternative sites for a terminus closer to the centre.

Both Nine Elms and the London & Southampton gained rapid notoriety as a result of an unfortunate event within a few days of opening. The first section of line, a twenty-three-mile route from Woking Common to Nine Elms, opened in May 1838. The service included seven intermediate stations, an early indication that the London & Southampton – for all its main-line pretensions – realized that shorter journeys were the more likely source of income. A week after the opening, the annual four-day Epsom horserace meeting was held, which included the running of the Derby, and an advertisement was placed in *The Times* to the effect that trains would be run 'to a point on the railway south of

Kingston which is nearest to Epsom'. Eight special services were
provided but the railway failed to mention that the racecourse
was actually six miles from Kingston station. That omission may
explain why thousands more people than expected turned up at
Nine Elms very early in the morning on the first day of the races,
besieging the little terminus. *The Times* estimated the crowd of
potential race-goers at 5,000 and reckoned there were ten times
more 'applicants' for the seats than the number available, which
inevitably meant most would remain 'disappointed'. The angriest
of these started pushing against the station entrance, which had
been shut to keep them out, and having yanked the doors off their
hinges, swept onto the platform and hijacked a first-class train that
was waiting to leave. It took several hours before the crowd could
eventually be cleared by the Metropolitan Police. Nevertheless, the
London & Southampton had learnt that there was a good market
to cater for race meetings and a few weeks later advertised services
to Ascot via Woking station. It was a tradition that outlived the
various vicissitudes in the history of the railway – and even today
lots of smartly dressed race-goers travel by train bound for Ascot
to avoid the terrible traffic jams leading to the racecourse.

That incident, which attracted considerable publicity, certainly
put the new railway on the map and patronage was strong right
from the start. Passenger numbers built up to 1,000 a day within
the first six months of operation, more than three times the original
estimate in the company's prospectus. The railway even provided
services on Sundays (other early railway companies banned them
on religious grounds), because the directors felt, as they put it, that
they should not prevent the public from enjoying fresh air, exercise
and relaxation on the Sabbath. In fact, they were smart enough to
see the money-making potential of Sunday services, as Londoners

needed little incentive to seek relief from the fetid air of the capital on their only day off work. Interestingly, the railways in the UK are unusual in having separate Sunday timetables, which is not the case with most Continental railways.

The London & Southampton was undoubtedly one of the better-run early railways, with a route that was built to a high standard. John Herapath, the editor of the *Railway Magazine*, then a flourishing weekly publication, remarked on the quality of the railway, emphasizing the brilliance of the locomotives whose performance was 'particularly remarkable by the simplicity and excellence of construction and the ease and rapidity with which they perform their journey, often at the rate of between 40 mph and 50 mph'.[1] This was as fast as any contemporary railway and demonstrated the value of employing a reputable and experienced contractor like Brassey. Helped by the healthy revenues from passenger traffic, and continued good work by Brassey, the line was extended to Southampton in May 1840, with the usual celebrations. A group of directors and VIPs took the train from Nine Elms and three hours later were greeted in Southampton by a twenty-one-gun salute.

Soon after the line to Southampton opened, a branch to Gosport was envisaged and it was at that point that the company's name was changed to the London & South Western Railway. The reason was that while the good burgesses of Portsmouth were delighted that they would have access to the line, they were disappointed that it was being built on the wrong side of the harbour, requiring their residents to reach the line via a ferry trip to neighbouring Gosport. While they could just about put up with that iniquity, later remedied with a new branch into the town itself, they could not tolerate the idea of being served by a railway named after a rival port. Realizing the commercial imperative of attracting Pompey folk, the directors hastily agreed to the change even before the completion of the branch.

Despite the focus of the original promoters on main-line services, it was the short-distance traffic that was to be the mainstay of the London & South Western, both in terms of income and passenger numbers. A branch from what is now Clapham Junction to Richmond opened in July 1846, serving affluent villages such as Putney (where the local shipping company had objected to the proposed railway as the line put its steamers out of business), Barnes and Mortlake. This extension quickly developed into a thriving part of the railway company's business as it soon provided a quarter of its passengers travelling to or from London.

In its advertising, the London & South Western sought to highlight that Nine Elms was about the same distance to the Royal Exchange in the City as Euston was, and nearer than Paddington. It could not, however, disguise the fact that the station was inconvenient for most of its passengers. There were often long queues to catch boats to the City and the road journey was slow because of congestion and more expensive due to tolls. The station's location put off business travellers, and rivals made money operating stagecoaches from the City to some of the areas served by the London & South Western, mostly because passengers disliked having to transfer to and from ships.

A move closer to the centre of London was inevitable and a search, which had started as soon as the railway opened, ended when land in York Road near the south end of Waterloo Bridge was found that was nearly two miles closer to the City. This had, in fact, been the proposed site for the terminus of the Richmond & West End Railway, initially an independent company but which was subsumed into the South Western to create the Richmond branch. The 'West End' part of its name had proved too ambitious as it had to abandon any notion of crossing the river to reach its initial target of Piccadilly in the heart of London.

The Waterloo extension was an ambitious project that required the tracks to run over 290 arches through an already built-up area. Finding a route was difficult as the line had to skirt round an existing gas works and, crucially, avoid Lambeth Palace. More than 700 houses were demolished and the final cost of £1.25m for just two miles of railway and the modest station building represented about a quarter of the company's capital. The task of acquiring the properties was made easier by the fact that the land needed for the extension was almost entirely owned by various arms of the Church, and the ecclesiastical authorities were much more amenable to railways buying their land than the great traditional property owners north of the river. There was, too, much more empty land on the marshy wastelands of the south bank, which had never been developed and was cheaper to purchase as a result. In a canny move, the directors of the South Western insisted the embankment should have four tracks, rather than two, to accommodate future growth, but ultimately even this would not be enough.

The work, which included construction of an intermediate station at Vauxhall, was carried out remarkably quickly. Full Parliamentary permission was obtained in 1847 and within a year trains started running into the new terminus. Such rapid progress was partly due to the lack of any substantial construction at the station itself, which had a frontage but little else in terms of passenger facilities. Waterloo Bridge, the name initially given to the station, was originally designed as a through station with vehicle ramps on either

1. The viaduct built for London's first railway, the London & Greenwich, which runs for nearly 3.5 miles and remains the longest set of arches in Britain.

2. Spa Road, the original temporary terminus of the London & Greenwich Railway, which started operating in 1836.

3. This was the second station built at London Bridge, but this rather pleasant building, which housed trains for the London & Greenwich Railway as well as three other railways, lasted only five years as it was demolished to make way for a larger structure to cope with the rapid growth in passenger numbers.

4. The Camden Town Engine House, which powered the rope used to haul trains from Euston up the incline in the station's early years until locomotives able to do the job were introduced in 1844.

5. The elegant entrance to the Primrose Hill tunnel, seen here under construction in 1837 for the London & Birmingham, was a requirement by Eton College, the owner of the land beneath which it was built.

6. Nine Elms station, which opened in 1838 as the terminus of the London & Southampton, was replaced a decade later by Waterloo. It is now the site of the New Covent Garden vegetable market.

7. (*above*) Bishopsgate, the precursor to Liverpool Street as the station serving East Anglia and originally called Shoreditch, was supposed to be temporary but remained in use from its opening in 1840 until 1875. It now houses Shoreditch High Street station on the London Overground.

8. (*left*) Three railway bridges were built across the Thames in the 1860s to connect new stations with south London. This one, shown around 1880, leads to Cannon Street, with its characteristic two towers that were used to pump water.

9. (*above*) The wonderful clean lines of the two arches at King's Cross were for many years marred by various pieces of clutter at the front as shown in this 1860 picture, less than a decade after its opening.

10. (*right*) Several of the London terminuses were built on the site of slum areas like this one at Somers Town, which was razed to make way for St Pancras and the adjoining goods depot.

11. (*above*) A pair of
moveable wooden frames
were used to construct
the roof of the train shed
at St Pancras, which was
completed in 1868.

12. (*left*) The vaults under
St Pancras were designed so
that beer barrels, brought in
from the Midlands, could
be easily moved around
and, consequently, this
determined the size of the
distance between the columns
supporting the tracks and
platforms above.

13. St Pancras station, which housed the Midland Grand Hotel, c.1880, viewed from the southeast, with the Great Northern hotel, part of King's Cross, on the right. Famously, the clocks of the two adjoining stations never showed precisely the same time.

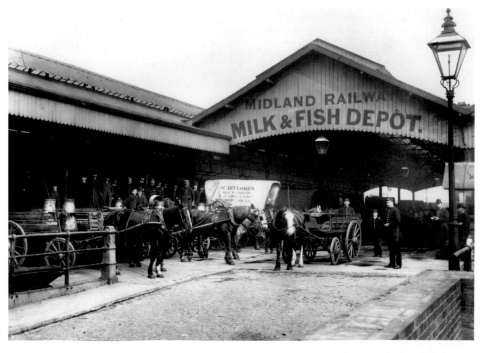

14. Most terminus stations were linked to nearby goods depots where freight was transferred by road or canal to parts of the capital.

15. (*above*) The much-lamented Doric arch at Euston, completed in 1837, served no purpose other than as an expression of the importance of the London & Birmingham Railway, a symbol that the iron road had arrived in the capital.

16. (*left*) The Great Hall at Euston, through which passengers passed on their way to the trains, was built at an inconvenient location and had to be demolished, along with the Doric arch, to allow for extension of the platforms in the redevelopment of Euston during the 1960s.

side. The London & South Western wanted the line to reach either the West End or the City, preferably both. Why bother, therefore, erecting a grand building if it wasn't going to be a permanent terminus?

The London & South Western directors expected to extend the railway to a terminus located on the Thames just south-west of London Bridge, giving much better access to the City.

Indeed, Parliamentary authorization had already been obtained for such a scheme. Therefore the design of Waterloo Junction station included a spur on the western side that was intended to lead to a line under the Thames through to a site just east of Parliament Square, which was being laid out at the time. The Waterloo & Whitehall Railway had obtained Parliamentary approval for a pneumatic railway in 1865 and had begun dredging the Thames just upstream of Waterloo Bridge in preparation for laying prefabricated metal tubes through which the railway would have run. More than £70,000, an impressive sum raised from investors, had already been spent before the company ran into financial difficulties after the collapse in 1866 of Overend, Gurney and the scheme was abandoned. A probably apocryphal tale suggests that part of the trench dug on the north side of the river is now the wine cellar of the National Liberal Club in Whitehall Place.

The London & South Western's misplaced optimism about its chances of continuing further east and north meant that for the rest of the nineteenth century Waterloo Bridge (the name was not changed until 1883) underwent haphazard expansions, earning it the reputation among Londoners of being the most badly organized station in the capital, as well as – unfortunately for passengers – the most heavily used. Initially, there were just four platforms sheltered by an undistinguished roof built in two spans; unlike at the previous terminus stations, they were all used for both arrivals and departures.

There was a modest frontage on Waterloo Road built in the classical style with a main arch and two adjoining smaller ones, and a pediment emblazoned with 'The South Western Railway' as there was not even sufficient room for the company's full name. The plan for the City extension was killed off by a financial crisis soon after the opening of the station, but the London & South Western retained hopes that it would eventually find a terminus closer to the City than Waterloo. While that lingering ambition was partly why it took so long to improve the station, the other reason for the lack of investment in the new terminus was that the financial burden of building the extension had stretched the company's finances almost to breaking point. A small building for offices was erected on the southernmost platform and outside a cab yard and approach road were added to run to the main entrance in Waterloo Road. Further offices were added in the 1860s but there was no clear overall plan and the station was poorly laid out. None of these structures survive as the present Waterloo station was built in the first decade of the twentieth century (see Chapter 12).

Passenger services to Nine Elms ended as soon as Waterloo opened and the station became a freight depot – unusually for the time, Waterloo didn't have a freight depot because access to the Thames was blocked by a brewery. Nine Elms did, like Bricklayers Arms before it, continue to be used by Queen Victoria given its proximity to Buckingham Palace. The station building was badly damaged by bombs in the Second World War, leading to its demolition in the 1950s, and it is now the site of the huge New Covent Garden wholesale market for fruit, flowers and vegetables – all now brought in, however, by road.

The operating procedure at the mouth of Waterloo station was irritating for passengers and added to its poor reputation. In the early days, no trains entered Waterloo with their engines. Instead, trains heading towards the station were halted in the throat just outside where there was a short wooden platform. A railway worker would then attach a rope to the coupling between the engine and the train, and he would stand, perilously, on the footboard of the first carriage holding the other end of the rope. As the engine pulled the train forwards, he would pull the coupling open with the rope, letting the engine run into a siding, while the points would be changed by a signalman to allow the rest of the train into the station where it would be brought to a halt by the guard applying the handbrake. It was ingenious, though cumbersome and dangerous, but allowed the engine, after refuelling and rewatering, to be quickly reattached at the front in order to take the train on its next journey. Equally irritating for passengers was that all trains entering and leaving Waterloo stopped at Vauxhall, a mile away from the terminus, where an army of ticket collectors would go along the train at great haste checking every compartment, which inevitably added to delays. This was made necessary because at Waterloo, unlike most other terminuses, passengers were allowed to enter the platforms and the trains without any prior ticket check.

The first major extension of Waterloo Bridge was a small adjoining station completed in 1854 whose purpose can be gleaned from the name of the organization that built it, the London Necropolis Company. London had long faced a growing problem over what to do with its dead. No extra space had been allocated in the capital for graveyards and the consequence was horrendous. Graves had to be constantly reused with bodies crammed into them and the previously buried corpses being exposed and scattered over the ground. There was even a macabre trade in second-hand coffin wood, which was used for household fuel in poor neighbourhoods, and many tons of human bones were shipped out of the capital and crushed to be used as fertilizer in the North.

The simmering crisis came to a head in 1848–9 when a cholera epidemic resulted in nearly 15,000 extra deaths, in addition to the capital's normal annual total of 50,000. In the wake of a public health campaign, the London Necropolis Company was established by Sir Richard Broun and Richard Sprye, two entrepreneurs with railway connections, to create a vast 2,000-acre cemetery near the village of Brookwood, twenty-five miles from Waterloo on the Surrey–Hampshire border. It would, they said, be sufficient to cater for London's needs for the next 500 years (indeed, my mother who died in 1999 is buried in the Swedish section there). The only feasible way that the bodies could be taken there from London was a one-way trip by rail. The cemetery was near the South Western main line at Woking where a branch led to two newly built stations – North for Nonconformists and South for Anglican. Later a special station, Brookwood (Necropolis), which still had separate sections for the different religious denominations, was built on the main line.

At the London end, there was a small three-storey station just off Westminster Bridge Road designed by William Tite, who had also been responsible for Nine Elms. Oddly, there were two sizeable living rooms on the ground floor intended for a caretaker. On the intermediate floors, there were separate entrance halls, mortuaries and waiting rooms for different classes of funerals and at the top, which was on the same level as the railway, there was a group of eight first-class waiting rooms, toilets and the private platform. A lift for the coffins, worked by a powerful steam engine, linked all the floors.

Great efforts were made to ensure that the mourners and the deceased were kept out of the view of the other passengers using Waterloo Bridge, whose numbers had soon grown to more than 10,000 per day. A private access road enabled the hearses to be unloaded in private and for mourners to arrive at the station without having to encounter other passengers. There was even a separate exit into York Road, which meant hearses did not have to reverse. While the mourners were kept discreetly away from the rest of the station, the purpose of the building was in no way disguised. Quite the contrary. Over the main arch, 'Cemetery Station' was emblazoned on a wooden board and when a bit later an office block for the company was built on the side of the main entrance, above the windows on the various floors there were large inscriptions that read respectively 'NECROPOLIS', 'Brookwood cemetery', 'funerals furnished' and 'central offices'. The company's badge was even starker, featuring a skull and crossbones, surrounded by a rather happy snake eating its own tail. The trains were divided into three classes and, indeed, segregated for different religions and even denominations. The first funeral train ran to the cemetery in November 1854, and the first people to be buried there were stillborn twins born to a Mr and Mrs Hore of Borough.

The train service built up quickly to one per day, carrying up to forty-eight bodies in what later was known irreverently by railway workers as the 'Stiffs Express'. The process of organizing the train and ensuring mourners were placed in the right carriages was a complex affair. Those attending a first- or second-class service were each allocated their own waiting room, while the third-class mourners were put in one large waiting room on the first floor. Many of the latter were relatives and friends of people who had died in workhouses, hospitals and prisons, as several of these organizations had contracts with the London Necropolis Company to handle all their deceased. Then, each party would be called through to their own separate compartments on the train to which, at the back, were attached the hearse vans for the coffins whose class determined the level of ornamentation on the train's compartment doors. The London Necropolis Company prided itself, according to one of its brochures, that its arrangements kept classes separate: 'the funeral trains draw up alongside the 1st class Waiting Rooms and Mourners pass straight into the reserved carriages'.[2]

The company had hoped there would be at least two trains per day and passive provision was even made for the possibility of a third, but, in fact, apart from the odd special, there was only ever a daily train and the company never achieved its hoped-for level of service. In the best year of business, it only carried 4,100 bodies, an average of just a dozen a day and fewer than 10 per cent of deaths in London, suggesting that its hopes of dominating the capital's funeral market never materialized.

The train left London every weekday at 11.35 a.m., taking just under an hour to reach the cemetery. There was a slightly earlier service, at 11.20 a.m. on Sundays, which was a strange provision since at the time several train companies avoided running on what were the church hours and few people chose to have funerals on the Sabbath. The Sunday train was dropped in 1900, but otherwise, for the most part, there was a daily service from the inauguration of the operation in 1854 until the 1920s, and thereafter, broadly, one every other day until 1941.

Remarkably, for all but the last couple of years of the service, the fares remained the same as this had been specified in the Parliamentary Act that established the railway. First-class passengers paid six shillings (30p) return while in second and third the fares were three shillings and sixpence (17.5p) and two shillings (10p) respectively. There was, too, a differential rate for coffins, starting at two shillings and sixpence (12.5p) for a pauper, increasing to five shillings (25p) for an 'artisan' and £1 for all others. Chaplains and other ministers of religion travelled free, as did any officers of the Necropolis Company. The fares were so much cheaper than the normal ones charged between these stations that, according to John Clarke, the author of the history of the Necropolis Railway, 'many avid London golfers, suitably disguised as mourners, used to travel by the Necropolis Train to play at one of the nearby golf links, and save on their railway fares at the same time'.[3]

Numerous famous people made their last journey courtesy of the London Necropolis Company, notably Friedrich Engels, the founder, with Karl Marx, of communism, who died in London in August 1895. After a service with around 150 people at the Necropolis station, he was taken by train to Woking where he was cremated (as Brookwood did not have a crematorium) and his ashes scattered later at Beachy Head. Oddly, Karl Marx's daughter, Eleanor, who died three years later, was also taken by the company to be cremated at Woking. Probably the best-attended funeral was that of Charles Bradlaugh, a Liberal politician and noted atheist who had supported Indian independence. When he died in 1891, an estimated 5,000 people, principally from the Indian subcontinent, including the twenty-one-year-old Gandhi, were taken by the Necropolis Company for his burial at Brookwood.

The original Necropolis station was demolished at the end of the nineteenth century when London & South Western finally decided to replace the ramshackle Waterloo with a station befitting its status as London's busiest (described in Chapter 11). The old Necropolis station was collateral damage, as it stood in the way of the new buildings. That, however, was fortuitous for the London Necropolis Company, which negotiated an excellent deal with its bigger neighbour. The London & South Western had to provide not only a new – and larger – station at its own expense, but also a new train, £12,000 compensation for the loss of the old building and a 999-year lease at a nominal rent on its new building. Moreover, mourners were to be allowed to return from Brookwood on any London & South Western service for the price of their outward fare.

The new Necropolis station was a pleasant, narrow four-storey building in a classical style with Ionic columns linking the first and second floors under an ornate arched roof. A curious circular entrance was big enough to allow a horse-drawn hearse to be driven up an incline to reach a driveway and the platforms. While the lower levels contained mortuaries, offices and workshops, the top floor was adjacent to the company's private first-class platform and contained the '*Chapelle Ardente*, the special chapel which provided a private resting place for coffins in the most ostentatious surroundings'.[4]

There was a second platform for the third class, linked to a smaller building on the other side of the tracks. Therefore the two classes (there was no second-class accommodation) were completely separated, except that all the hearses had to go through the entrance at 121 Westminster Bridge Road where the station building survives today but with nothing to reveal its origins. The station was rightly described by a contemporary newspaper as 'probably unique, comprising within its walls a Railway Station, a Private Chapel, Mortuary Chambers, Waiting Rooms, Offices etc. The whole of the panelling of the various apartments for the use of Mourners together with the stairs is of English oak, while the furniture and the decorations are of special design. The Chapel is sumptuously, and artistically furnished, and has an oak catafalque in the centre, and oak stalls for the Clergy and congregation.'[5]

This station, apart from the four-storey building on Westminster Bridge Road, was obliterated in a bombing raid in April 1941 and it was only then that the funeral trains, which had continued in the early months of the war, finally ceased. The London Necropolis Company considered rebuilding it after the war but decided that this type of service, facing so much competition from road transport, was now 'obsolete'.

Seeing the early success of the London Necropolis, the ever-entrepreneurial Great Northern set up its own funeral business. The company found a large 150-acre plot of land at Colney Hatch, the site of a huge lunatic asylum, and teamed up with the local landowner to create the Great Northern London Cemetery Company. This new venture deliberately targeted the lower end of the market, charging just six shillings (30p) to carry a coffin, and a return fare of one shilling and sixpence (7.5p) for each mourner for the six-mile journey from King's Cross to the cemetery. Burial, too, was cheaper, at around half the £1 charged at Brookwood.

The funeral train service began in 1861 and ran along a new branch line to East Barnet Lane station where there were waiting rooms and chapels beside the cemetery. At the London end, a special station was constructed in a building separate from the rest of King's Cross just off Maiden Lane (now York Way). Called Great Northern Cemetery station, it included a spire and Gothic arches, as well as a morgue. A lift carried the coffins up to the platform but the facilities for mourners were nowhere near as comprehensive as those at Waterloo. The service was not a great success; it never ran more than two trains a week and as a result was loss-making for the Great Northern. The company, ever businesslike, withdrew its support, the service was scrapped and the stations at both ends demolished. The vast cemetery, however, remains to this day.

In 1866, just to make things more complicated, Waterloo acquired a third station, Waterloo Junction (now called Waterloo East), which was built as a through station by the South Western's rival, the South Eastern Railway, whose trains ran on to the newly opened Charing Cross (or later to Cannon Street). This provided a gateway to the West End and the western side of the City for the large numbers of commuters arriving from south London and Surrey. But rivalry between the two train companies meant journeys were not as smooth as they could have been. While the stations were connected by a short footbridge, the London & South Western and the South Eastern could not agree on joint ticketing arrangements, forcing passengers transferring between the two to queue for a second ticket. It was a typical example of how bad relations between railway companies inconvenienced passengers and added to the cost of their journey. Oddly, though, the London & South Western enjoyed far better relations with the London & North Western, which started a service between Waterloo and Willesden Junction via Addison Road (now Kensington Olympia) – an excellent way into the West End and the western side of the City – creating a rare link between the rail networks on the two sides of the river.

Expansion at Waterloo continued apace and soon it had more platforms and ran more daily trains than any station in the UK. Each new group of platforms was named, like the station itself, in honour of great military triumphs and as a celebration of Great Britain's Imperial power, then at its height.

In 1878, for example, two new platforms that were officially known as 'South Station' were soon being called 'Cyprus Station' to mark the fact that the island had become a British colony in June that year. The next group of six, which were used for services to Richmond and Windsor, became known as 'Khartoum Station', a rather strange choice given it marked the massacre in 1885 of British and Egyptian troops in Sudan. Effectively, these new sections operated as separate stations rather than as an integrated whole creating yet more inconvenience for passengers. In the mid-1880s, two office blocks were built at the entrance on York Road on land cleared of around 400 small houses that were occupied by an estimated 2,000 people, about half of whom were rehoused in tenements provided by the railway company, demonstrating that the neighbourhood around the station had remained poverty-stricken and squalid despite its heavy use.

There was no disputing the fact that Waterloo, with all its messy additions, was a terrible muddle despite – or maybe because of – the huge numbers using the station. The fundamental problem was that the London & South Western took a long time to accept that Waterloo was as far as its trains would go, as the twin barriers of the River Thames and the recommendations of the Parliamentary Commission made it difficult, if not impossible, to get closer to the centre of London. Although, as we will see in the next chapter, no fewer than three stations were built on the northern bank of the Thames, each served by a railway bridge across the river, Waterloo continued to serve a large swathe of south London and places further afield, which had rapidly growing numbers of commuters and their families. The London & South Western Railway's success at building new routes serving this region was the reason why numbers into Waterloo kept on growing.

As a result, Waterloo grew far faster than any other London terminus. As early as 1861, there were 114 trains arriving every day and this rose to 350 over the next twenty years, disgorging around 50,000 passengers a day (though barely a fifth of today's total). Thanks to an 1890 article in *Titbits* magazine, a popular weekly that specialized in providing technical information in a readable form, evidence of how busy the station was at the time is available in great detail. The magazine reported that, as well as the trains, 740 (horse-drawn) omnibuses and 3,480 cabs per day served the passengers using the station. There were animal, as well as human, passengers, too. With so many race meetings in the area covered by the London & South Western, there was a regular traffic of up to five trains per day made up entirely of horseboxes that were sent to various stations serving racecourses and stables.

Although Waterloo was primarily a passenger station, freight deliveries had to share the same platforms because, as we've already seen, there was no separate goods depot, and more than 3.5 million gallons of milk went through the station annually – in precisely 220,779 churns according to *Titbits*. The magazine also informed its readers that there were 2,760 gas burners or lights, which consumed 47.5 million cubic feet of gas to keep the station lit, though by all accounts it was still a gloomy place, with countless eerie dark passages lined with bare brick walls. The Lost Property Office was extremely busy, handling 23,158 items in 1890, sixty-three per day.

There were eighteen platforms, served by the four tracks – expanded to six in 1892 – leading into the station and, as a result, delays were frequent, especially when there were breakdowns or poor weather. Platform numbering was a great source of annoyance for passengers, because of its inconsistency. While some numbers referred to a platform face – for example, 3 and 4 would delineate the separate tracks accessed from the same platform – on several others only the platform itself would be numbered and therefore passengers would not know from which side their train was departing. Just to add to the complexity, since the various sections of the station were treated as separate, known officially as North (Khartoum), Central and South (Cyprus), two of them had platforms numbered 1 and 2. The confusion was so notorious that in Jerome K. Jerome's popular 1889 comic novel *Three Men in a Boat*, the intrepid threesome turn up at Waterloo looking for a train for Kingston and are so bemused that they only manage to reach their destination by bribing an engine driver to divert his train. More seriously, poor management of the station was in evidence when large and regular contingents of soldiers heading for Southampton Docks during the Boer War of 1899–1902 added to the chaos.

By 1884, all the terminus stations north of the river, except Fenchurch Street, were connected to the Circle Line, giving their passengers an easy way of continuing their journeys. By contrast, Waterloo had no underground connection and its link with the West End and City, Waterloo Bridge, was a permanent bottleneck. About a quarter of the daily 50,000 people arriving wanted to reach the City, and while the South Eastern took in about half of them, the rest had to struggle onto the slow and overcrowded omnibuses or simply walk. On two occasions ambitious plans were put forward for an overhead railway, like the one along the docks in Liverpool that opened in 1893, but the idea was rejected as too expensive. However, to accommodate this affluent and crucial clientele, London & South Western decided to back the construction of a subterranean link with the city, a concept that had been mooted for some time.

The first Tube line, the City & South London running between Stockwell and Bank, had opened in 1890, showing that the concept of a railway dug deep down under London and powered by electricity was viable. The proposal for the Waterloo & City line, which was built by a company whose board was dominated by London & South Western Railway directors, was approved in 1893 and opened five years later. It became London's second Tube line and was the only one that remained as part of the railway network when British Railways was created in 1948, and did not become part of London Transport until it was eventually absorbed in 1994. Known colloquially as 'The Drain' because of its notoriously leaky tunnel, the one-and-a-half-mile line runs between Waterloo and Bank station in the heart of the City with no intermediate station. Because of the spread-out nature of Waterloo station, from one side it was reached by a long incline that was so steep that the railway company sanded it in wet weather to prevent people falling in the Stygian gloom.

There was, too, better news in 1906 when the Baker Street & Waterloo Tube line was opened. This had its origins in the defunct Waterloo & Whitehall Railway and its various successors, none of which saw the light of day. It had, though, taken thirteen years for it to be built since the passage of the Parliamentary Bill authorizing the line was delayed by numerous difficulties. There were both financial and technical difficulties, and it was only when the scheme was taken over by the Underground Electric Railway Companies of London, controlled by the brilliant but mysterious Charles Yerkes, that funds were found to complete the line, which, with connections through to Piccadilly Circus, Oxford Circus and Baker Street, immediately proved its worth. Bakerloo, an obvious conjunction of the line's official name, was first put forward by an *Evening Standard* headline writer and, despite some misgivings from some of the more puritanical members of the public concerned about the slightly risqué aspect of the name, was soon adopted officially by Yerkes's company.

All these various additions and new connections were not enough to solve Waterloo's fundamental problem. Hamilton Ellis's description of the station was apt: 'the old outfit was getting lumpy like a diseased potato'.[6] By the end of the nineteenth century, it was, in Alan Jackson's words, 'an untidy and confused collection of platforms, passages, stairways, cab yards and offices, the despair of any stranger'.[7] It had to go. Reluctantly, the directors of the London & South Western realized that there was no alternative to building a new station that would be far more efficient for both passengers and train services, but it would take a decade into the new century before Londoners benefited from this decision.

EIGHT

THE THREE
SISTERS

IN THE SPACE of the first six years of the 1860s, another short railway boom saw the construction of three major stations in remarkably quick succession. Built by rival companies on the north bank of the Thames, they all served south London and its hinterland via new bridges over the river. The 1846 Commission had been a modest attempt to coordinate and rationalize London rail services; this spate of building, however, was the ultimate expression of Victorian laissez-faire economics, which resulted in London having the most terminus stations in the world. The spur to the creation of these new terminuses was, as ever, the desire of the railway companies to bring services as close as possible to the centre of the capital, particularly to the City and the West End with their potentially huge passenger markets. These invading forces, however, rarely acted in concert but, rather, were ever eager to do each other down, and establish a dominant position or, more important, at least ensure none of their rivals did so.

This new mini railway mania, which was largely concentrated in the capital, was sparked by Parliamentary authorization being granted to the initial section of the Metropolitan Railway, the world's first underground line, running from Paddington to Farringdon. This was seen as an important development in opening up parts of London and consequently triggered a renewed interest in railway building in the capital. Suddenly, all kinds of proposals to build lines, many in breach of the restraints imposed by the Commission in 1846, were being brought to Parliament. A terminus at Victoria, which effectively became two adjoining stations, another at Charing Cross and a third at Cannon Street were all approved by Parliament during a hectic three-year period from 1858. Overall, there were proposals for some 219 railways within London and its environs in the 1860s, covering a total of 882 miles, a ratio which reveals that the majority were for short connecting links between various existing lines. Not all these lines were authorized, let alone built, but several important routes in the capital including the Great Northern branches to Barnet, which is now part of the Tube, the South London line from Bermondsey to Battersea via Brixton, and extensions to the Great Eastern and the North London date from this period. By the end of this mini-mania, today's London rail network was nearly all in place.

This spate of railway development did not meet with universal approval. The most controversial aspect was the construction of a key link over the Thames through Blackfriars. The first section of the Metropolitan Railway completed in 1863 had its terminus at Farringdon, which could also be reached by Great Northern services running underneath King's Cross station. The London, Chatham & Dover, whose services at the time terminated at a station called Blackfriars, which – unlike a successor of the same name – was on the south bank of the Thames, saw this as an opportunity to run services further north using the Metropolitan's tracks.

Amazingly, the Chatham obtained Parliamentary authorization to build Blackfriars Bridge and to run a line to Ludgate Hill, a few hundred yards further north, which opened in the summer of 1865, and the following year the connection with the Metropolitan was completed, giving London its first north–south connected rail route. This was a controversial development not just because it breached the boundary established by the 1846 Commission, but, even worse, the new line wrecked one of London's most iconic views, St Paul's looming over the rest of the City as one descends Fleet Street from the west.

The damage to the cityscape appears to have been spotted too late, only eliciting protests after the ugly railway bridge at first-floor level, cutting the view of the cathedral from the west in half, had been erected. Somehow, the Parliamentarians who had given the go-ahead for the line seemed to have missed this aspect of the scheme. It was only when the trains started running along the track, belching out smoke, that Victorian environmentalists seemed to have cottoned on to the damage. One contemporary critic did not hold back, saying the bridge 'has utterly spoiled one of the finest street views in the metropolis; and is one of the most unsightly objects ever constructed, in any such situation, anywhere in the world'.[1] *Punch* magazine took up the cudgels, saying, 'St Paul's had best be converted into a terminus. What else will it be fit for when every railway runs right into London?'[2]

These were influential voices that formed a backdrop of constant and at times successful opposition to railway projects. *Punch*, first published in 1841, was a constant thorn in the side of the railways, exposing rightly the sometimes shady dealings of railway managers and owners, and attacking their poor safety record. Above all, though, *Punch* 'denounced them [the railways] for their destruction of ancient buildings and damage to the countryside'.[3] The outrage at the construction of the line ensured that any further attempts at linking lines through central London, proposed by several companies, would never see the light of day. In fact, given the rules set by the 1846 Commission, the fact that this connection between the Metropolitan and the Chatham was ever built is remarkable. Perhaps Parliamentarians recognized its importance as the only main-line link between the networks of north and south London and they were justified when it played a key role in the two world wars carrying troops and freight through the capital.

After the line opened on New Year's Day 1866, the Chatham made good use of this new route. Frequent passenger and freight trains ran through to Farringdon via a short tunnel and there were even services that continued on to the Great Northern's tracks north of King's Cross. Indeed, the Great Northern and the Midland also made use of the new line, resulting in the establishment of all sorts of interesting cross-London connections such as Herne Hill to King's Cross and Barnet to Victoria.

After being closed in the 1960s and reopened in 1986, today this route through the City is a key part of the very busy Thameslink service. However, the bridge blocking the view of St Paul's was, fortunately, demolished when the reopened line was routed through a cut and cover tunnel.

It is worth noting that Ludgate Hill, St Paul's, Holborn Viaduct and Blackfriars were, at various times, all terminus stations in the City, although none are today. Situated just over the bridge, Ludgate Hill was the initial terminus for the London, Chatham & Dover's services from the South but only for a few months. It had four platforms and, according to the *Illustrated London News*, had 'no great pretensions to dignity of style, but it presents a lively appearance, with its turrets in each corner, and its decorations of parti-coloured brickwork above the arched doorways'.[4]

Once the through line was complete, many of the Chatham main-line trains terminated and started at Holborn Viaduct. This equally modest station had six short platforms with each one only capable of taking a half train length. It opened in 1874 to relieve congestion at Ludgate Hill and operated services to Kent, including some that connected with ferries, notably to Vlissingen in the Netherlands (oddly anglicized as Flushing). The frontage consisted entirely of a hotel opened three years later, and though run by a separate company, it was so well integrated with the station that hotel guests found it hard to find the entrance.

After the closure of the Snow Hill tunnel, which was directly below the station, in the First World War, Holborn Viaduct principally served suburban traffic. It was, though, never a popular terminus and its use declined between the wars and after the Second World War, during which the hotel, then being used for offices, was obliterated by a German bomb. As passenger numbers continued to fall, the station lost its train shed, which was replaced by a nasty plastic canopy. British Rail had long failed to see the advantages of cross-London links but suddenly changed tack as a result of the intervention of Ken Livingstone, the then leader of the Greater London Council, and decided to reopen Snow Hill. That sounded the death knell for Holborn Viaduct, which closed in 1990 and was replaced by the nearby through station, City Thameslink.

St Paul's, which was called Blackfriars after 1937 and was located near the present site of the recently rebuilt station of that name, was both a through station and a terminus, with three 'bay' (dead end) platforms on the side. It was a small and rather mean terminus, which is all that the permanently struggling Chatham could afford.

Jackson describes it rather cruelly: 'In pink-red brick, it huddled apologetically against the viaduct [Blackfriars Bridge], trying hard to look dignified by displaying stumpy towers in each corner'.[5] Oddly, the frontage featured a rather random and eclectic set of the names of fifty-four towns and cities across the world that could somehow be reached from the station, though some, such as Brindisi, St Petersburg, Basel and Geneva, would have needed rather more than one train to reach whereas others, such as Westgate-on-Sea, Chatham and Crystal Palace, were, effectively, just a few miles along the tracks.

The station could, though, boast one proud innovation. The three bay platforms were fitted with what the company called 'hydraulic buffers of enormous resisting power'. This was claimed as a new development that would prevent any damage to the station, even if a 200-ton train were to crash into the buffers at 10 mph; of course, they have now become standard at terminus stations and bay platforms across the world. The opening of the station in 1886 was timed to coincide with the completion of a new Blackfriars railway bridge as the original proved to be unable to deal with the heavy loads crossing it. The current bridge, which incorporates the second railway bridge, now has platforms along its whole length, which were built as part of the Thameslink programme in the 2010s.

Of far more lasting significance than these lost terminus stations were the other three incursions across the river, ending at Victoria, Charing Cross and Cannon Street stations. Victoria, the first of these to be authorized by Parliament, was a good example of how railways developed in this period. Its genesis is a complex story involving half a dozen competing railway companies that sometimes cooperated on mutually beneficial projects, but inevitably eventually fell out.

The station's origins can be traced to the support given by the London, Brighton & South Coast Railway for a line built by a new company, the West End of London & Crystal Palace Railway, to a terminus called Pimlico. The destination accounts for the rather fanciful 'West End' in the company's title, although the terminus was actually located on the south side of the river adjoining Chelsea Bridge, overlooking Pimlico on the north bank. Pimlico station, which opened in 1858, had all the hallmarks of a temporary structure, as it was made of wood and had no facilities for passengers. The intention was always to build a bridge over the river, a plan devised by yet another railway company, the Victoria Station & Pimlico Railway. Like the 'West End', it was effectively a front company for the London, Brighton & South Coast, which provided nearly half the capital needed to build the bridge together with a short line north of the river.

The route of the railway was over the defunct Grosvenor Canal, part of the old Chelsea Waterworks, which meant that the land was cheap to buy as it had long been unused, and a recent Act had banned its use even for water extraction. The owner of nearly all the required land, including the canal, was the Marquess of Westminster, who unusually among contemporary aristocrats was supportive of railway projects. Perhaps he recognized that the character of the area was changing anyway from a purely residential zone to one that included shops, offices and businesses. Or more likely he was suffering a temporary cash shortage. The proposed new terminus was just a stone's throw from Buckingham Palace and was at the western end of the recently created Victoria Street, which gave the station its name. This was almost in the West End, as defined at the time as the boundary of London's built environment, and definitely closer to it than any other station until the opening of Charing Cross a few years later. There were three other railway company backers, which each had an interest in having access to the new terminus, even though they already had their own – the Great Western, the London, Chatham & Dover and the London & North Western. While they cooperated to see the Bill authorized in Parliament, they soon argued over how much access each would have in the new terminus.

The Act to build the line was quickly obtained even though it breached the 1846 Commission's recommendations. Belgravia and Pimlico had recently been laid out with the elegant and spacious houses, backed by mews for the horses, that still dominate the area today, and having a station on their doorstep was seen as advantageous by some of the affluent new residents. Others, however, worried about the smoke and noise emanating from the railway, and during the Parliamentary process the railway company had to agree that the track should be shielded from local residents by a large glass and steel roof enclosing much of the track on the north bank of the Thames. These influential Nimbies also managed to ensure that the sleepers on which the rails rested were cushioned with rubber in order to reduce the noise of the passing trains, that no goods trains would call at the station and even that shrubs would have to be planted on the approaches to the bridge, which was required to have aesthetically designed parapets.

John Fowler, one of the most eminent engineers of the day, who would later go on to design the Forth Bridge, was chosen to oversee the work despite the fact that he was simultaneously in charge of building the first section of the Metropolitan Railway a couple of miles away. Work on the Victoria Railway Bridge, the first dedicated railway bridge across the Thames (it preceded Blackfriars by four years), started in June 1859 and, remarkably, the inaugural train ran over it exactly a year later. Initially, there were just two tracks but, within a few years, four more were added due to heavy use of the line. A century later, in 1968, it was rebuilt with ten tracks, and became the busiest railway bridge in the world with more than 1,000 trains per day.

The cost of the huge train shed required by Parliament in the face of concerns from the residents meant there was no money left over to provide an impressive station frontage – that would only come with a refurbishment of the station and its associated hotel in the early twentieth century. Therefore, apart from Fowler's train shed, which survives today, there was only a wooden frontage and palisade that was meant to be temporary but actually lasted forty years. Designed by the company's resident engineer, Robert Jacomb-Hood, the station was built on the level, not least because raising it on a viaduct like several other terminuses in London would have created more noise for the local residents.

The western side of the station, which was for the trains of the London, Brighton & South Coast Railway, opened in October 1860, four months after the bridge became available. The delay had been caused by concerns from the Board of Trade inspector that the signalling system had not been properly installed. From the outset it was a big station, with seven platform faces and ten tracks under the roof, which, rather than a Barlow-style single span, was supported by the west wall and two rows of iron columns. Conscious of the risk of a derailed train hitting a support, as had happened in 1850 at Bricklayers Arms, one row ran along the middle of the wide cab road in the centre of the station, which was between two platform faces, ensuring that no rogue train could hit them. Having a cab road inside the station was a feature of other London stations such as Paddington and Waterloo and was in fact considered *de rigueur* in all subsequent terminuses to enable convenient transfers for people with large amounts of luggage.

With no notable façade to speak of, the most prominent feature was the Grosvenor Hotel in Buckingham Palace Road. Unusually for a railway hotel, it was built by an independent company with no connection to the railway. Opened in 1862, the 300-room hotel added a touch of architectural merit to the station with its frontage in rusticated stone blocks and carved stonework, though the latter proved an unfortunate choice since the little ledges soon became encrusted with soot from the steam locomotives. The hotel has a strong Gallic style, with its French Pavilion mansard roof, and opposite there is another homage to our neighbours across the Channel with a statue of the Allies' First World War military leader, Maréchal Foch. The hotel's pride and joy was its lift, the first in a London hotel and known by staff as 'the ascending room', which might have been because guests preferred to use the stairs for the descent.

All this was for the London, Brighton & South Coast Railway. Its three railway partners in the enterprise, however, were eager to use the site and received Parliamentary permission for a second station. Although built adjoining the east of the first station, it was separated for its whole length from the Brighton station by a wall and it was operated as a completely distinct terminus. This caused no little confusion among passengers who asked for Victoria station and were unaware which train company served their destination.

The 'Brighton side' was regarded as superior given it was the departure station for many travellers heading for the fashionable seaside resort or to their country homes in Sussex. The London, Chatham & Dover, on the other hand, was used much more by the working class, particularly for dockworkers and merchant seamen travelling either to the East End of London for the docks or Chatham for the shipyard. This subtle distinction clearly amused Oscar Wilde as it was the basis of a humorous exchange in his 1895 play *The Importance of Being Earnest*. The main protagonist, Jack Worthing – aka Ernest – relates how he was found as a baby in the cloakroom at Victoria station, stressing it was *on the Brighton side* in order to try to bolster his credentials as a gentleman, only to elicit a famous putdown from Lady Bracknell, who was never going to be won over: 'The line is immaterial.'

This second station, which opened in August 1862, again had no features of note, being constructed in yellow brick with stone facings, and was described by Jackson as 'plain, even severe, in appearance'.[6] The entrance was in Wilton Road, where the Chatham, which had at last obtained its much sought-after terminus, quickly erected a series of office blocks to cement its presence. Given its initial heavy use by all three railway companies, the station was soon extended and by 1869 had nine tracks and nine platform faces. While the second station was primarily for the use of the London, Chatham & Dover Railway, the Great Western and the London & North Western both ran services from Victoria to a variety of destinations. After crossing the river, they made use of the other new bridge over the Thames at Battersea and junctions on the West London Railway to connect with their respective main lines. Therefore, while the station was oriented to the south, passengers from Victoria could reach destinations to almost all points of the compass but may have been deterred by the fact these trains had to cross the Thames twice, which made for a slow trip. The Great Western started running services as soon as the Battersea Railway Bridge was completed, running to Southall in west London, Slough, Reading and, later, even Bristol and Birmingham. As the

Great Western was still using the 7ft o¼in gauge that Brunel had supported, the easternmost platforms on the Brighton side of Victoria had a couple of platforms with tracks that could accommodate both its trains and those using standard gauge.

The London & North Western, which had contributed to the construction of Battersea Bridge, only ran trains in a circular route using the West and North London lines to reach Broad Street via Willesden Junction. It is doubtful if anyone would have chosen such a convoluted way to travel between the West End and the City. These strange roundabout services were part of a wider battle between these companies, which were all trying to establish supremacy on certain routes ahead of their rivals. Skirmishing like this was largely a waste of time and money; most circuitous services were quickly withdrawn through lack of patronage, although a few survived until the First World War when there was a rationalization of the railway timetable. On the face of it, none of the investments towards the construction of Victoria by railway companies, which were already well established elsewhere in London, seemed to make sense. Their interest can best be explained by that ever-potent force, rivalry. They were testing the water, assessing whether there might be scope for takeovers that could result in rapid expansion. However, Board of Trade wariness of mergers between major railway companies and the failure of most of these services meant that the railway companies' expansion plans were not realized, and their money was lost.

It was not long before a second terminus obtained a foothold on the north bank of the Thames, stimulated, as ever, by competition between the main railway companies in south London. This was Charing Cross, a bare mile and a half to the east of Victoria and built by the South Eastern Railway, the third major force in south London railways other than the two main users of Victoria, which had long sought to reach the West End. And unlike any other railway company, it did.

The South Eastern had discovered that more than half its passengers arriving at London Bridge were heading for the West End, which, with no Underground as yet, entailed a slow journey on the crowded roads. The company had long wanted a more convenient terminus than London Bridge, which was fine for the City but too far from the West End. It was not unusual for people to spend as much time getting from London Bridge to Trafalgar Square on crowded and unsavoury roads as their train journey had taken from distant parts of south London or even beyond. When the Chatham obtained permission to build Victoria, the South Eastern tried to acquire running rights into the station. However, the Chatham had already agreed to share the terminus at Victoria with the London, Brighton & South Coast Railway and the two combined to reject any attempt by the South Eastern to muscle in on the site.

Reaching the West End, however, was only part of the South Eastern's ambitions. The company also sought to improve its access to the City with a station at Cannon Street, via a new bridge across the Thames. This would provide a connection for South Eastern services at London Bridge with terminus stations in both the City and the West End, as well as with a through station next to Waterloo station, the aforementioned Waterloo Junction. The South Eastern managed to achieve all of this in the 1860s, which, together with the opening of Victoria by its rivals, represented a massive increase in railway capacity in the capital and created a series of overground rail links between these various stations in the heart of London.

After being rebuffed in his request to make use of Victoria, Samuel Smiles, the secretary of the South Eastern, looked at four possible sites for a West End terminus, including a couple in Battersea, south of the Thames, and two on the north side, Pimlico and Hungerford Market in Charing Cross. In a booklet published to raise capital for the venture, Smiles made it clear in a thorough – and for the time incredibly sophisticated – analysis of the market that Hungerford Market was the preferred option because of its potential to attract various types of passenger. Dismissing the Battersea options because its population 'is almost entirely composed of the poorest classes', he also rejected Pimlico as too affluent since it 'is inhabited chiefly by the more aristocratic classes, who, as is well known, travel by railway at certain stated times of the year only', by which he meant for holidays and trips to their country houses. Charing Cross, on the other hand, would be perfect. The booklet cited the imaginary case of a father whose wife and children lived in Reigate, Dorking or Tunbridge Wells for the benefit of country air and how the siting of the new terminus would allow him to travel with ease two or three times per week from his permanent residence in Oxford Street or Regent Circus.

The West End at the time was not merely a place of entertainment as it is today. It had a sizeable resident population and was slowly becoming gentrified as its worst slums were being cleared for new roads and railways. Therefore, Smiles argued, 'a central West End terminus would be of much convenience to the highest classes of society – the nobility, the gentry, members of Parliament and their families, who principally reside at the West End of London – by enabling them to arrive in town during the season, and to leave it when it is over for their residences, or for sea-bathing quarters, or for the Continent'.[7] Like the Chatham, the South Eastern ran train services to connect with ferry services to France, and it was desperate to offer its international passengers a more convenient terminus than London Bridge. The competition was so intense, both companies would try to ensure that their passengers reached Dover ahead of the other. According to a contemporary local paper, 'idlers' on the pier at Dover would place bets on whether the train from Charing Cross or from Victoria would arrive first out of the tunnel near the entrance of the station.

The choice of location for Charing Cross station was made easier by the fact that Hungerford Market was in decline, making the land cheaper. Stallholders in this traditional market dealt in fresh produce that, as well as fruit and vegetables, included fish, which could be brought in directly by the fishermen from the wharf below. Housed in a relatively new building designed by Charles Fowler, who was also the architect for the market at Covent Garden, Hungerford Market was connected to the south bank by a suspension bridge for pedestrians built by Brunel. Famously, it is thought to be the first place in the UK where ice cream, produced by an Italian stallholder, Carlo Gatti, was sold. Fowler's building was damaged in a fire in 1854 and the market was struggling in the face of competition from Covent Garden and Billingsgate, which made it an ideal site for the purposes of the South Eastern.

Authorization for the near two-mile connection from London Bridge across the Thames to the new terminus was obtained in 1859 by the Charing Cross Railway Company, again essentially a front for the South Eastern. The line curved to the south-west to avoid Southwark Cathedral, which required using a small corner of the grounds of St Thomas's Hospital. Although this was a tiny parcel of just one sixth of an acre, this purchase was to prove costly for the South Eastern because the governors of the hospital were able, under the provisions of the Act enabling the construction of the line, to compel the railway to buy the whole of the hospital and its associated grounds. Rejecting £20,000 which the South Eastern had offered for the small piece of land, the hospital sought to obtain £750,000 (equivalent to around £100m in 2020) for the whole site, but after arbitration had to settle for £300,000, still a taxing amount for the railway.

To accommodate the new tracks, London Bridge station had to be partly demolished and a railway viaduct built above, creating a station on two levels, only the upper part of which was a terminus. The tracks through Southwark and Lambeth, by way of Waterloo Junction towards Charing Cross, were, as had become usual, built on a set of 190 brick arches. Again, a heavily built-up area of rookeries had to be demolished, displacing a couple of thousand people, as well as some 7,000 bodies from the burial ground of St Mary, Lambeth, which were taken by the London Necropolis Company to Brookwood.

Hungerford Bridge built across the Thames to reach Charing Cross station was another monstrosity. Brunel's footbridge was removed by the railway company, which sold the chains and ironwork to be recycled for the celebrated Clifton Suspension Bridge in Bristol. Designed by the South Eastern's engineer, Sir John Hawkshaw, Hungerford's over-engineered lattice iron structure was in a style known as 'pony truss'; it gave the appearance of being designed by a short-sighted ten-year-old with a Meccano set. The ironwork, which to make matters worse was painted in red oxide, was so heavy and thick that trains passing along the bridge almost disappeared from view. The arched brickwork support on the central supporting pier did little to improve the appearance of the bridge as it was equally banal and leaden. The bridge's only redeeming feature was its utilitarian functionality. It carried four tracks, which proved essential for the density of traffic. Adjoining it were the narrow footpaths on each side that replaced Brunel's far more appealing footbridge, a legal requirement that the railway was forced to provide and did so grudgingly, charging users a halfpenny to cross the river. Perhaps the bridge's enduring quality was its solidity since it remains in place today, thankfully shielded now by elegant new matching independent suspension footbridges on either side; a Millennium project that greatly improves the riverscape in this area popular with tourists.

Hawkshaw's train shed at Charing Cross was rather better but, as we shall see, would suffer a disastrous fate. It was high, an impressive 100 feet above the rails, and topped by an arched roof that made it appear enormous, especially when viewed from the opposite bank. The roof, together with the similar one he built at Cannon Street, was described by a contemporary writer as 'colossal sheds of stations… that mar the river's banks, that soar and project like Brobdingnag poke-bonnets'.[8] However, their high roofs did the trick, helping to keep the stations free of smoke and soot from the steady flow of steam locomotives in and out of these riverside stations. In fact, at dawn in the winter months, thanks to the proximity of the Thames, the station was often wreathed in fog that lingered long into the day and caused considerable operational difficulties as trains moved very slowly while fogmen sat feeding braziers lit next to the tracks to help the drivers see their way through.

As the station was built on an incline rising from the river, there was plenty of space in the arches underneath, which was long used as cellars for wine merchants. There were half a dozen platforms as well as the customary cab road and a small concourse overlooked by a large clock on the inner wall. Agreeing to meet people 'under the clock at Charing Cross' became a music hall joke with a louche undertone. The *Railway Magazine* commented that 'half feminine London used to wait there at night for its young man, and the other half said that was who it was waiting for'.[9] Apparently, when Cannon Street opened in September 1866, this second group of women discovered that the first-class compartments of the trains between the two stations provided an ideal and cheap venue, at a fare of only sixpence (2.5p), for a 'quickie', as the journey took seven minutes and the windows had excellent blinds. Unfortunately, though, once the stop at Waterloo Junction, which opened in 1869, started being used on most journeys, the number of drawn blinds on these trains noticeably declined. They would easily have found elsewhere to go, however, as the area around Charing Cross was not salubrious and had long been a red light district. Rudyard Kipling lived nearby on his return from India in 1889, attracted by the low rent and cheap eateries in Villiers Street alongside the station, which inspired him to write his first novel, *The Light That Failed* (1891), a story of unrequited love.

Charing Cross was planned as an international station from the outset. Therefore, at the end of the westernmost platform, there were facilities for customs, including a room for searching baggage and accommodation for customs officials that featured a bedroom and sitting room for the chief officer. These amenities were needed for checking passengers on the boat trains from Dover and Folkestone, which, as they were dependent on the tide, could arrive at any time of the day or night, and gave an international flavour to Charing Cross with signs reading 'Herren', 'Damen' and 'Bagages' prominently displayed alongside their English equivalents. The South Eastern transferred all its international services to the station and Thomas Cook responded by setting up an ornately decorated office, matching the style of the hotel, on the Craven Street side of the forecourt. The South Eastern made efforts to speed up its international services and connections, and just before the outbreak of the First World War, the quickest journey between London and Paris could be made in just six and a half hours.

The rapid connections with the Continent gave Charing Cross a key role in the war. For high-ranking officials, ministers and crucial service personnel, it was the starting point of the journey to France and, if their trip was particularly urgent, they could make use of a special Pullman train that was held in constant readiness for emergency use. In the opposite direction, Charing Cross was the London receiving station for the ambulance trains bringing the wounded back from the Western Front who, thanks to the boat trains, sometimes arrived on the same day as the battle where they had been injured. From the station, they were transferred to the nearby hospital of the same name.[10] After the war and the restructuring of the railways into four big groupings, international services transferred to Victoria, which was by then, like Charing Cross, part of Southern Railway.

The highlight of Charing Cross station was the obligatory station hotel, which in keeping with the fashion of the time was large and luxurious. There were 250 bedrooms in the seven-storey hotel that was spread across a wide French Renaissance-style frontage almost adjoining Trafalgar Square. It was designed by Edward Barry, the son of Charles Barry, the architect for the Parliament building under construction at the other end of Whitehall. Until the 1950s, the outside of the attic rooms and the mansard roof were in the same style as similar buildings in Paris, which gave it a really French flavour, but sadly this was lost when the top floor was rebuilt in a more conventional Georgian style.

Thankfully, perhaps, the interior was not quite as extravagant as the Midland's but, in fact, it was almost equally impressive in a more restrained way, exuding 'a feeling of serious dependability, class and timeless style'.[11] Like the Grosvenor, Charing Cross had a lift, which was so slow it was fitted with comfortable seats. The hotel was such an instant success that a ninety-room annexe, connected to the main building by a footbridge over Villiers Street, was added in 1878 and it contributed considerably to the railway's profitability, earning in the initial years a handsome 20 per cent rate of return on the investment.

The original Charing Cross monument had stood at the top of Whitehall for three and a half centuries, as the grandest of a dozen similar crosses erected across the country by Edward I in honour of his deceased wife Eleanor. The cross was destroyed by the Puritans in 1647 and Barry was charged with erecting a replacement. He managed to copy the design from an indistinct print of the original held in the British Museum, but his effort was actually even grander and more ornate than the original. At seventy feet tall and built from Portland Stone, it is an elaborate monument that stands among the taxis in front of the station but is passed unnoticed by most Londoners and visitors, being rather overshadowed by the hotel itself and Trafalgar Square nearby.

Though well connected to stations on the south bank, the South Eastern was keen to try to improve services to the north by building a direct connection to one of the stations along Euston Road. There were numerous attempts between the opening of Charing Cross in 1864 and the end of the century to connect to the rail network north of London, as its rivals at Victoria and the Chatham at Blackfriars had managed to do. Several schemes even obtained Parliamentary authorization but foundered through a failure to find sufficient investors. The North Western & Charing Cross Railway, a joint venture by the South Eastern and the London & North Western, envisaged a line running between Charing Cross and a newly created junction near Euston, built by the cut and cover method used for the recently completed Metropolitan Railway. Passed by Parliament in 1864, even a guarantee of a 5 per cent rate of return did not convince investors, probably rightly, that it was a feasible proposition given the disruption construction would have caused. Like so many other projects, it collapsed in the financial crisis of 1866.

Next, a similar proposal, the London Central Railway, which this time would have linked Charing Cross with the Midland's tracks out of St Pancras, was authorized in 1871 but the requirement to build new streets on the route of the line and an onerous vibration clause deterred investors. The Euston plan was revived in 1885 but foundered when Edward Watkin, the extremely bullish head of the South Eastern, and Richard Moon of the London & North Western could not reach an agreement over the capital arrangements – even though both railways were prepared to put up £500,000 towards the estimated £1.5m cost. In the event, it was a deep Tube connection, in effect the only realistic option by the late nineteenth century, that provided a convenient link for passengers when the Charing Cross, Euston & Hampstead Railway opened in June 1907. However, unlike the previous plans, there was no rail connection that would have enabled trains to transfer between the two stations and given London a third through route to add to those using the rail bridges at Battersea and Blackfriars.

Looking at these plans from a twenty-first-century perspective, it is astonishing that such schemes were even considered and approved by Parliament, given the disruption they would have caused, and the expense of building them without any state support. Even though they failed, the fact that they came close to being built shows the amazing inventiveness and foresight of the Victorians. There is some parallel with even more damaging plans in the 1960s to build a circular motorway around London just two or three miles from Charing Cross, which were defeated by public opinion and the high cost.

Charing Cross's prestigious location made it the subject of attention, over the years, from envious property developers. Right from its creation in 1889, the London County Council sought for a long period to buy the station and demolish it to make way for a new road bridge across the Thames that would also have linked the northern and southern tramway networks. The Strand would have been widened and a bypass for Whitehall created through the land occupied by the station. The idea was to replace it with a new station on the other side of the Thames, but the cost of the scheme proved prohibitive.

There were continued attempts to demolish the station in the interwar period, even though it had proved its worth during the war. A Commission set up in 1925 to examine various options for new bridges suggested that the station and Hungerford Bridge could be replaced with an even more unsightly double-decker bridge for both road and rail and a new station. While this proved too expensive, a threat hung over the future of Charing Cross for the rest of the decade with a revival of the road bridge plan. Southern Railway, which by then owned the station, had reached an agreement with the Ministry of Transport, which was willing to

pay for 75 per cent of the scheme. However, it was only the reluctance of Sir Henry Cautley, the chairman of the Commons Select
Committee that considered the matter, to agree to a large new
terminus at the bridgehead of the south bank that prevented the
plan from progressing and eventually the Ministry of Transport
withdrew its offer.

An attempt was made in 1936 to revive the double bridge plan
as Southern Railway was anxious to redevelop both the station and
the hotel, but this time it was Westminster City Council and the
Metropolitan Police that combined to prevent the scheme from
being considered in detail. If nothing else, this saga, stretching
over half a century, demonstrates how planning in London for
such big projects is a haphazard process with decisions ultimately
made in an opaque manner by a variety of organizations at both
the local and national level. The very many passengers who today
use Charing Cross for commuting have cause to be grateful for this
rather arbitrary process.

Hawkshaw's roof proved to be less solid than his bridge. Just
before Christmas 1905, work was being carried out to renew part
of the roof when the men on the scaffolding above the station
heard a sudden noise. They soon realized that the enormous
roof was beginning to sag in the middle and started to flee. The
station was hastily evacuated just before a seventy-foot section of
the roof and the huge windscreen at the river entrance crashed
onto the stationary trains below. The side wall on the western side
also collapsed, demolishing the next-door Royal Avenue Theatre.
Thanks to the warning signs, which resulted in a partial evacu-
ation and the fact that the collapse was in the middle of the day
rather than rush hour, only six people were killed. The subsequent
inquiry suggested that the structural integrity of the original roof

was compromised by the failure of a supporting wrought-iron bar. A fault with the initial welding had been exacerbated by the extra weight of the scaffolding that had been erected for the maintenance. The station had to be closed for three months while repairs were undertaken, and an entirely new roof, a simple utilitarian flat design, was erected.

The collapse of the roof did have a fortuitous side effect. The station had been in need of refurbishment and, following the completion of the new roof, the amenities at the station were greatly improved, with the creation of a new large booking hall and waiting room. It also resulted in a better connection with the Underground, which was under construction at the time. Amazingly, the Underground company had been required to pay £60,000 for the privilege of providing the South Eastern with a good connection through a passageway, yet another example of how competition rather than coordination is responsible for the disjointed way the rail network was built in the capital. After the roof collapse and the temporary closure of the station, the Underground company suggested that the forecourt could be dug up and the station built from top down, rather than the other way round, saving money and improving the design.

The third of the South Eastern's ambitions, a City terminus, was already under way while Charing Cross was being constructed. The South Eastern had obtained permission to build a station in Cannon Street, a road in the south of the City that runs parallel to the Thames from near St Paul's to the Monument at the north end of London Bridge. It was the perfect location on the north bank of the Thames overlooking the river, just a couple of minutes' walk from the Bank of England in the heart of the City. It was, yet again, rivalry and, in particular, the Chatham's scheme to obtain permission to cross the river and link up with the Metropolitan that was the spur to its construction.

Inspired by the Chatham's success in obtaining permission for its bridge at Blackfriars, the Charing Cross company, acting on behalf of the South Eastern, obtained Parliamentary authorization in 1861 for a station in Cannon Street. Apart from the bridge, the scheme only needed three quarters of a mile of track running off a junction with the Charing Cross line just to the west of London Bridge and for once there was no need to carry out extensive demolition. The site in Cannon Street had once been a medieval ironworks that had fallen into disuse and there were only a few derelict structures to pull down to make way for what became a very impressive station.

The station, the bridge and the new line were all designed by John Hawkshaw. Work began in the summer of 1863 and took three years to complete. The bridge, a simple structure, was much easier on the eye than the Meccano-set Hungerford. There were no messy girders above the rails and there were, at the insistence of the local authorities, footways on both sides that, for a brief period until 1877, were used by the public for the small consideration of a halfpenny, but were soon needed for extra tracks. On the north bank, the bridge led onto a huge viaduct, consisting of 27 million bricks, to carry the tracks into the station where Hawkshaw's train shed was a 700-foot-long structure covered by an imposing glass and iron roof with a semi-circular frontage between two domed towers. It had no central support span, making it a striking precursor to Barlow's effort at St Pancras, built just a couple of years later.

The towers formed the most notable landmark and were filled with enormous water tanks used to power the lifts down to the vast vaults below, and then for carriage cleaning after electric power was installed. The shed gave cover to the nine tracks and five spacious platforms, as well as the usual cab road. At the Cannon Street end there was an expansive concourse and, typically, a hotel, which was smaller and more modest than any of those at other London stations and may have accounted for its lack of success. Known as the City Terminus Hotel, it had five floors and was 'a high Victorian jumble of Italianate and French Renaissance styles'[12] designed, like the Charing Cross Hotel, by Barry. From the outside it looked rather a mess, with banks of chimneys, mansard roofs in the northern corners, balconies on some of the floors, an Italianate water tower on the south-eastern corner and much artificial stone cladding. The hotel was initially run independently but it struggled and was soon taken over by the South Eastern when the name was changed to Cannon Street Hotel. The accommodation may not have been popular, but its spacious public rooms were well used for meetings and banquets. Indeed, rather better known than the hotel's architecture is the irrelevant but notable fact that a meeting held there in July 1920 set up the Communist Party of Great Britain.

The star turn at the station was the public lavatories, a novel facility for a train station, which were looked upon with envy by rival railway managers. They were, in fact, a great money-spinner thanks to a novel device invented by Joseph Bailey. To prevent the lavatory attendants from pilfering the pennies, he patented a 'registering lock'. When the door was opened by the attendant and the penny entered into the mechanism, it would move a dial half a notch and the cycle would be completed by another half a notch when the user left. At the end of the day the inspector would then be able to ensure the attendant handed over the right money. When Mr Oakley, the manager of King's Cross station, inquired about the system, he was surprised to find that receipts for July 1872 were £58 11 shillings and tenpence – representing a staggering 14,062 passengers caught short, or 453 per day.

On the south side of the river, there was an incredibly complex junction as Cannon Street was effectively at the end of a short branch line but most trains, even the international ones, travelling between Charing Cross and London Bridge called there. Known as the Cannon Street triangle, three lines headed west towards Charing Cross and four went east to London Bridge. Another set of tracks, allowing trains to run between those two stations directly, made up the third side of the triangle. All this was built on arches and out of necessity there were tight bends in order to minimize the land take, which was a major expense. A sophisticated signalling system was installed that was 'interlocked'– a very modern innovation for the time; in other words, the aspect shown by the signals always matched the direction in which the points were set, ensuring that drivers could always rely on a green signal being accurate.

The finished station was a proud addition to the cityscape viewed from across the river. According to Jackson, 'A great train shed yawning over the Thames, high brick walls, proud towers and a wedding-cake hotel across the street frontage combined to give the old Cannon Street a special aura.'[13] Unfortunately, as he pointed out, German bombs and the requirements of longer trains have meant that 'this architectural magic has all but vanished'. Much of the original structure, including the hotel and the original roof, are long gone. Despite this, the station is still recognizable thanks to the two domed towers, even though it now has a backdrop of various oddly shaped skyscrapers due to the massive developments in the City triggered by the Big Bang in the 1980s.

With the completion of Cannon Street in September 1866, the South Eastern had access to four main London terminuses and ran profitable services between them, greatly relieving the local City roads of a significant proportion of their traffic. Nearly all the services from Charing Cross called at Cannon Street and at Waterloo Junction (now called Waterloo East) when it opened, and this local traffic was a useful source of further revenue for the South Eastern. In 1867, the first full year after it started operating, Cannon Street handled 8 million passengers, of whom nearly half were simply travelling between the West End and the City. The number of journeys between the two terminuses on the north bank reduced considerably once the District Railway, which had a station at Charing Cross linked by a passageway from the station, opened between Westminster and Mansion House in 1871, and virtually disappeared once the whole Circle Line – known at the time as the Inner Circle – was completed in 1884 with a stop at Cannon Street, despite attempts by the South Eastern to advertise its 'open air route'.

Regardless of the occasional push to use the station for long-distance services, Cannon Street has, throughout its history, essentially been a rush-hour terminus for suburban commuters, leaving the concourse largely deserted in the middle of the day. In 1878, there were 165 trains entering the station in a two-and-a-half-hour morning peak period, virtually one per minute, which must have made passengers thankful for the high roof and the occasional cleansing breeze from the Thames. A decade later, it was busier still and extra tracks and another platform had to be added.

It is noticeable that none of these three stations built in the 1860s had large associated goods yards. Since they were serving a region south of London, most journeys were short and there was little scope for freight. Even the seaports were modest operations compared with London's docks, where most imports from abroad, as well as coastal shipping from the North, would arrive, and there were few mineral resources in the South to be exploited. Moreover, having a goods station in the centre of London would have taken up large tracts of expensive land. The station on the south bank of the Thames called 'Blackfriars' was later converted to handle only goods after the Blackfriars railway bridge was completed. Consequently, these stations, primarily aimed at south London and its commuting hinterland, focused on the market for short passenger journeys. In this respect they were fantastically successful and adapted their marketing strategies accordingly. In particular, they developed the concept of season tickets, giving frequent travellers considerable discounts. These were available for periods from a week to a year, and the South Eastern offered incentives such as purchasers being able to buy a second 'lady's ticket' for wives, since almost invariably the commuters were men.

However, while comfortable profits were made on the busy lines, these companies had overstretched themselves by building all sorts of uneconomical short connections and lines to less populated areas largely in order to keep rivals off their territory. Thus weakened, embarking on their most expensive projects ever, the construction of huge terminuses on expensive land in the centre of London, was a foolhardy enterprise. These schemes may have benefited Londoners, improving the train services and leaving a legacy of impressive buildings, but few of the shareholders of these companies profited. Indeed, quite the opposite. Most lost much of the money they had put in. The driving force behind the decision by railway companies to build these stations was the fear of losing out to rivals and of being left out, unable to access not just London but other great cities, which also gained numerous large stations during this period as the big companies battled for better access to them.

As well as rivalry, there were other more opaque forces driving this rush to build major stations. There was the continued appetite for aggrandizement by the railway companies, which were the largest capitalist enterprises in the land and wanted people to know it, but one also has to ask who benefited from this spate of grand construction projects? As with today, there was the self interest of construction and contracting firms, run by men such as Thomas Brassey and Samuel Peto, who, together with the managers of the major railway companies and the professionals who helped draw up schemes, formed a 'railway interest' that established itself during the railway mania of the 1840s. It was mirrored in Parliament by a large group of probably around 100 MPs, many of whom had directorships or substantial shareholdings in railway companies. This was a tight-knit band of powerful men who often worked on schemes together and all moved in the same circles, meeting socially or through shared business interests.

After the collapse of the railway mania, fewer private investors were ready to risk their savings on railway ventures. Because of this shortage of capital available from the public, the contractors began to accept payment for their work in the form of shares or bonds, essentially taking the risk from the success of the venture. They also invested directly in proposed schemes. Therefore, as John Kellett, the author of a seminal book on the effect of railways on the development of Victorian cities, puts it, this relatively small group of men had 'all the elements for a powerful lobby, whose prime interest lay in works of demolition and construction' and included 'regiments of solicitors, counsel, and land and law agents [who] all stood to gain from the promotion of further schemes'.[14] Analysis of railway projects shows, incidentally, that lawyers pocketed around 5–7 per cent of their total costs. Added to this group were engineers and surveyors, some of whom earned astronomic levels of fees from railway development. Most notably, John Fowler received £300,000 (around £30m in today's money) for his work on two projects for, respectively, the Metropolitan and District railways. For many of these schemes, it was the contractors, or even solicitors, who originated proposals, rather than the railway companies themselves.

The role of the railways, led by this small elite, in reshaping London cannot be exaggerated. In the 1860s, according to Kellett, 'it is arguable that no other group of men exercised, to the same extent, such a conscious power to alter cities in the nineteenth century'. Local authority efforts to make improvements to slums 'appear by comparison small in scale and dilatory in action'. London was, indeed, the most changed with the construction of these terminuses. Even the building of new roads by the Metropolitan Board of Works 'did not require such extensive uprooting of homes and businesses, or demolition of property, as the railway operations of the 1860s'.[15] This is perfectly illustrated by the high rate of demolitions in this period, which, as well as the new terminuses along the river, also includes the building of St Pancras station. According to the 'Demolition Statements', which were by then a mandatory requirement on the railway companies, there were 37,000 displacements of working-class inhabitants between 1859 and 1867, around half the total forced out of their homes in the whole Victorian railway building period.

The construction of these stations was an enormous burden for the railway companies. Land was obviously expensive; the clearing of existing housing was also costly, as well as being unpopular, and the amount of capital required stretched their finances to breaking point and even beyond. Cannon Street and Charing Cross alone, with their short extensions, cost a combined £4m (around £400m today) and Victoria, which was something of a bargain thanks to the cheapness of the land, £1m including the bridge. Note, too, that by and large the land costs of these companies were less than those of railways operating in the north of London. As we have seen, most of the land they acquired was from the Church, which was a far easier landlord to deal with than the big aristocratic owners north of the river – the Marquess of Westminster being a notable exception. Happily, too, the land south of the river is mostly flatter than the hills to the north, requiring less tunnelling; a considerable saving given it was often the most expensive part of a railway scheme. On the downside, there was the cost of the bridges across the Thames.

The way the money was raised, and the identity of the key investors, was part of an opaque and at times decidedly illegitimate process. The cost of Charing Cross, for example, ended up being three times the capital that was legally raised as the expense was underwritten by contractors. People listed as shareholders who were fronting schemes were often men of straw who had no pecuniary interest and were acting for others. The use of front companies, specially created to build these small sections of line and the terminuses themselves, was another aspect of a process that was far more complex than presented. Most of the money came from sources with a vested interest, such as contractors and solicitors, since by this stage smaller investors were not attracted to railway investments. While ostensibly the companies claimed that their investments would be profitable, they tended to put in massaged figures that underestimated costs – matched by overoptimistic assessments of the likely traffic, a process that is all too familiar to those who analyze today's megaprojects. And these really were megaprojects. The £4m expended by the South Eastern for its two terminuses and their railway connections represented 0.5 per cent of the whole of the UK's annual Gross Domestic Product in the 1860s.

Not surprisingly, these costs together with continued rivalry pushed several of the companies into near bankruptcy, sparked by the financial crisis of 1866 caused by the collapse of Overend, Gurney. The London, Chatham & Dover was the first to get into trouble, going bankrupt in 1866, and had to be refinanced, with the consequent loss for the existing shareholders. The London, Brighton & South Coast, too, teetered on the edge of bankruptcy the following year and emerged only thanks to cutting back on planned extensions and being forced to cooperate with the South Eastern, which also had to reduce its investment projects. The Great Eastern, which was about to embark on the construction of Liverpool Street, covered in the next chapter, also found itself in difficulty at this time, but recovered sufficiently to start work on its terminus in 1870. All these railway companies that were struggling as a result of overreaching themselves must have looked on enviously at the omnibus companies that were competing with them on many London routes and earning decent rates of 10–12 per cent for their shareholders. 'It is tempting to argue,' say the authors of the history of London's transport, 'that the railways bestowed the largest social benefit upon London by enabling it to grow outwards, yet derived the smallest economic reward.'[16]

Indeed, the ultimate cost was heavy. The effective merger of the services of the London, Chatham & Dover with those of the South Eastern in 1899 was an illustration of the weakness of both companies' financial position. Although legally they remained separate entities, the merged operations had a monopoly in Kent and therefore the companies were able to rationalize their services, cutting costs and improving the timetable.

It is quite possible that the railway companies would have done better had they not pushed as far as they could into London. A witness giving evidence to the 1846 Commission was unequivocal: 'Many of the railway companies would be better satisfied to have no more termini in the metropolis, provided all others could be kept out.' However, he pointed out, there was a whole group of professionals whose interests were undeniable: 'I do not know that this applies generally, neither do I think it would be the same with surveyors and lawyers, engineers and architects; they would wish very much to have these stations carried out.'[17] His words were prescient.

There was also a damaging cost to all this concentration on building terminuses as other investment suffered. Hamilton Ellis pointed out that the South Eastern's focus on building its two new terminuses diverted funds from improving its rolling stock, which was 'filthy and poverty stricken'.[18] Nevertheless, the dark and dingy carriages did not stop people from flocking to the railways to use these new facilities. Nor did the extra 'terminal' taxes that some of the companies began to impose on the carriage of goods for journeys that started or ended at these new stations. These were justified on the basis of the extra expense resulting from the construction of these stations, but attempts to impose a similar charge on passengers were blocked by the secretary of the Railway Clearing House, the body that allocated fares between companies when they used a rival railway's tracks.

The overall effect of the establishment of these stations, together with the construction of lines in and around London, which continued apace thanks to the mini railway mania until the 1880s, when today's network was pretty much completed, led to the creation of a commuting culture. The growth this engendered was impressive. While in 1854, walking was still the norm, with around 200,000 people travelling on foot to work every day, and just 6,000 commuters, half a century later, in 1904, there were 318,000 rail commuters. Although many of these were relatively high earners, such as clerks and other office staff, in the east the Great Eastern, which in the 1870s was at last building a station that was more convenient for City workers, set out deliberately to attract a different type of clientele.

NINE

THE WORKERS'
STATION

THE RAILWAYS SERVING the East of England were an impoverished group, not least because the region was poor railway
territory mostly given over to agriculture with a low population
density. The potential for attracting Londoners to make shorter
train journeys had been neglected by the rival companies and they
struggled to establish successful markets for longer journeys. The
biggest of these companies, the perennially cash-strapped Eastern
Counties, had a terrible reputation for poor punctuality and delay.
W.M. Acworth, who wrote an amusing history of the railways,
called it the 'pariah of companies'. He related how 'a strapping 16
year-old' had been refused a child's half-price ticket by an inspector
only to insist 'that he was under twelve when the train started', and
Acworth went on to misquote Thackeray: 'even a journey on the
Eastern Counties must have an end at last'.[1]

Even though the north-eastern suburbs were already more
extensive than those in other parts of the capital, the Eastern
Counties Railway had ignored this potential market for short-distance travel through a policy of running infrequent services

combined with high fares. It was, therefore, little surprise that the Board of Trade, which was generally reluctant to allow mergers of large railway companies, broke with normal practice to wave through the plans to create the Great Eastern even in the face of a wide range of objectors concerned about giving too much regional power to a particular railway company. The main component of the new company was the Eastern Counties but it also included four other sizeable railways and a number of their subsidiaries and associated companies, which did indeed result in the creation of a regional monopoly, an unusual feature at the time.

The decision to build a large station on the edge of the City was predicated on a change of attitude. The Great Eastern would now focus on the commuter market as a route to prosperity. As we saw in Chapter 5, Bishopsgate was an inconvenient terminus, both poorly located and too small, but despite various attempts in the 1850s to find another site, the poor financial state of the Eastern Counties and concern from City interests stood in the way of progress.

That changed quickly once the amalgamation went through in 1862 and the directors examined potential sites for the new station. While the Great Eastern had also taken over a few services that ran into Fenchurch Street, there was no potential for expanding this little terminus nestled in a far-off corner of the City, and negotiations with the North London Railway to make use of Broad Street got nowhere. Finsbury Circus was briefly considered as a possible terminus, as was a site in Wormwood Street, a couple of hundred yards south of the present Liverpool Street station, but both were rejected as impractical.

The only feasible site was on the east side of the North London's terminus at Broad Street, which meant that once again the capital was about to get two adjoining stations run by separate companies and operating to a different set of destinations without any coordination. The large new station just inside the City boundary at Liverpool Street required only a mile of new line but, beset by problems, took a decade to build amid a host of difficulties. The site eventually chosen had once been the gardens of the Bethlehem Hospital, which was demolished in the seventeenth century. The first major decision was to reject the idea of bringing in the line at the same upper level as Broad Street whose tracks ran along a viaduct, but rather to build the terminus at ground level. This idea was favoured as it would enable rail services to connect with the underground Metropolitan Railway, which at the time was still regarded as a way of connecting rail services arriving at the major main-line stations such as Paddington and King's Cross. In the event, the crowded lines of the burgeoning Underground meant the link was little used and eventually abandoned in 1907.

The long delay between approval of the plan for the station in 1864 and its completion was partly due to the Great Eastern's parlous financial state; like so many other railway companies, it nearly went under after Overend, Gurney's collapse. However, progress was also slowed by the need to construct a tunnel under the City streets. In order to bring the tracks down to ground level, the extension had to be built on the steep gradient of 1 in 70 down from Bethnal Green, bypassing the existing Bishopsgate station and then running in a tunnel under Commercial Street and Shoreditch High Street. The sharp gradient for trains leaving the station was, as at King's Cross and Euston, an operational headache, right up to electrification of services in the 1960s.

The Great Eastern's last chairman before the creation of the Big Four railways, Lord Claud Hamilton, was a fierce critic of the layout:

'The result has been a great inconvenience to the travelling public... every one of our heavily laden trains has to commence its journey at the bottom of an incline.'[2] Hamilton blamed the bean counters for the decision not to build a viaduct, which would have required more expensive demolition. The railway managers at the time, he wrote, would have greatly preferred a high-level station but this was vetoed by the directors who had been brought in to rescue the company in the difficult 1860s. They included Lord Cranborne, who as Lord Salisbury would become a three-time prime minister towards the end of the century, and Sir Edward Watkin, who was director of a number of railway companies and the long-time chairman of both the Metropolitan Railway and the South Eastern. Incidentally, Lord Salisbury was in the habit of using a private railway carriage to take him home to Hatfield House, his family seat, from King's Cross after the final Parliamentary business of the day.

For all the cost-saving efforts of the accountants, the line's construction still required the demolition of two major buildings: the City of London Theatre and a large gas works. In addition, 450 tenement dwellings housing 7,000 people were also razed to the ground. Some of these houses were occupied by as many as seven families and were among the worst in the capital. Once again, displaced tenants were given little by way of compensation. The most fortunate received between about thirty and fifty shillings (£1.50–£2.50), depending on family circumstances, while others got nothing and, not surprisingly, most simply decamped to neighbouring slums.

In this case, however, there was something of a quid pro quo, though not one that was of much benefit to those summarily evicted from their homes. As a trade-off, the railway company was required to provide early morning workmen's trains at a discounted fare.

The London, Chatham & Dover had been the first railway company to provide these services, which were written into the Bill authorizing its extension across the Thames to connect with the Metropolitan, mentioned in the previous chapter. The railway company was required to run two services every morning from each terminus on its roundabout route between Victoria and Ludgate Hill via Brixton 'for the exclusive accommodation of artisans, mechanics and daily labourers, both male and female, going to their work or returning from work to their houses', according to the *Illustrated London News*. These were early trains, running at 4.55 a.m. and returning at 6.15 p.m., though when other companies introduced these tickets, the journeys back home in the evening could be taken at any time.

This requirement on the Chatham had been a proviso of the Act authorizing the line and specified the fares and times of the trains. This provision of workmen's trains began to become standard practice when new lines were authorized by Parliament as politicians realized that railways had previously enjoyed far too much leeway over the services they provided. The Great Eastern, fearful it would be forced to rehouse all the people displaced by its extension into the City, agreed to a particularly onerous condition to run workmen's services from Edmonton and Walthamstow to Liverpool Street for a return fare of just twopence – a bargain for round-trips of seventeen miles and fourteen miles respectively. This was an important moment in the history of London and the railways according to John Kellett, as it placed unprecedented obligations on the rampaging railways. He argued it was 'the first major attempt to force a commercial company to offset the social costs incident to an urban terminal scheme by providing… a bulk service at low margins of profit per unit; a significant new development and one which had far-reaching effects upon the growth of later nineteenth-century working-class suburbs to the east and north-east of London.'³

Train services began running from the partly completed Liverpool Street station in early 1874, but it was another eighteen months before the completed terminus was finally opened. The large station was laid out in a kind of L shape on a ten-acre site, with short platforms for suburban trains on the western side and longer, main-line platforms to the east. Passengers reached the platforms via the angle of the L, and the station layout conformed to the idea that arriving and departing passengers, as well as those travelling on the suburban or main line, had to be separated, which was confusing and the cause of much complaint. Both sides of the station could be accessed via ramps from the street, another inconvenience caused by the decision to site the platforms below street level, rather than on a viaduct, as at Broad Street next door.

Due to the odd layout of the station the platforms were covered by a long, high iron and glass roof with two aisles and two naves. The roof was the station's best feature, 'lofty and delicate-looking, it imparts grace to the interior'.⁴ According to the architectural transport historian Oliver Green, 'the great transept over the suburban concourse and main line platforms gave the centre of the station a cathedral-like quality, later enhanced by an elaborate four-faced Gothic clock which hung over the tracks'.⁵ There was another clock, too, over the platforms and both, despite their old-fashioned appearance, were electrically operated.

There were three main buildings at the front, all in an unexceptional French-Gothic style with white Suffolk brick and stone dressings, but the only aspect of interest was the clock tower and its spire. The station suffered from the lack of an architect, as Jackson rather cruelly explains: 'Edward Wilson, an engineer [for the Great Eastern], drew up the designs for the terminus and any architectural assistance was at a humble level. The style is restrained Gothic, seemingly taken straight from a copy book of do-it-yourself architecture.'[6] Wilson was clearly constrained by the Great Eastern's financial struggles, given that the extension had cost £2m, a massive amount for a company that had recently faced bankruptcy. While most of this was spent on engineering, a substantial proportion had to be paid to the owners of the land from which the unfortunate tenants had been summarily evicted at a few days' notice. As with the stations mentioned in the previous chapter, the work was carried out by a front company, the Great Eastern Metropolitan Station & Railways Company.

Although the hotel wasn't opened for another decade, it was worth waiting for. Completed alongside the frontage of the station, it was designed by two sons of Charles Barry, the architect of the Houses of Parliament, in a vaguely French Renaissance style. A later section was added alongside Bishopsgate at the turn of the century (designed by Sir Robert Edis, who was also responsible for the Hotel Great Central at Marylebone). This new annexe made the Great Eastern Hotel the largest in the City of London, with a luxurious style that matched that of its older rivals. Its opulent interior, with much marble and brass on display, included the rococo Hamilton Hall, and the Abercorn Rooms which comprised two Masonic temples – one Grecian and the other Egyptian. The glass-domed restaurant was another notable space as it featured dancing sylphs painted in 1903 by Ingham Bell.

The second section of the hotel was built over platforms 9 and 10, which provided it with a railway-served basement that was used every night for deliveries of food and other supplies. This was part of a mysterious area of the gloomy and grimy station that clearly long haunted the chronicler of London stations, Alan Jackson. He recounted how as a child on his way to visit relatives, he walked through this 'murky and mysterious place where there was an equally grim subway that led to the eastbound Metropolitan platform', and added that he never passed through it 'without a shudder, as both subway and "backs" had entered his subconscious and formed the scenery of many a frightening dream'.[7] He later discovered that there was a train that arrived every night just past midnight carrying ballast for the permanent way, coal and food for the hotel. This 'ghost train', as it was called by the staff, departed carrying hotel refuse and ash from the locomotive coaling bays.

The path to financial redemption for the Great Eastern was through the development of its suburban network. It was no accident that the first trains from Liverpool Street ran to Enfield and Walthamstow, while main-line services continued to operate from Bishopsgate. The opening of the terminus saw a great expansion of suburban services, new lines north of Bethnal Green and a rationalized network with direct routes to places such as Edmonton and Tottenham, and additional branches, notably to Wood Green.

This network was to be the bedrock of the Great Eastern's business since it had little main-line or goods traffic. Services along these suburban lines expanded rapidly as the railway stimulated the construction of housing in much of north-east London. The workmen's trains to and from Walthamstow and Edmonton actually ran on to Enfield Town, eleven miles from Liverpool Street. This led to considerable migration to outer suburbs where cheaper rents made up for slightly higher rail fares. Workmen's trains were soon introduced on other lines and rapidly the character of these suburbs changed. By 1884, 8,000 people per day were going to work on these trains, which was by far the most such traffic of any of the major London terminuses. As with the inaugural Chatham workmen's service, these were very early trains starting at five in the morning to get passengers to work by six.

The general manager of the Great Eastern, William Birt, rather sniffily seemed to deride his own railway's influence when giving evidence to a House of Commons inquiry into housing in 1884. He explained to the MPs about the change that had occurred to the swathe of north-east London covering Stamford Hill, Tottenham and Edmonton:

> That used to be a very nice district indeed occupied by good families with houses of £150 to £250 a year with coach houses and stables, a garden and a few acres of land. But very soon after this obligation was put upon the Great Eastern to run workmen's trains... speculative builders went down into the neighbourhood and, as a consequence, each good house was after another pulled down, and the district is given up entirely now to the working man.[8]

Perhaps his rancour was personal because he had lived there himself and he recounted sadly how he had been forced to move after all his friends and neighbours had gone.

While the Great Eastern complained about its obligations to run workmen's trains, its services continued to expand. Liverpool Street was becoming so busy that what had once been derided as a white elephant, far too large for its requirements, was, just a decade after opening, becoming full. The company chairman quite accurately boasted that the Great Eastern could fill a thousand trains daily in and out of Liverpool Street, but the station could only cope with half that number. The railway began buying up parcels of land between the station and Bishopsgate, which runs north–south alongside the terminus, and in 1890 construction of what became known as the East Side station began. Times had changed, however, and no longer could railway companies simply cleave their way through sections of London with no regard for the local residents, however poor they were. Parliament imposed much more onerous requirements on the company when compared to the construction of the original station. The Great Eastern was forced to provide alternative affordable fixed-rent accommodation for the 1,071 officially displaced people, most of whom moved into new tenement buildings constructed at the railway's expense. Although the Great Eastern had been buying up properties along Bishopsgate for some time, it eventually needed Parliamentary authorization to complete the accumulation of land which was so expensive that it represented two thirds of the £1m cost of the station expansion.

Designed by W.N. Ashbee, the Great Eastern's head architect, the new neo-Tudor-style section marked a move away from the Italianate, Renaissance and Gothic that up until then seemed to be the only styles considered suitable for London terminus stations.

In his book about the station, Nick Derbyshire, British Rail's chief architect who designed the new Liverpool Street station in the 1980s, praised 'the quality of the brickwork and the detailing [which] was of a much higher standard than that of Wilson'. He added: 'there was much carving of stone and brickwork and the office building, Harwich House, built adjacent to the new concourse had attractively carved brick panels, depicting cherubs carrying out typical railway jobs'. The extended part of the hotel was different in style, too, 'more florid and Flemish, and tourelles, turrets and steep gables made their appearance'.[9]

The extra platforms allowed more trains, which were essential, and the new concourse had a more spacious and lighter feel than the cathedral-like older section. The layout, however, meant the station was essentially divided into three sections as the two suburban parts were separated by the longer main-line platforms. In order to make the station more manageable, a high-level bridge was added, but as Jackson writes, 'this main footbridge was by no means straight, none too wide, and at two different levels'.[10] Indeed, I remember using it in my trainspotting days and it was ugly and confusing, and as Jackson says, 'from it many a curse must have been uttered because of it and many a train missed'.

There was, though, one redeeming feature, praised by Jackson: 'three little tea rooms jutted out from it, offering refreshment and relaxation for the weary'.[11] These were, indeed, fine additions that were equally beloved by Betjeman, who wrote: 'I know of no greater pleasure for elevenses in London than to sit in this teaplace and watch trains arrive and depart.'[12] These odd Gothic gazebos were a strange, eccentric even, addition to the station but were famous for the aroma of tea and buttered toast that wafted out of their open windows, mixing with the smoke and steam on the bustling platforms.

The expansion of the station to accommodate eighteen platforms, at the time the most in London, allowed a considerable increase in the number of daily trains. In particular, a new and somewhat superior type of 'workman' was now being accommodated: the clerks and other office staff who had to be in the office by 9 a.m. Their trains were typically a bit more expensive than the earlier ones, costing threepence (1.25p) return between 7.00 a.m. and 7.30 a.m., and fourpence (1.7p) between 7.30 a.m. and 8.00 a.m. As the main employment opportunities in central London shifted from factories and warehouses to offices, these later trains ultimately proved even more popular than the ones aimed at manual and artisan workers. By the turn of the century, while the twopence return workmen's trains were being used by 19,000 people a day, the cheap trains were bringing in 35,000 clerks daily and Walthamstow was being called 'largely the home of the half-fare traveller'. Class restrictions on these trains were relaxed with second class being made available to this huge influx of clerks, but first class, where the seats were covered with oilskins, was reserved solely for women passengers. While there were long-distance expresses to Ipswich and Norwich, and to the Continent via Harwich, commuters accounted for most of the Great Eastern's business. The promise to handle more than 1,000 daily train movements was exceeded by the turn of the century, when there were nearly 1,100 every weekday.

The Great Eastern was able to turn its finances around by becoming 'the Poor Man's Line', as it began to be called. Even though, as we have seen, the attitude of some of its managers towards this growing number of passengers was begrudging, the company did put on extra trains and try to accommodate the demand. This was in stark contrast to the Great Northern, operating from King's Cross, which was much more reluctant to do so but which found itself being forced into making considerable investment. The Great Northern's business model was very different from that of the Great Eastern as its main profits came from main-line goods traffic and, to a lesser extent, long-distance travellers. Consequently, the growth of commuters came as a surprise to the Great Northern, which had done nothing to stimulate the market. Compared with the twopence to fourpence bargains for early travellers on the Great Eastern, commuters from Hornsey paid eightpence in third class for a return journey of just over five miles. Even when

1. Liverpool Street station, seen here around 1885, became the centre of a network of lines used by working-class and lower-middle-class passengers living in suburbs such as Enfield and Walthamstow, which grew rapidly thanks to special cheap services for workers.

2. Paddington, the ultimate cathedral of steam, pictured c.1900.

3. Broad Street, seen here around the turn of the century, was the biggest London station to be demolished, making way for the Broadgate development that also encompassed neighbouring Liverpool Street in the 1980s.

4. Fenchurch Street, tucked away in a side street in the City, is probably London's least well-known terminus but remains heavily used by commuters.

5. (*above*) From its opening in 1854, trains departed Necropolis station, next to Waterloo, taking many of London's dead to Brookwood in Hampshire. It closed during the Second World War after the building was hit by a bomb.

6. (*left*) Waterloo, which was redeveloped over a ten-year period, was reopened in 1922 with a Victory Arch celebrating Britain's triumph in the Great War.

7. Waterloo has had a long connection with racing, taking racegoers to meetings and used by trainers to transport their horses around the network.

THE MOST POPULAR RENDEZVOUS IN THE CITY

GREAT EASTERN HOTEL LIVERPOOL S.ᵗ STATION LONDON, E.C. 2.
OWNED AND MANAGED BY THE LONDON & NORTH EASTERN RAILWAY
FOR PARTICULARS OF TARIFFS APPLY RESIDENT MANAGER

8. Luxurious hotels were built at most of the major London stations, greatly improving the standard of hotel accommodation across the capital.

9. The arch at Victoria, which became 'The Gate of Goodbye', famously photographed by F.J. Mortimer in 1917.

10. After the First World War, Victoria replaced Charing Cross as the principal station for services to Europe and most notably was the terminus of the Golden Arrow, which took people to Paris in as little as six hours.

11. The *porte cochère* at Marylebone station, the last terminus to be built in London and famously described by Betjeman as resembling a 'public library from Nottingham'.

12. The main concourse at Euston, which had no seats for passengers when it was completed in the 1960s, was widely criticised for its modernist architecture, in sharp contrast to the elegance of the old station that had been demolished.

13. The new concourse at London Bridge, which was completed in 2018 as part of a £1bn redevelopment that has greatly improved links between the two parts of the station and allowed for a substantial increase in passenger numbers.

14. The land behind King's Cross and St Pancras, which used to be railway sidings and yards, has been extensively redeveloped but several historic buildings such as the gasometers, warehouses and the coal drops have been repurposed.

15. King's Cross station, which had a poor internal design, now boasts a superb new side entrance with this lattice-work roof after a £500m redevelopment completed in 2012 that also saw the clearing away of the 1960s additions at the front.

16. The statue of Sir John Betjeman – who saved St Pancras station from demolition – on the upper section of the redeveloped station, opened in 2007 and now used by the Eurostar trains to and from Europe.

workmen's trains were introduced, fares were still fourpence from Finchley, around half the distance of some of the Great Eastern journeys available at the same price. The Great Northern belatedly responded to this demand, building up its suburban network and adding more early workmen's trains. Predictably, the expanded network stimulated suburban housing development but mostly for the middle classes since rail fares were more expensive and therefore only the relatively affluent workers could afford them. The section between Finsbury Park and King's Cross was particularly busy and, according to the historians of London's transport network, 'all this extra traffic involved the Great Northern in heavy expenditure for the track had to be doubled, and then trebled, to accommodate it, and on that route out of London this entailed tunnelling as well as widening'.[13]

Interestingly, the authors are bemused that the Great Northern risked its profitable long-distance traffic by encouraging these peak-time commuter trains that came to dominate the services at King's Cross. Was it, they asked, driven by the sheer weight of numbers of commuters clamouring to get on the trains, or were there more directly self-serving reasons? 'Or do the land and property speculators enter the picture? Were they able to bring pressure to bear on the Great Northern directors?'[14] Railway companies, with the exception of the Metropolitan Railway, were, in fact, banned from land speculation around their stations but the authors are implying that directors might have got round this by agreeing private arrangements with developers. This was perfectly possible. Although the 'railway interest' that was such a powerful force in the mid-nineteenth century had somewhat dissipated and weakened, a study of railway schemes and investments in this period still shows that there was a relatively small group of men

– and they were all men – who both instigated and benefited from these schemes. It is quite likely that a few would have had property interests on the side.

The effect of these services, together with the associated expansion of suburban lines, is unarguable. They stimulated a mass migration from the overcrowded parts of inner London, known today as Zone 1, and even parts of what is now Zone 2, such as Hackney and Stoke Newington. This not only ensured the filling up of the outer suburbs but greatly relieved housing pressure on the inner ones. Indeed, it is difficult to exaggerate the impact on the suburbs, particularly those served by the Great Eastern. The population of Tottenham doubled in the ten years to 1881, and then did so again in the following decade, reaching just under 100,000. In the same twenty-year period Edmonton's population almost tripled to 36,000 and Walthamstow experienced the greatest growth, going from just 11,000 in 1871 to 97,000 thirty years later. Interestingly, the growth in places further out, such as Enfield, occurred in the first couple of decades of the twentieth century, as the suburbs closest to London filled out first.

The Great Eastern was unique across the capital in providing such a large number of these cheap train services. In his study of London railways, H.P. White concludes that during the second half of the nineteenth century, the north-eastern suburbs 'had become the most homogeneous, now being almost exclusively peopled by unskilled workmen, artisans and lower-paid clerks. All this was largely the result of policies continuously pursued by the Great Eastern Railway after its formation in 1862.'[15]

In south London, there were some workmen's trains provided by the railway companies but by and large their fares were more expensive than those of the Great Eastern and consequently had less impact on the provision of working-class housing. Other railways, notably the Great Western, the Midland and the London & North Western, never attempted to exploit this suburban market with the result that there was a very different pattern of development in the parts of London served by their trains. The Great Western, in particular, was uninterested and its efforts to develop this market half-hearted. In the early days, the large amount of traffic from Windsor and Ealing rather took the company's management by surprise but its directors were disappointed when stations at Hayes and Acton generated little income, especially from the sort of City commuters who could afford higher fares. Kellett argues that this is because the company did not price fares properly and failed to 'assess the attitudes of landowners on the Great Western's route, survey the possible market for season tickets [or] define, even approximately, who the "city people" were likely to be… and whether they would find accommodation at the rents they could afford'.[16] Moreover, Paddington, he argued, was a remote West End station, whereas southern and south-eastern commuters could access terminuses that were on the fringe of the City.

Despite their intense use and heavy ridership, the workmen's trains were initially only operated with great reluctance by the railway companies, which had to be forced by law to provide them. Their long-term impact on these companies was complex as there were both benefits and costs. As we have seen, these services undoubtedly contributed to the spread of London through working-class migration to the suburbs, which resulted in a great improvement in many people's housing. However, there was much debate about whether the railway companies themselves benefited from the operation of these workmen's trains, which they were constantly complaining about having to run. One of the arguments against their provision was that it was impossible to police who used these cheap services. One senior railway official complained of seeing a party of revellers in full evening dress using an early morning train, presumably on their way home after a good night out. It was clearly impossible to ascertain who were bona fide users and who were freeloading, but quite frankly anyone prepared to get up early enough to take these trains deserved a cheap ride.

More significantly, there were issues about the behaviour and mores of the people who used the trains. According to Henry Oakley of the Great Northern in evidence to an 1884 Parliamentary inquiry, they were dirty and put off other customers who, of course, paid more: 'the condition in which they are after a day's work at bricklaying, or other work, is such that it disturbs the coats, at all events, if it does not ruffle the tempers of other passengers'.[17] Moreover, he went on, they apparently spat on the floors, smoked offensive pipes, rather unbelievably cooked herrings in the waiting rooms, cut off the leather window straps and, worst of all, hung about waiting 'with evil consequences' for some of the young female workers.

Most important for the railway companies was the issue of profitability, balancing, as one manager put it, the interests of the poor workmen with those of the poor shareholders. There were numerous claims that these trains did not bring in sufficient profit, but when asked to provide concrete evidence, the results were uncertain. There were indeed costs involved, with trains sometimes having to be used for two peak-time return journeys, which meant that the outward morning journeys were virtually empty. Therefore, even a heavily loaded train might mean only, on average, a 50 per cent loading. The train companies complained that they were uneconomic, but rather negated their argument by providing more than necessary, which suggested they were clearly profitable. They claimed this was necessary because of the high demand, but presumably they must at least have paid for their operating costs if not more since the Great Eastern developed these services far beyond the required statutory minimum as did many other railways. According to Professor Jack Simmons, the railway historian, 'most London railways came to provide far more workmen's services than they were obliged by statute – ten times as many, in all, by 1883'.[18] Nobody had forced them to do that.

With the opening of Liverpool Street, London had a dozen terminuses facing every direction of the compass and it seemed unlikely, given the high costs, that any more would be built. But that sensible assessment ignored the ambitions of Edward Watkin and his desire to create a main-line railway across much of England and through a tunnel to France. And inevitably that required a major station in London, the last one to be built.

TEN

A TERMINUS
TOO FAR

I N A RATIONAL world, London, with a dozen terminus stations already by 1874, would not have needed another one a quarter of a century later. However, there was nothing rational about the development of railways in the capital, as we have already seen. Instead, it was haphazard and largely driven by rivalries and a push for short-term profitability. Marylebone, terminus station of the Great Central, was a symbol of that system and the eventual failure of both railway and station was an inevitable consequence of its flaws.

Between the completion of Liverpool Street and the opening of Marylebone twenty-five years later in 1899, London's railway system had filled out with new lines, several short branches and numerous additional links allowing new connections, a process underpinned by London's late mini railway mania. However, competition rather than cooperation remained the order of the day. London, despite its size, should never have ended up with so many terminus stations; one reason why it did was the creation of the Inner Circle (Circle Line), which linked them altogether. Its construction was recommended by a Parliamentary committee in 1863, although a circle line had become almost inevitable once the 1846 Commission had blocked the construction of railway terminuses in central London.

Again, forget rationality. It would have been sensible in 1863 to have simply given the Metropolitan Railway powers to build the rest of the Inner Circle following the successful opening that year of the first section from Farringdon to Paddington. The Metropolitan had already set in motion plans to extend eastwards towards the City and westwards to South Kensington. But the Victorian obsession with competition meant that another company, the Metropolitan District, known as the District to avoid confusion, became involved in the construction of the Circle. The District was awarded the contract to build a line from South Kensington to Westminster, a difficult engineering task, complicated by the need to divert a river and made considerably harder by the hostility of the local aristocratic landowners. As a result, construction went seriously over budget leaving the District with no funds to extend east beyond Westminster. After a delay, partly caused by the construction of Sir Joseph Bazalgette's Thames Embankment, as well as an inevitable funding shortfall, the District reached Mansion House. At the other end, the Metropolitan got to Aldgate and served Liverpool Street through the connection, mentioned in the previous chapter, that had been specially created to link with the Great Eastern services.

Then building work stopped and the situation descended into farce. The fundamental problem was the intense rivalry between the Metropolitan and the District and their respective leaders, Edward Watkin and James Staats Forbes. The two men had such a visceral personal dislike of each other that they could barely be in the same room let alone thrash out deals. Watkin, who controlled the South Eastern Railway as well as the Manchester, Sheffield & Lincolnshire Railway, was appointed chairman of the Metropolitan in August 1872, at about the same time that Forbes assumed the same role at the District, which he had joined as general manager two years previously. The two had form. They had headed rival railways in Kent that fought a long territorial battle, with an outcome that weakened both railways and even has an impact on commuters today as the Kent railways remain slow and have a complex route structure, with many towns having two stations that used to belong to rival companies. Watkin's South Eastern Railway and Forbes's London, Chatham & Dover wasted considerable amounts of shareholders' money in a battle for domination. Watkin was abrasive and secretive while Forbes was smoother, 'but their disputes were acrimonious, bitter, personal, and obsessive to the point of damaging their own companies'.[1] It wasn't until 1899 that the two companies merged, by which time both Watkin and Forbes were in their dotage.

Given that both the Metropolitan and the District were ailing financially, an obvious solution would have been to work together and eventually merge. Instead, the two men stalled further progress because they were both waiting for the other to go bust so that the survivor could take over the whole service. The Underground service at this stage was not separated from the rail network in the way that it is today; the companies operating on the subterranean tracks believed that trains would come on and off the main lines at terminuses such as Paddington, King's Cross and Liverpool Street, and run through to a variety of often far-away destinations. The District, for example, at one point ran services from Ealing to Southend with a stop at Barking to change from electric to steam power, and several railway companies such as the Great Northern and the London, Chatham & Dover ran services over the Metropolitan's tracks between Blackfriars and King's Cross, linking a number of destinations on either side of the river.

Therefore, the two companies that were in the process of forming the Inner Circle were used to running on the tracks of other railway companies, but the hostility between the two meant that it was difficult to thrash out reasonable deals to accommodate each other. Once the District completed its tracks to Mansion House in 1871, the company started operating trains all the way round this horse-shoe-shaped line on the Metropolitan's tracks to the temporary terminus at Moorgate. The Metropolitan also ran trains, which made for a ten-minute frequency, demonstrating how useful the line immediately became. However, the Metropolitan disliked the arrangement and was forever putting obstacles in its rival's way. At one point such was the antagonism that the District parked an engine and a coach in a siding belonging to the Metropolitan and chained it there in order to establish its right to use those particular tracks. The Metropolitan tried, and failed, to drag the locomotive out by force and the dispute had to be resolved in the courts.

Not surprisingly, this enmity further delayed construction work and it took another thirteen years before the Circle was completed. Even the creation of a separate 'completion' company between the two failed to break the deadlock, and it was only when Forbes and Watkin were forced to cooperate following an arbitration process headed by Sir John Hawkshaw (of Hungerford Bridge fame) that the final connection was made and completed in 1884. The whole thirteen-mile circular line, linking twenty-seven stations including most of the north London terminuses, cost an estimated £11m, which even accounting for inflation would translate into around

£1,100m in today's money, all paid for by private investors. It was a great bargain, given that Crossrail, the new railway under London, is costing at least £18bn.

There was still no truce between Watkin and Forbes, however. They did, apparently, sit together at the opening journey on 17 September but made sure that no photo was taken of them. When public services started the following month, there was turmoil because of the companies' mistrust of each other. They had agreed that the Metropolitan should run clockwise around the outer track and the District would operate in the opposite direction, but they both tried to run too many trains and consequently services were often late. Moreover, there was a dispute over the allocation of fares and over a section of track built without permission by the District between High Street Kensington and South Kensington stations. Worse, both companies operated ticket offices at many of the stations and they competed for business, failing to inform passengers which train might offer the shorter journey. If anything was a metaphor for the way that rail services developed in the capital, it was this endless dispute between the Metropolitan and District railways that dragged on into the opening years of the twentieth century.

There was, though, no doubting that the Circle Line – a name that was not used until the 1930s and not shown on the Tube map until 1949 – was immensely helpful for passengers continuing their journeys from the national rail network, as well as those changing trains between the various terminuses. The competition between the District and the Metropolitan ensured there were no train paths available in the timetable for other companies and that helped create the impetus for the construction of London's last terminus station, Marylebone.

The key figure, yet again, was the ubiquitous Watkin. He was a man of limitless ambition as demonstrated by the fact that he had hoped, at one stage, to link the railways of England with those of France via a tunnel under the Channel and, specifically, to run services between London and Paris. Watkin controlled three railways – the Manchester, Sheffield & Lincolnshire, the Metropolitan and the South Eastern – which together could offer a through route from the North-West to the south coast, and possibly beyond.

The South Eastern Railway started building the first mile or so of this Channel tunnel in 1880, but within a year work had stopped due to a lack of money and the intervention of the British government. The military was concerned that the tunnel could be used by an invasion force, an unlikely scenario given that the entrance would have been easy to block off or blow up. There are, in fact, doubts about whether Watkin, by the time he turned his attention to building the Great Central, still harboured hopes of running through trains from Manchester to Paris. He was extremely guarded and his intentions in relation to the Channel tunnel and the Great Central were unclear. While most writers suggest his plan was still for a continuous international railway, there is no evidence that he ever thought this would be possible after the tunnel had been abandoned a full decade before plans for the Great Central were authorized by Parliament, and nearly two decades before the line was completed.

For many years after taking over at the Manchester, Sheffield & Lincolnshire, Watkin, who had joined as general manager as far back as 1854, sought to find a way for the company to reach London. The company was rather disparate and impoverished, with a main line that linked Grimsby with Sheffield and Manchester, good for transporting fish and coal but little else. Reaching London, as we have already seen, was the ambition of any forward-looking provincial railway and Watkin, with his extensive holdings in railway companies, was not one to sit back and shy away from greater ambitions.

The Manchester, Sheffield & Lincolnshire Railway had contracted with the Great Northern and the Midland to carry goods and passengers into London but that really only highlighted the fact that it was losing valuable custom to its rivals. Watkin's attempts to persuade his fellow directors to build a line to the capital were rebuffed several times after he became chairman in 1861. Gradually, though, by the end of the 1880s, they began to relent and his connection with the Metropolitan opened up the possibility of the two companies sharing a forty-two-mile stretch of line from Aylesbury into London. That still left a fifty-mile gap from Nottingham to Aylesbury, and crucially two miles from a junction near Finchley Road station to a new terminus that he decided would be in Marylebone just south of the Regent's Canal. These last two miles into the capital were necessary to give the railway any chance of long-term viability, as a reasonable connection to central London was now widely recognized as essential for any railway. Certainly, it had to be at least as good as, and preferably better, than the connections offered by other stations.

Unfortunately, these last two miles were to prove not only exceedingly expensive but almost fatal to Watkin's plans. It was cricket, in the guise of the Marylebone Cricket Club, that looked like being an insuperable barrier. Watkin, rather naïvely, had underestimated the power of the MCC and its aristocratic members, and the opposition they could mount. His initial proposal, which required the acquisition of part of Lord's Cricket Ground, owned by the MCC, and possible purchase of the whole ground, an idea that clearly was a red rag to a bull for the Establishment, was thrown out in 1891 by Parliament in the face of opposition from the cricketers as well as predictably from the Midland and the Great Northern. *Punch*, never a friend of the railways, published a cartoon of W.G. Grace leading his cricket team out to meet the enemy, the Great Central, with Watkin at its head.

During the course of the debate over the second Bill, which was eventually passed in April 1893, Watkin made a series of commitments to allay the concerns of both the MCC and local artists, who occupied many of the pretty villas of St John's Wood. He gave a commitment to the MCC that any damage to the pitch would be covered up and restored as new in the winter close season, and no spoil would be carried through the genteel streets of north-west London. He also bought off the rival railway companies by promising them access to his line.

Three cut and cover tunnels were built under Lord's, which involved digging up the entire ground at the end of the cricket season in September 1896. The work was timed to perfection with not a day's cricket lost as the pitch was restored to the MCC on 8 May. In fact, the cricketers received a bonus and were richly rewarded for their indulgence. The neighbouring Clergy Orphan Asylum along Wellington Road, the main road towards Finchley, had to be demolished and rebuilt at Bushey at the expense of the Great Central and to the joy of the orphans who found themselves in much more salubrious surroundings. When the cricket pitch was restored, the MCC also benefited from the gift of nearly two acres of land that was formerly part of the Asylum's grounds; consequently Lord's was extended to Wellington Road, allowing the MCC to create a whole new practice pitch at the east end of the ground that today houses its Academy. All that Lord's lost permanently was a small parcel of land, about 130 feet by 330 feet, that was never part of the cricket pitch. Many other conditions were imposed by the owners of the land in St John's Wood before they acquiesced to the Parliamentary Bill. Large walls were to be built to conceal the railway, no advertisement hoardings were to be erected, coal yards were to be roofed in and, just as with Euston, almost three quarters of a century before, there was an insistence that the railway buildings had to be ornamental in character.

South of the tunnels under Lord's, the tracks crossed the Regent's Canal on a particularly wide bridge, intended to accommodate fourteen tracks for a project that was never built. This would have been a line that would have run over the canal from Royal Oak, just outside Paddington station, through to the City and to the Royal Albert Docks. In the event, despite Parliamentary powers having been obtained several years previously and renewed numerous times, the idea, which would have been extremely expensive, never came to fruition.

While the MCC managed to survive the construction of the railway pretty much unscathed, that was not true of the local area. There was massive disruption to, inevitably, the poorer parts that stood in the way of the new line. Unlike the area north of the canal, Marylebone was not a neighbourhood of pleasant villas. Quite the opposite, in fact, as the section south of the canal was one of the most insanitary and overcrowded parts of London. Although by this time many of London's worst rookeries had disappeared, not least thanks to the efforts of the railways, building the two miles of railway and the new terminus at Marylebone led to the displacement of 4,448 'persons of the labouring class'. We know the precise total because various pieces of legislation passed during the previous quarter of a century had placed far more onerous requirements on the railway companies to rehouse people whose properties they demolished. Every displaced person had to be identified and accommodated, but the initial effect was to make the slums in Lisson Grove even more overcrowded. Of this total, more than half, 2,690, were given basic accommodation in a series of six five-storey apartment blocks just off St John's Road built by the Wharncliffe Dwellings Company, named after Lord Wharncliffe who had replaced Watkin in 1894 as the chairman of the Great Central. The railway funded the construction of these blocks – which were themselves replaced in the 1960s by the Greater London Council redevelopment of Lisson Grove – rehoused other displaced people and built a school and vicarage for St Paul's Church.

Much of this land was acquired for a large adjoining goods depot that included carriage sheds, a coal yard and fish and milk wharves to transfer produce onto barges on the Regent's Canal. The vast space, a total of twenty-eight acres, making it the biggest goods yard in London, was also intended to provide extra platforms for the adjoining station, but given the failure to attract much custom, these were never built.

All these extra requirements for land and the need to mitigate the impact of construction placed an almost impossible burden on the already cash-strapped Great Central. Its predecessor, the Manchester, Sheffield & Lincolnshire, had been known as the 'Money Sunk and Lost' in the newspapers, which played with acronyms as part of their vendettas against railway companies; the Great Central would soon be known as 'Gone Completely'. The cost of construction outside London had already been greater than expected due to the high standard of many embankments and no fewer than eight viaducts, interspersed by long tunnelled sections through cities such as Nottingham and Leicester. But it was the London section that nearly brought down the company. Indeed, the Great Central was so short of funds it had to use a type of hire purchase agreement to obtain rolling stock, which involved leasing the locomotives and coaches from a Rolling Stock Trust rather than a direct purchase from the manufacturer. It was, oddly, an arrangement that nearly a century later was used to underpin the structure of the privatized railway when in the 1990s British Rail's rolling stock was sold to three leasing companies.

Marylebone became the fourth station after Euston, King's Cross and St Pancras to be located on New Road, London's bypass built in the eighteenth century, although this section was by then called Marylebone Road. Like Euston, it was not on the Circle Line but was soon connected to the Tube network. Not surprisingly, therefore, Marylebone station was a modest affair. So modest, in fact, that it was not even granted an architect as it was designed by Henry Braddock of the company's engineering staff.

Hidden from Marylebone Road by a very large hotel, its architecture was constrained by the Great Central's budget. With three storeys and built of red brick, it certainly had no pretensions. The best feature was the *porte cochère* of iron and glass that spanned – and still does – the eighty-two-foot road between the station and the hotel, which meant people could pass between the two, protected from the elements. It was the finest entrance to any London station, but that was the only fancy part of the building. Indeed, its whole design seems to have been an attempt to blend in with the local housing by incorporating Flemish gables and Tudor-style red brick with terracotta dressings, matching many of the nearby squares.

Beyond the booking hall, there was a huge concourse, twice the width of the platforms and track, as originally there were to have been up to ten platforms. In the event, there was only enough money to build four and, as mentioned above, the low usage meant the others were never built. Alan Jackson says the resulting station building 'would have been creditable as council offices for a minor provincial town but was hardly worthy as the London terminus of a railway that aspired to be in the first rank'.[2]

The first goods train to use the new line ran in July 1898 but delays to the completion of the station meant the celebration marking the inauguration was not held until 9 March 1899. In his speech, Lord Ritchie, the president of the Board of Trade, accurately predicted that it was an event that London was not likely to see again. Among the 700 guests was Edward Watkin who had been forced to resign the chairmanship of the Great Central five years previously after suffering a stroke.

The accompanying hotel was as impressive as dear old Marylebone was mundane. Watkin had wanted to build a plush luxury hotel to attract overseas visitors but he was frustrated by lack of money, and the finance was provided by Sir John Maple, the eponymous owner of the furniture company. The Hotel Great Central, designed by Sir Robert Edis who had also been responsible for the extension to the Liverpool Street station hotel, was built around a large central forecourt. Externally, the frontage on Marylebone Road was of golden terracotta with a central tower that few now notice on the ever-busy road. Betjeman says the style was 'Flemish Renaissance' while Jackson suggests 'Jacobean'. Over the main entrance, there were two reliefs portraying women, the first featuring a helmet and a battle-ready brassiere, the other hatless and draped but with, strangely for these prudish times, an exposed breast. Jackson was bemused: 'Goodness knows what should be read into this little bit of symbolism'.[3]

Betjeman could not hide his admiration for the nine-storey hotel and even expressed envy for his Nottingham-based cousins who could arrive at the station, cross the road under the great *porte cochère* and be 'dazed by its marble entrance hall, the wide stone staircase, and the painted tympana of nymphs and goddesses. They would have heard a string band in the distance, the sound coming from the glass-covered courtyard where it played and where palm trees shaded tables for tea.'[4] There was plenty more. The Wharncliffe Rooms, equally as grand as Liverpool Street's Abercorn Rooms, and the great dining hall were lined with mahogany supplied, of course, by Maple's store. The heavy cutlery was from Sheffield and there were vast chandeliers, lit by electricity, in every public space. And in a piece of miscellany that would probably stump any pub quiz enthusiast, on the roof of the hotel there was a cycle track. This was probably intended as a spectator diversion rather than for the use of overweight hotel guests, as fitness fanaticism was not a feature of late Victorian life when, rather, an elegant round stomach was seen as a sign of affluence.

The Hotel Great Central was on a larger scale than most of its rivals at other London stations with 700 rooms, enough to accommodate 1,000 people, although it is doubtful that they were ever all full. Like many of the other railway hotels, it struggled during the 1930s Depression and was turned into offices just before the Second World War, later becoming the headquarters of British Railways as 222 Marylebone Road (and, oddly, in 1995, it once again became a luxury hotel, called the Landmark).

The modesty of the station was rather in contrast, too, to the type of train services that the Great Central sought to provide. The aim was to run a superior train service for discerning passengers who would enjoy a good on-board meal. C. Hamilton Ellis, the flowery railway writer, was on his best form when he described his journey on the Great Central. The trains may have been lightly loaded, he wrote, but they were smartly timed and 'internally they were the most comfortable, while they perpetuated the old Sheffield Company's partiality for gorgeous decoration. Jason fought for the Golden Fleece in mezzotint panels on the dining car ceilings and as you lounged on a splendiferous pew of carved oak and figured plush, the sun, shining through coloured glass deck lights, gave a delicious bizarre quality to the complexion of the lady opposite.'[5] He added that even those trains that did not have restaurant cars were furnished with a buffet, an innovation at the time.

Despite the emphasis on passenger comfort, the rather out of the way location of Marylebone and the slowness of the services hampered the Great Central's ability to attract passengers. Its services to destinations such as Sheffield and Manchester were slower than those of its rivals and were only marginally faster on the East Midlands routes to Leicester and Nottingham.

There were only fifty-five people on the three trains that ran on the first day and things did not really improve. Contemporary newspapers noted rather unkindly that it was not unusual for the clutch of porters greeting an arrival of a train to outnumber the passengers alighting. Trains were speeded up, making use of the quality of the track and the absence of level crossings – there was just one on the whole line – but the efforts were to no avail.

The disadvantage of the rather remote location of the station was reduced by the advent of the Bakerloo Line in 1907 with a station that was, all too briefly, called Great Central but later renamed Marylebone. This replaced an earlier idea: a connection leading off the Metropolitan Railway that would have run under the hotel and emerged on the west side of the station. It would have been far more useful than the Bakerloo as trains could have run on directly to the City, in the way they currently do at Baker Street, and possibly even to south London, without passengers having to change onto the Underground. The Great Central even obtained Parliamentary authorization for the link but it never materialized because of opposition from the Metropolitan, as well as the hotel (think of the noise troubling the eminent guests), and the penurious state of the company.

Therefore, for all the emphasis on passenger comforts, it was largely freight that used the well-engineered and elegant railway that Watkin and his successors had built. In 1903, four years after opening, there were still only fourteen daily passenger trains, most of which went to Manchester. Marylebone was so poorly used that a cruel joke emerged: a Roman Catholic complains to his confessor that 'there is nowhere in London I can meditate in peace and quiet' only to elicit the response 'Have you tried Marylebone, my son?' Marylebone was probably too small to be called a white elephant, but it effectively was one from the start. Its services duplicated those of other railways, providing very few new journey opportunities, and therefore Marylebone and the Great Central could be seen as the swansong of the crazy competition that led to London having by far the largest number of terminus stations of any city in the world.

The Great Central struggled under the weight of the £11m cost of the new line and its London terminus, which was nearly four times its original £3m budget. Despite efforts at promoting the long-distance train services, passenger numbers remained stubbornly low and under a dynamic railway manager, Sam Fay, the emphasis changed. A new section of line linked the station with the Great Western Railway's route to High Wycombe and a series of suburban stations were opened on the route as well as on the section from Neasden to Northolt. These innovations were the start of a strategy that saw Marylebone switch its focus from express trains to commuter services. The station's best and busiest days were when football matches were being played at Wembley stadium, which opened in 1923. A special station on a diverted section of line was built in anticipation of the British Empire Exhibition held over the two subsequent years but the crowds on these days were not enough to make up for the lack of passengers the rest of the time. Although the suburban ridership built up steadily, the station was always underused and, as we will see in Chapter 12, not only lost its main-line services when the Great Central closed on the recommendation of Beeching but also narrowly escaped being shut altogether in the 1980s and its lines turned over to the use of motor coaches.

ELEVEN

LONDON'S
UNIQUE DOZEN

A ND THAT WAS it. There were to be no more terminuses, and London's railway network was effectively complete by 1906–7 when three new Tube lines opened in quick succession. Yes, there would be a few extensions to the Underground network, mostly between the wars, and the odd new suburban connection on the national rail network, but it would not be until 1969 that a new Tube, the Victoria Line, was opened by which time parts of London's rail network would be under threat from Beeching's cuts that, fortunately, in the capital at least, mostly never materialized.

Pause for a moment and consider what happened in the remarkable four decades between the opening of London Bridge and the completion of the new Liverpool Street station. Leaving aside Marylebone, an outlier that was only built because of the larger-than-life figure of Edward Watkin, the other eleven surviving terminuses, together with the sadly demised Broad Street and several interim stations such as Bricklayers Arms, Bishopsgate and Nine Elms, were all built between 1836 and 1874. Several in that period were expanded or rebuilt, and in addition many had neighbouring or adjoining goods yards that took up far more land than the space earmarked for passenger use. All this took place in an area of about fifteen square miles of mostly already occupied land in the biggest and most prosperous city in the world, with a windy and troublesome tidal river running through the middle of it. As mentioned previously, several smaller terminuses, such as Blackfriars, Holborn Viaduct and Ludgate Hill, also emerged in the nineteenth century and have subsequently disappeared or become through stations.

Consider the sheer size, scale and import of this achievement: twelve megaprojects were completed in the space of forty years, a period that included a couple of financial crises that severely constrained the railway companies' ability to invest. And all this was accomplished entirely with private capital in the face of a diffident and at times downright obstructive government, which failed to outline a strategic view, and a Parliament riven with vested interests that led to a haphazard pattern of authorizations to build lines. Of course, the railway companies were big players in all of this, making decisions that would have a permanent effect on London. However, they were not the sole arbiters of their own fate. As we have seen in Chapter 8, their decisions to build and to invest were often influenced by property owners, developers, hoteliers and an assortment of professional advisers who also benefited personally from the construction of these enormous stations. The dismantling and renewal of the urban fabric, called by some authors 'creative destruction', carried out by the railways was on an unprecedented scale especially given the speed and extent of the process.

By 1890, the major railway companies had spent £100m on new terminuses, more than one eighth of their total raised capital, most of which was spent in London. They had bought at least 800 acres in the capital to build the terminuses and associated facilities, and according to Michael Freeman, the author of a book on Victorian enterprise, it was not just the direct ownership that was important: 'In the major cities, they had become owners of up to 10 per cent of the land in central areas and indirectly influenced the functional land use of up to 20 per cent.'[1]

Even after chronicling the stories of how these impressive structures came to be built in London, it is difficult to understand how the capital acquired such a remarkable collection of railway stations. Other cities and large towns across the world had a few, possibly a handful, of terminuses, or concentrated services on just one large central station, like the German *Hauptbahnhöfe* or the American union terminals.

This has left London with a dozen terminus stations, many of which have great architectural qualities but which are underappreciated both by Londoners and visitors because they tend to be tucked away in streets that offer no opportunity to view them with any perspective. Several, such as the three in the City – Cannon Street, Liverpool Street and Fenchurch Street – are tucked away in side streets with virtually no space in the forecourt from which to contemplate their design. The two adjoining stations, King's Cross and St Pancras, have been greatly improved recently in this respect, with the horrible clutter in front of the former having been removed, while the refurbishment of St Pancras has allowed its Gothic features to be viewed without the covering of a near century and a half's grime. Several of the frontages are blocked by hotel buildings and it is the train sheds behind that provide a chance to reflect on the scale and elegance of these stations. Sadly, as we see in the final chapter, some of these have been sacrificed at the altar of Mammon as office blocks have been built over the station concourse and platforms.

There are several key factors behind London's unique situation as the world leader in terminus stations. First, the capital was relatively well developed at the dawn of the railway era. Breaking through into the crowded heart of the city would have been difficult even without the intervention of the 1846 Commission, which effectively ruled out the idea of a station in the city centre. It was this intervention, combined with the recommendations of the subsequent 1863 Parliamentary inquiry into London railways, that paved the way for the construction of what became the Circle Line of the Underground. This was a rare and brilliant piece of planning, which at least partially lessened the inconvenience of having so many terminus stations by linking them and allowing for easy interchange between different rail services. According to the architect Terry Farrell, the Circle Line captures the spirit and character of London and offers 'the simplest and most singular definition of centrality that we have'.[2]

In a better-planned city, however, there might have been another circular railway further away from the centre, say broadly where the North and South Circular roads were built, to link up railways of the north and south, and which might have obviated the need for so many terminuses. Such a railway was built in several Continental cities, notably in Paris where the *Petite Ceinture* line was completed in 1867, and one in Berlin opened a decade later. In both Paris and Berlin, construction of the lines was encouraged by the military, eager to improve the protection of key cities.

Apart from the Inner Circle, there were other lines that together formed something of a circular route round much of London. By 1853, there was one that ran anti-clockwise from Blackwall on the north side of the river to Waterloo via Islington, Willesden Junction and Barnes; later the North Western Railway ran what it called the

Outer Circle from the District Railway station at Mansion House to Earls Court then via the West London Railway to Willesden Junction and the North London to Broad Street. Neither of these represented anything like a full circle and moreover required running on the tracks of a number of different railway companies, resulting in higher fares and infrequent services. It is only since London Overground built a section around south London in 2012 that we now have a full outer circle route around the capital, although for operational reasons passengers have to change trains at Clapham Junction. The absence of an outer circular route was largely due to a lack of rail links between the two sides of the river. Any such connection was hampered by the fact that only two railway bridges, at Blackfriars and Battersea, built relatively late in London's railway history, connected these networks. This meant that apart from the odd roundabout service, no railway company at the time served multiple destinations on both sides of the Thames, which drove the need for more terminus stations.

Reaching deeper into the centre was further complicated by established ownership structures. There were powerful institutions that raised objections: St Thomas's Hospital, as we have seen, added to the expense and complexity of building Charing Cross; and the City of London itself battled against railway incursion. Attempts to force railways to build new roads as part of Parliamentary authorization almost invariably led to schemes being unaffordable.

The other powerful force lined up against railway development was the aristocratic landowners who possessed nearly all the land required to build railways in north London. These were among the richest families in the country, such as the Russells and the Grosvenors. As Kellett points out, these were not naïve local landowners eager to cash in on a few acres of land whose use was about to be transformed from agriculture to railway, but wealthy traditional families who 'had several generations of experience of managing urban estates by the time the first railway approach routes were cut'.[3] Backed by armies of solicitors, land agents and supportive politicians, they were never going to be an easy touch. They had their friends in Parliament – in which many of them sat anyway – who ensured their interests would be protected. Consequently, their large London estates were left relatively untouched by the incursion of the railways, but when, exceptionally, they wanted to sell, they extracted a high price. The aristocrats, who were at the point of cashing in on their vast holdings as London expanded, were acting out of self-interest, concerned that allowing in the railway would cut land values. They wanted the pleasant squares and terraces that were filling up the likes of Bloomsbury and Westminster, not the type of development that was attracted by the railway.

There is an interesting subtext here, too, in that the investors in these railways were principally from the North; some had even invested in lines south of the river. As L.T.C. Rolt, the classic railway author, put it, the Doric portico outside Euston was a 'triumphal arch, bestriding the processional way of the first railway to march on London' and its arrival represented 'the victory of the engineers over the subterranean waters and quicksand of Kilsby [where a lengthy tunnel was built by the London & Birmingham Railway] and their passage through the great hewn defiles of Tring and Roade'.[4] The railways effectively marched upon London and took it by storm. The northern urban nouveaux riches and industrialists underwrote the extension of the railways southwards and they wanted to show off their new-found power through the Euston Arch. While the aristocratic landowners made money in the short term and quibbled about which bits of their estates they would release, the impression, literally and figuratively, left by the railways was of far greater duration and significance. Freeman sums it up neatly: 'Coupled with the extended voting franchise and the new constituency base of the Great Reform Act [of 1832] whereby many new industrial towns got political representation for the first time, the traditional landed classes appeared in some eyes to be under attack from all sides.'[5]

South of the river, the pattern of land ownership was different. The land was mostly owned by Church interests, such as the bishops of Winchester, Rochester and London. This meant that the railways for the most part only had to deal with one or two large ecclesiastical bodies, making land acquisition easier. Moreover, most of the properties housed poor people in insalubrious housing. The Church had no consistent policy on development, with the result that by and large it offered no objection to proposals for demolition from railway companies, not least because the bishops agreed with the notion that clearing these clusters of poor housing would improve the area. While this made incursion deeper into London easier than north of the river, the cost of acquiring the land was made more complex as there were many leaseholders with small parcels and as a result none of the schemes for terminus stations proved to be cheap.

All these factors contributed to the creation of the capital's array of terminus stations. There was one overriding factor, however, that ensured London came to have the most terminuses in the world and it can be expressed in one word: competition. The railways emerged at a time when capitalism was at its most raw and competition was seen as the most important way to restrict the powers of big companies. British liberalism, based on the philosophies of

John Stuart Mill and Adam Smith, which encouraged competition and the development of the free market, was the prevailing
ethos and the railways were hardly going to be allowed to set up
cosy cartels by governments that were on the lookout for any
restrictions on what they saw as the natural forces of the market.
Most railway managers at the time were eager exponents of this
cut-throat philosophy and all too ready to indulge in fierce competition with their rivals, rather than compromising over particular
routes or regions. They built uneconomic railways to steal market
share from existing lines, they imposed huge charges and damaging
restrictions on other companies seeking to use their lines and they
attempted takeovers that would have created monopolies.

Indeed, there was a fundamental contradiction in the way that
the railway market was created. Over time, railways veer towards a
natural monopoly because of the sunk costs of investment and the
simple convenience for passengers of having a single operator. But
the Victorian model, with its extraordinary emphasis on competition and an inevitable lack of cooperation, resulted in more
than 200 companies surviving to the early days of the twentieth
century. It was the First World War, during which the temporarily
nationalized railways were overused and suffered drastic underinvestment, that brought about consolidation of most of them into
just four private companies.

When the railways started to compete to get into London in
the middle of the nineteenth century, cooperation and collective
working wasn't a consideration. Not only would they have been
prevented from doing so by both government and Parliament, the
companies themselves wouldn't have seen it as desirable. It was a
dog-eat-dog world, in which the most ferocious mutt would win
out. Despite this, there were two types of instances of working

together. Companies could either create a terminus and then effectively rent out track and platform space (known now as train paths) to other companies or they could build a joint terminus to share. Both concepts were tried, and neither were successful.

The chequered story of the first London terminus station, London Bridge, perfectly illustrates the failure of the first approach. As we saw in Chapter 1, it was built and rebuilt within a few years of opening and it was used by several competing companies, one of which, the South Eastern, was so dissatisfied it built another terminus, the nearby Bricklayers Arms. By 1850, mergers left just two surviving operators at London Bridge, the London, Brighton & South Coast Railway and the South Eastern; but their enmity was so intense that, like warring siblings sharing a bedroom, they built a dividing wall down the middle of the station. It was their efforts to do each other down, together with the late entry of the London, Chatham & Dover Railway into the fray, that led to the creation of a string of stations along the north bank of the Thames. Victoria station, remember, was also divided in two by a wall separating rival operators.

There was similar rivalry north of the river, which helped create that other string of stations along what had been known as New Road. The impossibility of the Midland working with the Great Northern at King's Cross led to the construction of St Pancras, while Marylebone was an attempt to take business away from several existing long-distance railway companies. The construction of two other adjacent stations, Liverpool Street and Broad Street, was due to the failure of the Great Eastern and the North London to agree to share a site.

This isn't to say that London and its rail passengers would have been immeasurably better had there been more coherence and coordination behind the creation of the capital's terminus stations. However, it seems indisputable that some sharing of facilities and coordination between the companies would have benefited them and their customers. Certainly, the expense of building these huge structures on expensive land put the railways under great strain and the money might have been much better spent on improving other aspects of their service.

The long-term effect on London is more difficult to assess. There were few, if any, parts of the capital that were not changed, transformed even, by the railway revolution and the terminus stations form an incredibly important part of London's environment today. While the revolution didn't start there, the capital quickly became the centre of the nation's rail network and the principal destination for every self-respecting railway company. This plethora of termini nuses made London accessible from any part of the country and served to entrench its position as the biggest and most important city in the nation. With such a fantastic array of train services, its position was unchallengeable. Connections between regional cities were poor in comparison and frequently left to train companies that, because they were unable to access profitable routes to the capital, were less able to invest in their networks.

The expansion of London between the opening of the London & Greenwich in 1836 and the end of the nineteenth century cannot easily be disentangled from the growth of the railways during that period. It was a symbiotic process, with a complex interrelationship between economic growth and the spread of the railways, but it is undeniable that the effect was to transform almost every aspect of Londoners' lives in this period.

The simple fact of being able to travel to virtually every town and village across Britain was the most obvious and fundamental change – and at speed. By the 1850s, some trains were averaging more than 50 mph, meaning, for example, it was possible to reach Oxford from Paddington in just sixty-eight minutes. Further improvements quickly followed. In 1852, the 129 miles from London to Birmingham could be covered in two hours forty-five minutes (just under double the time it takes today). By the end of the century, Penzance, as near to Land's End as any railway ever got, could be reached from London 256 miles away in under nine hours, and for a time during a series of races in 1895, the 400-mile journey from London to Aberdeen could be undertaken in the same time. According to *Bradshaw's*, the timetable compendium, in 1899 the fastest train between London and Exeter ran at 50 mph, while for Liverpool and Manchester they were 45 mph and for Leeds 48 mph. It was quite feasible, therefore, for business people to travel to great swathes of the country for a meeting and return to London within the day. Moreover, with a network that served every town and most sizeable villages in the country, it was possible to reach pretty much any destination from London within a day.

Sometimes there was a choice of different railways serving the same destination. For example, there were numerous ways to go from London to Birmingham or Manchester, both being lucrative markets for rival railway companies. Even many smaller provincial towns had two or more stations served by different companies. It is no wonder that Sherlock Holmes's first action on being engaged for a new case is to bark at Watson to consult *Bradshaw's*. Not only had the railways speeded up journeys across Britain, but there was no alternative method of fast travel. The railways ensured that London was *the* place from which to do business and *the* city to live in for those making the most money from the increase in economic activity stimulated by the railways. Again, it is difficult to disentangle the cause from the effect, except to suggest that in countries where the capital city was less dominant, such as Germany and Italy, the railways were less centred around that city.

The railways accelerated the urbanization of the population with the proportion living in towns and cities in the UK doubling over the duration of the nineteenth century. Growth was particularly marked in London, which was by far the biggest city with a population of 7 million at the outbreak of the First World War. There were also fundamental demographic changes in this period, with a huge increase in clerical jobs to service the rapidly growing economy. As a result, new suburbs were built mostly for the middle classes who moved out of central London. It is quite possible to argue that the railways accelerated the process of social fragmentation between the classes as witnessed by the American expression 'the wrong side of the tracks', although, to put it in perspective, they really only exacerbated a feature of urban areas that long pre-dated their existence.

The increase in speed of travel was the catalyst for a series of other developments. We have already seen how construction of the terminuses led to the demolition of mostly slum dwellings that housed London's poor. Undoubtedly, tens of thousands of people were evicted by the first railways but no figures were made available until 1853 when legislation required railway companies to count them. These statements show that in the second half of the nineteenth century, the construction of lines and the new London stations displaced about 72,000 people. However, this is only part of the story because the railways did not always provide accurate figures. For example, after the North London extended into Broad Street, the company was forced to admit it had underestimated the number of people moved out of their homes by a factor of four or five; other companies may have made similar errors.

A more accurate estimate can be obtained from a calculation based on the land take of the railway companies that was at least 800 acres, although that does not include land acquired by companies in the extensive railway supply chain. Applying a conservative estimate of 150 residents per acre suggests that a minimum of 120,000 people were made homeless in London. Despite the increasing requirements placed on the railways, they were reluctant right to the end to recognize their responsibilities in this respect. Jack Simmons is scathing: 'The companies sometimes made arrangements for new houses to be erected on their land by housing societies. But there does not seem to be a single recorded case in which any railway provided satisfactory new housing, available before the destruction of the old... The railways contested every yard of this ground, never conceding defeat.'[6] The time lag between demolition and the provision of alternative accommodation meant that the occupants of the housing provided at the cost of the railway were rarely those who had been displaced. Even as late as 1907, when the approach to Paddington was being widened, the Medical Officer of Health for Kensington reported that the Great Western managed through technicalities to avoid rehousing nearly 300 of the 1,028 people displaced by the scheme.

This had repercussions across London, as Freeman explains: 'Railway demolitions in working-class districts in the centre of the capital triggered a chain reaction: the poor... displaced the artisans, who then dislodged the lower middle and middle classes from the exclusive suburbs to which they had retreated.'[7]

There was another great economic stimulus for London from the railways. The supply industry for the railways became a major factor in the city's economy. Four of the big companies – the London & South Western, the Great Eastern, the North London and the London,

Chatham & Dover – actually built their locomotives at works in the capital, which were all near their respective terminuses. There were three major manufacturers of signalling equipment based in London and others that produced lifts, seats, blinds, carriage trimmings and special paints and varnishes for the rail industry. Several printers were kept busy purely by producing handbills, advertising material, timetables and guide books. Together these companies employed vast numbers of people, as did the railways themselves, though officially this was listed as about 40,000 at the turn of the century; this seems somewhat low given the labour-intensive nature of the railways at the time, but this may be explained by the fact that it does not include many of the permanent way workers. Each terminus would employ several hundred people (nearly all men) in addition to the train drivers, firemen and guards.

The goods depots, like the stations, were frenetic hives of activity, and those that grew up on the site of former temporary terminus stations often focused on particular types of freight. After passenger traffic shifted to Waterloo, Nine Elms became the main transit point for imported foodstuffs from North America and South Africa. At times, enormous quantities arrived from south coast ports in batches. It was not unusual for fifty wagons of bacon from Canada to arrive in one day, and similarly large deliveries of frozen meat from the United States were brought directly from the refrigerated ships that had docked at Southampton a few hours earlier.

Maiden Lane became part of a huge complex behind King's Cross station, handling vast quantities of grain and flour, coal and bricks, principally from Bedford and Peterborough. Bishopsgate, replaced by Liverpool Street in 1875, was the last temporary terminus to be converted to a goods yard, but was probably the busiest as it mostly dealt with foodstuffs and provided easy access to several markets as well as the City. By the early 1900s, it employed 2,000 people working on three different levels at the giant twenty-one-acre site; it dealt with an average of eighty goods trains a day and about 1,100 horses and 850 road vehicles were based there to transport goods in and out of the depot. Interestingly, rather than replacing horses as a method of transport, the London railways actually used them extensively, so that by the end of the nineteenth century they owned 6,000 simply to haul carts to and from the terminus stations and goods depots.

As well as huge loads taking up whole wagons or even trains, the railways were a common carrier, which under law required them to take whatever freight or parcels customers offered them, including house removals and circuses. Therefore every terminus station had a parcels office and goods depot that had to deal with loads big and small, a great burden for the railway companies as the prices were set by regulation and many items were simply uneconomic. The companies tried to cut their losses by establishing monopolies over the carriage for onward delivery or collection but this led to countless disputes with road haulage companies.

Nevertheless, the most important commodity carried by rail remained coal. As we saw in Chapter 4, the railways changed the nature of the coal market; not only did they carry vast quantities into London, they also used enormous amounts, particularly to power steam locomotives but also for heating station buildings. Most of this was handled by immense depots and sidings usually two or three miles away from terminuses, although many stations had small coal stores. London's coal consumption grew fivefold in a fifty-year period from 1830, while the population only doubled; this was undoubtedly made possible by the railways. Moreover, the supply became much more reliable as the railways were not affected so much by the weather, notably fog, which often prevented colliers from sailing.

One of the most radical ways in which the railways transformed the life of ordinary Londoners was the improvement to their diet. This was made possible because railways could carry perishable foodstuffs that would arrive at market while they were still fresh. The best example was milk, which until the 1850s was mostly produced by cow-keepers who would have an animal or two in a basement or shed. At the time, there were an estimated 20,000 cows kept in the city and its immediate surroundings. The first milk arrived by train in London on the Eastern Counties Railway into Bishopsgate in 1845 but at first other rail companies showed little interest in this traffic. Interestingly, the process of transport effectively homogenized the milk, making it more difficult to separate the cream, and rather disparagingly it became known as 'railway milk', a slightly inferior product, in the way that coal had once been 'sea coal' as a result of the way it was transported. The trade grew steadily until the 1870s when the development of refrigeration equipment and the addition of chemical preservatives soon ensured that milk brought by train dominated the market and, thanks to these improvements, became indistinguishable from any other milk. As demand grew, so did the increasingly distant places that supplied it – Berkshire and Wiltshire in the 1870s, Somerset in the 1880s and Devon and Cornwall in the 1900s. Special freight rates were offered to dairy farmers by a number of rail companies to encourage this trade and beat off rivals who might offer a better deal.

Because milk was generally carried by passenger trains, much of this trade came through the new terminus stations, enabling it to be despatched onwards very quickly, rather than via the goods depots. Some early services, notably on the Great Western, became known as 'milk trains' and these daily specials carried far more churns than passengers. Given the rich dairy lands covered by the Great Western's routes, Paddington emerged as the biggest station for the handling of milk deliveries. A special milk arrival dock was built in 1881 and by the turn of the century more than 3,000 churns were being handled daily from places as far away as St Erth in Cornwall, almost 300 miles from London. Waterloo, as we saw in Chapter 7, also handled hundreds of milk churns every morning, which gave the station a characteristic smell of sour milk all day.

By the outbreak of the First World War, all but 4 per cent of milk in London arrived by train. Thanks to the railways' ability to bring fresh milk from far afield, consumption in the capital grew from six gallons annually per head in 1850 to twenty-one gallons by 1910, representing an important improvement in nutrition. The influence of this new trade spread far out into the countryside as rural life had to adjust to London's pace, as the authors of the seminal work on stations explain: 'The milk train became an essential fact of rural life altering its rhythms by demanding the co-ordination of milking times with train departures.'[8]

There were numerous other ways that the railways helped improve Londoners' diets, such as enabling far greater supplies of meat and fish to be brought to the capital. Before the railways, livestock was driven to Smithfield, on the edge of the City of London, where it was traded and then slaughtered in insalubrious small abattoirs nearby. Once the line to King's Cross was opened, the trade moved to Copenhagen Fields, a mile north of the station, but then gradually more and more animals were slaughtered near where they had been reared and transported to the capital as meat, a trade that again was boosted with the advent of refrigeration in the last quarter of the century.

The carriage of fish was equally transformed. Indeed, fresh fish had not been widely available in the capital but now it could be taken by overnight train to London from almost any destination. Some of this arrived at the terminus stations in goods wagons attached to passenger services. As a result, and partly through the growth in popularity and widespread availability of fish and chips, fish became a staple in poor people's diet.

Other food had seasons; there were strawberry specials in June and July, plums were carried in August and September and at various times there were cargos of everything from tomatoes and cucumbers to potatoes and marrows. The Great Western provided flower specials in the summer. London had previously been very dependent on market gardeners in the Home Counties who flourished thanks to the rich alluvial soils in the Thames Valley. But the railways enabled far longer carriage of foodstuffs, ensuring that many more farmers could have access to the lucrative London trade. The market gardeners suffered more than just the loss of their immediate business. Some of their land was bought up by the railway companies as they built lines into the capital and much more was subsequently incorporated into the developments that the advent of the railway spawned. The main trade in the other direction, away from London, was of horse manure and night soil to provide fertilizer for the rapidly growing number of farmers catering for London's almost insatiable demand.

While the main emphasis of the railway companies was often on attracting people into London through their terminuses, there was a considerable market in the opposite direction, especially for leisure and sporting activities, notably racing. Since most people worked six days a week, the railways had to overcome any resistance to Sunday trains from the strong Sabbatarian lobby, which by and large they managed to do by the end of the 1840s. The scale of Sunday travel out of London grew rapidly with 42,000 people leaving from the six main stations on a Sunday in August 1857, the majority on specially arranged 'excursion' trains. Spurred on by the railways, it was in this period, too, that some businesses allowed their staff to have Saturday afternoon off as well as Sunday. According to Jack Simmons, a lobby group, the Early Closing Association, 'encouraged those who were given this new leisure to use it for health recreation in the open air'.[9] The railways responded by providing 'Saturday only' services from their main stations and some, such as the Edgware, Highgate & London Railway (which became part of the Great Northern), published booklets on what to do on these leisurely Saturdays.

The reduction in Saturday working encouraged out of town weekends; by the 1880s fast trains ran from London to all the principal seaside resorts of the South-East, often at a reduced fare. For those who could not afford to go that far, there were the London parks, one of the great achievements of the more enlightened Victorians in the mid-nineteenth century. The new parks – Battersea, Finsbury and Victoria – were all easily reached by rail and drew hordes of people at weekends. Other attractions for day trips, like Greenwich, Virginia Water, Epping Forest, Hadley Wood and many more, proved magnets to people eager to get out of the polluted London air. Day trips by rail were such a widespread phenomenon that it was mentioned rather pompously in Parliament in 1910: 'people are acquiring the habit of going long distances from London by railway in order to walk in the country'.[10]

As we have seen in Chapter 7, the railways were vital for horse racing as they not only carried the punters but the horses and the riders as well. London was ringed with a series of eight racecourses, all of them with stations nearby. Alexandra Park was the nearest, and the only one north of London, but it was Waterloo, serving both Kempton Park and Sandown Park, that was the most used for racing. Inevitably, competition crept in. The Great Western tried to serve Ascot through its Windsor branch and the South Western responded with trains from Waterloo to Ascot via a new branch completed in 1856. Epsom ended up being served by two stations: Epsom Downs opened in 1865 by the London, Brighton & South Coast Railway, and Tattenham Corner built in 1901 by the recently merged South Eastern & Chatham, with, respectively, a remarkable eight and six platforms that were used for just a few days a year.

But it was not only racing. Sporting fixtures became mass events thanks to the railways' ability to deliver huge numbers of passengers in a short space of time. In particular, the growth of football in London was stimulated by the relationship between the railways and the clubs. Several, including Charlton, Tottenham and Chelsea, moved to grounds that gave their fans easier access to the railways. My own team, Queens Park Rangers, was granted land cheaply by the Great Western for their ground at Park Royal.

And then there were day trips to London. Shopping was the big attraction, but so were the museums that had been built in South Kensington, the theatres and the music halls. That ring of terminuses around the centre of the capital now gave easy access to the various large shops that started emerging in the second half of the nineteenth century. Their location was influenced by the ease of access to the railways. William Whiteley, for example, decided to build his eponymous department store at Bayswater close to Paddington, and others imitated him by siting their shops on the

Metropolitan, with rapid connection to the main-line stations – notably at Kensington High Street where Barkers, Pontings and Derry & Toms opened within a few years of each other.

For those staying overnight, the railways not only provided a significant proportion of the hotel accommodation available to visitors but also set the standard for other hotels. The railways both created the possibility for people to come to London and provided the accommodation for them to stay. As we have seen, almost every one of the terminus stations – Waterloo and Fenchurch Street were the exceptions – had its accompanying hotel and as time went on these got bigger and grander as well as more luxurious. As a Victorian writer put it in 1875 in *Building News*, when all but one of these terminuses had been completed, 'Railway termini and hotels are to the nineteenth century what monasteries and cathedrals were to the thirteenth century. They are truly the only representative buildings we possess.' The early fourteenth century, as we saw in Chapter 6, was seen as the apogee of the Gothic style. This umbilical attachment between hotels and stations was particularly marked in the UK. While some Continental railway stations did have hotels, it was in Britain that it became almost mandatory for any large station to have one, not just in London but throughout the railway network and especially at the seaside resorts it served.

London Bridge, where the 150-room Terminus Hotel was only built in 1861, was the first to dispense with its hotel, which was never profitable and was converted into offices in 1893. Cannon Street lost its unsuccessful hotel in the 1930s, the same year when one of the best, the Midland Grand Hotel in St Pancras, shut its doors. In fact, most of the hotels suffered in the interwar period, particularly in the Depression, and after the Second World War they lost their luxurious cachet when they became part of the nationalized British Transport Hotels. During the past couple of decades, however, they have enjoyed a great renaissance thanks to the desperate shortage of hotel accommodation in the capital. Most have been fully refurbished, with the restoration of many original features, and have become part of luxury hotel chains with names like Andaz London Liverpool Street, the Amba Hotel Charing Cross and the St Pancras Renaissance Hotel.

It was rather strange that hotels became the sine qua non of all these terminuses when the stations provided few other facilities and were planned in a way that was not particularly suited to their use. The designs were borrowed from other buildings, such as churches or town halls, and repurposed with little thought as to what passengers needed. Nearly all were built with separate platforms for arrivals and departures, often with a large number of central tracks that were for carriages waiting to be formed into later trains.

At stations, the railway companies were slow to allow outsiders to provide services but they eventually became home for a variety of traders and their walls were papered with vast amounts of advertising. The most familiar addition was the bookstall, which became an indispensable part of stations as reading was the obvious pastime for long journeys. The first reaction of the railway companies to the interest of passengers in reading was to chain copies of the Bible to lecterns at the principal London terminuses, but soon they brought in booksellers to offer their wares. However, the railways quickly realized passengers needed rather more than that. Possibly the only claim to fame of that little lost terminus, Fenchurch Street, is that it was the site of the world's first station bookstall, which opened in 1841 and was run by William Marshall, the founder of an eponymous firm of newspaper distributors. More significantly, a few years later W.H. Smith & Son, named after William Henry Smith, the son of the original founder Henry Walton Smith, was awarded a contract to sell books and other material for the London & Birmingham Railway and opened a stand at Euston. It was an instant success and similar stalls opened at all the main stations along the line and every London terminus had at least one, and sometimes several, such outlets.

As with everything to do with the railways, the introduction of bookstalls in stations proved more complicated and controversial than might have been expected. Almost instantly, there were complaints about the nature of the material being sold at these bookstalls. According to the busybodies who must have spent considerable time inspecting these apparent dens of iniquity, 'it was alleged that the presence of a bookstall attracted large numbers of beggars, thieves, ladies of the night and other undesirables'.[11] Undoubtedly, some of the material in these bookstalls was as risqué as a Victorian trader dared to offer. Bookstall concessions were often leased out to injured ex-railway employees or their widows, whose taste in literature may have been somewhat downmarket and who were canny enough to realize that selling what were known as 'French novels', of the kind that respectable citizens would not be seen buying from their regular bookseller, could be lucrative. The term 'railway literature' became one of abuse, as did 'yellowback' because it was the predominant colour of these books' covers. *The Times* went to the trouble of sending a reporter, Samuel Phillips, to the bookstalls in 1851 and found 'with few exceptions unmitigated rubbish encumbered the bookshelves of every bookstall we visited'.[12] Articles like these provoked the ire of that large group of Victorian moralists who saw it as the duty of the upper classes to uplift, educate and improve, and they considered novels in general, and those on sale at railway stations in particular, as frivolous and even reprehensible. This was deeply unfair as the railway journey was a perfect time for people to read and, if anything, spread the habit to the lower middle and even upper working classes who might previously not have had the opportunity to sit down with a book. Publishers such as George Routledge and John Murray responded to these complaints by issuing material specifically aimed at rail passengers that was deemed suitable, which was selected 'to disperse sound and entertaining information and innocent amusement, by which he hoped to counteract and supersede the trivial, and often immoral, publications at present destroying the taste, and corrupting the morals of Railway Readers, more especially the young'.[13]

While it was unfair to blame the bookstalls, it was unarguable that the large railway terminuses did, at times, attract the wrong type of character, particularly, though by no means exclusively, prostitutes and those preying on them. This was part of a wider phenomenon of stations having a harmful impact on the local area rather than, as many of these stations' promoters had hoped, leading to its improvement. There was an odd dissonance between the luxury hotels that were incorporated into many of these station buildings, and the deterioration of the areas that surrounded them. This was particularly true of the terminus stations providing long-distance services, which attracted a proliferation of cheap hotels, shoddy cafés and tatty souvenir shops. In fact, as we have seen, the areas cleared for the terminus stations were often already run-down and the failure of the railways to provide housing for those displaced merely added to their impoverishment. Travellers far from home were easily tempted by the availability of cheap drink in the noisy and anonymous public houses and the illicit sex that was widely on offer. The most prominent red light district, with a series of small brothels, developed near Waterloo because it was the transit point for so many sailors and soldiers. The areas around Paddington, King's Cross/St Pancras and Waterloo all developed a red light district based in nearby cheap hotels. In turn, this attracted pimps and other petty criminals, particularly pickpockets who were not short of potential victims among the unprepared country people arriving in the Big Smoke.

One almost universal aspect, which was helpful for the more affluent travellers, was the availability of cab roads, several of which ran right through the station, to enable arriving passengers to continue their journey. Many of these survived until well after the Second World War – I remember my father driving me through Paddington station on a Sunday in the 1960s for a quick bout of number taking of Kings and Castles before lunch, barely needing to stop on the road between platforms 7 and 8 as we paused by these elegant engines.

As well as hotels, bookstalls and cab ranks, the stations gradually built up a wider range of other amenities. Toilets eventually became commonplace after the example set by Cannon Street. Tea rooms, cafés and restaurants, and waiting rooms separated by class and gender all became accepted features of these stations. There were vast numbers of official porters to carry luggage for passengers with ticket collectors at platform entrances (although not, as we have seen, for many years at Waterloo) and a wide range of offices dealing with such matters as lost property, policing, left luggage and telegraphs.

The rebuilding of Waterloo at the zenith of the railway's dominance offers an insight into what the railway companies expected to provide in their terminus stations in the early years of the twentieth century. There was no doubting that the station, which dealt with 50,000 passengers daily in the winter and more than 80,000 in the summer, when the number of trains rose from 800 to more than 1,000, was inadequate for the task. Its history of random patched-on additions that were not properly melded with existing facilities had created a mess that was compounded by the continuous and extensive growth in passenger numbers. It was a brave but overdue decision in 1897, made after much fraught debate by the directors of the London & South Western, to start afresh with a completely new station rather than, as had been suggested, to make partial improvements. However, subsequent delays caused by lack of money and the sheer size of the task, which needed work to be carried out in distinct phases, resulted in the whole process, from planning to the realization of the new station, taking nearly three decades.

The plan developed by the company's chief engineer, J.W. Jacomb-Hood, who had visited the United States to look at their latest terminus stations, was for twenty-three platforms built on a new superstructure with a steel-framed frontage with every conceivable facility required by a modern railway. In the event, the roof covering the north (or Windsor) section of the station was retained, which reduced the platforms to twenty-one. It would, though, turn a ramshackle mess into what O.S. Nock, one of the classic railway authors of the mid-twentieth century, proclaimed was 'one of the really great stations of the world'.[14]

TWELVE

SETTLING DOWN
AND DODGING
THE BOMBS

THE BRIEF EDWARDIAN period at the start of the twentieth
century was a time of consolidation for the country's railways
before the upheaval of the First World War. The completion of the
Great Central meant no more main lines were needed or, more
importantly, built. Rapidly rising passenger numbers prompted
the railway companies to concentrate on improving services and
tackling bottlenecks. Poorly built lines were improved, curves
straightened, junctions made more reliable and, crucially, safety
improved. Several London terminuses gained extra platforms or
were improved in other ways. During this period, the London
Underground system expanded, a development that was welcomed
by the more far-sighted companies that no longer saw them as
a threat. The tram system was at its peak and, with the electric
traction now universal, they did take business away from suburban
rail services, as they were cheaper and often more local.

As we shall see later, electrification of the capital's suburban
network started in the first decade of the twentieth century and

continued slowly over the following years; indeed, some lines were not electrified until the 1960s and others, notably those out of Paddington and Marylebone, are still waiting for the process to be completed. At the outbreak of the First World War, London's expanded railway had about 400 stations with a further 150 on the Underground network. While some were little used, they would soon be the catalyst for suburban development in the capital, boosting the numbers of passengers arriving at the terminus stations, which continued to grow right up to the outbreak of the Second World War.

Although there would be no new terminus stations in London, rebuilding Waterloo created another cathedral of steam. The renovated building was celebrated as the pinnacle in station design; it was spacious, with an airy concourse, efficient and able to handle vast numbers of passengers arriving together on numerous trains. It was also practical, easy to use and had lots of facilities.

The reconstruction of Waterloo was a complex task made more difficult by the need to keep London's busiest station running throughout the project. As a result, the scheme, which was carried out in distinct stages, took nearly three decades to complete. There were any number of vested interests to buy off since demolition of half a dozen streets was needed to make way for the new station, which would occupy an extra six and a half acres of land. Negotiations with the London Necropolis Company over the demolition of its station were tortuous and, as we saw in Chapter 6, resulted in an excellent deal for the funeral company. The local Lambeth vestry gained a new library and a residence for the librarian, and both All Saints Church and its school were replaced at a joint cost of £8,500. Alan Jackson notes that the Protestants were rather glad to see the back of this 'High Church' with services that were 'among the most ritualistic in Britain and it was thought that these popish practices would not be restarted in a new church'.[1]

Another £30,000 was demanded by the London County Council to pay for future road schemes and even the fire station had to be moved. For rehousing obligations, the London & South Western was required to provide six blocks of flats to house 1,750 people and, to the relief of the local respectable classes, many of the brothels and squalid pubs had to be demolished to make way for this new development. In their place, a new haven for servicemen, the Union Jack Club, was created on the other side of Waterloo Road (which still exists today; I have spoken there at meetings of retired railway people) with plenty of hostel accommodation.

Parliamentary permission was obtained in 1900 and clearance work began immediately, but it was not until 1909 that the first phase covering the old South (Windsor) station was complete. Rebuilding continued over the next thirteen years, interrupted, inevitably, by the Great War when the station was very heavily used by troops. As part of the reconstruction, the rail connection between Waterloo and Waterloo Junction – which was eventually renamed Waterloo East in 1977 – was severed. The bridge that carried the line over Waterloo Road is now used as the pedestrian walkway between the two stations.

The new terminus was opened officially on 21 March 1922 by Queen Mary, as her husband, King George V, had caught a 'chill' and was unable to attend. It was regarded as London's best station. The most striking feature on the outside of the building was the Victory Arch, erected to celebrate the defeat of Germany in the First World War. Given that the French were our allies in that conflict, it is ironic that the station itself was named after an earlier victory against our near neighbours. Indeed, it might have benefited the *Entente Cordiale* if the station had been renamed, especially as in the 1990s Waterloo became the London terminus for Eurostar trains for the first ten years of international high-speed rail services.

The Victory Arch, the work of the London & South Western's chief architect, James Robb Scott, is a strange amalgam of triumphalism and pacifism. It features on the left, with the inscription '1914', Bellona, the goddess of war, looking wild and angry, carrying a flaming torch and an unsheathed sword ready to reap death and destruction, while on the other side, above '1918', is a figure of peace enthroned on the earth and holding a palm branch. Surmounting both is Britannia, far above, and consequently probably less noticed than the rest of the arch, holding aloft the torch of Liberty, and just below her are stone panels carved with the names of various theatres of the recent conflict, such as Mesopotamia, Egypt, Italy, France and, strangely, the Dardanelles. The arch, which has four bronze plaques with the names of all the London & South Western's employees killed in the First World War, was part of a frontage in a style known as Imperial Baroque. However, because the station is rather hidden behind much foreground clutter only a minority of people arriving on foot will be vaguely aware of its presence; as Betjeman notes, 'they can only cross the road to look at it at the risk of their lives'.[2]

The main pedestrian entrance was from York Road where a wide flight of steps led to an impressive archway and to the great curved concourse, which is 700 feet long and was overlooked by a huge indicator showing the departure time, platform number and stations served for every train. There were numerous staircases leading to the Tubes and the Waterloo & City Line (still run by the railway company) below and to the tram stops on Waterloo Road. Opposite platform 1, the easternmost platform, there was a sixty-foot-long cloak and baggage room that was wide enough to take in barrowloads of ocean-bound luggage without having to unload them.

The famous men's toilets, located just a few yards further on, were reached from a staircase opposite platform 3. At 820 feet long, these subterranean facilities were described by the *Railway Magazine* as the finest in England, with a marble floor of black and white tiles, white glazed walls, bathrooms, a hairdressing salon and a huge number of urinals and toilets produced by the Scottish-based company Shanks. The display cases and counters were mahogany, as were the frames around plate glass mirrors. It was all so grand that the area was known as 'the Gentleman's Court' in the discreet terminology of the age. There was, of course, a permanent attendant and the advertising for the station promised that 'if desired, the air could be changed every five minutes by the action of electric fans'.

A huge luggage hall was located opposite platforms 4–6 – easily accessible for the cab rank – and it stood next to the even more enormous booking hall, which was Edwardian in style. It had a floor of coloured glass tiles and Doric marble columns supporting a plain but high, curved ceiling, which ensured it was airy and spacious. Half of the sizeable elliptical teak booking office was housed here, with the rest being on the concourse, and there were counters on both sides to serve the passengers. The booking hall gave onto a general waiting room with a separate one for ladies travelling first class, for their protection. The latter could only be reached through the booking hall, while the third-class ladies' waiting room gave onto the concourse. Ladies' toilets, adjacent to their respective waiting rooms, were also segregated by class and only the first-class facilities included a bath and dressing rooms.

Next along was another sizeable refreshment buffet with a small semi-circular counter and small round tables; passengers choosing to eat and drink here could enjoy the various marble hues of the walls and the Roman-style mosaic floor. All the food facilities were run by a private company, Spiers and Pond Ltd, a firm that improbably had its roots in the 1850s gold rush in Australia.

Continuing westwards and crossing the cab road between platforms 11 and 12, there was some symmetry as there were duplicates of many of these facilities. This indicates that while the rebuild resulted in one integrated station, it was not possible to entirely cover up its history as three separate stations, which had been, rather half-heartedly, attached. Next, therefore, was another, smaller, booking office that adjoined another refreshment room decorated in rich Baroque style with panelled marble extending almost ten feet up the wall, which was partially hidden by drooping curtains, as well as several bays for statues surrounded by rectangular columns. Alongside was the Windsor Room, which, according to John Fareham, the author of the history of the station, 'with cream walls, extensive mirrors, a floor of polished oak parquet and fittings of mahogany [was] clearly aspiring to stimulate Royal patronage... [and] consciously harked back to the Edwardian age with fluted pilasters atop columns in shades of grey and white with two domed pay-boxes containing curved glass windows either side of the door'.[3] Betjeman described it as 'Edwardian deluxe at its most refined'.[4]

The rest of this block, through to platform 21, was taken up with shops, including a W.H. Smith, a tobacconist and a bank, the National Provincial, which was the first to be opened in a London station. Soon, there would be a cinema showing 'news films' on an hourly loop, which could be interrupted by train announcements. In among additional waiting rooms, more ladies' lavatories and another 'Gentleman's Court', far less spacious than the other and again with no class distinction, there was an additional left luggage office that became notorious because of the discovery, in 1924, of part of a woman's body in a suitcase. The ticket for the case had been found by the suspicious wife of a philandering murderer, Patrick Mahon, who had killed his pregnant mistress. Following the discovery of the rest of her remains in a cottage that had been the scene of their trysts, he was hanged. In fact, left luggage offices became something of a convenient way of disposing of murder victims in the interwar period, as there were similar incidents at several other stations, notably Victoria and Charing Cross, where the murderer suffered the same fate. In May 1927, the stench from a suitcase alerted the left luggage attendant at Charing Cross and the body of a woman who had been asphyxiated was found. The taxi driver who had delivered the suitcase led the police to a man called John Robinson who, having admitted to strangling the woman over a money dispute, was hanged three months later in Pentonville Prison. 'Trunk murders' became so commonplace that George Orwell listed them as a distinctive feature of the interwar years.

Waterloo's new concourse was overlooked by a huge four-sided clock that was part of the 'Synchronome' system of 240 clocks across the station. These were all connected to one electrically driven pendulum master device that was synchronized daily with Greenwich. This system ensured all the clocks showed the identical time and as they were all 'slaves' they required very little mechanism to operate, ensuring they were reliable and took up very little space. Meeting under the clock at Waterloo became even more of a commonplace than the equivalent at Charing Cross.

Between platforms 15 and 16, there were stairs and an escalator to a rather strange two-storey block known as 'The Village', which served the station's 450 staff and included the stationmaster's office, staff canteens and the ever-busy lost property office. Upstairs, above the concourse opposite platform 11, there was the Surrey Dining Room, panelled in English oak in the Georgian style, with leaded windows overlooking the hurly-burly of the station. Able to seat 150 people, it was used for private banquets, and next to it was a small ladies' café that did light lunches and teas. Scattered around the station were a series of administrative spaces for the railway company as well as an inquiries office. Writing in the 1960s, Jackson is full of admiration for the only station that was rebuilt between the wars and describes it as 'an oasis of civilisation' and 'to enter the concourse after crossing the windy wastes of the south Bank is to experience a dramatic change of scale, to feel human again'.[5]

Built at the height of the railways' dominance, with a price tag of £2.3m, the new Waterloo set a standard for future station redevelopments that was not always met. In the ensuing four decades, only Victoria changed markedly when part of it was rebuilt, but, in addition, several stations were damaged during the Blitz. With the consolidation of the railway companies – battered and suffering from underinvestment after the Great War – into the Big Four in 1923, major new schemes were off the agenda. Instead, the four companies, still privately owned though less intent on rivalry, were more focused on improving services and reducing journey times.

One key way of achieving this was electrification. By the turn of the century, London already had three electrified Underground lines, and in the next ten years the existing subsurface lines – the District, Metropolitan and Circle – and three new deep Tube lines were added to the electrified network, all of them powered by a third rail system. London Bridge got its first electrified trains in

December 1909, run by the London, Brighton & South Coast Railway and powered by overhead line equipment, which was later replaced on all Southern Railway trains by the third rail system. This was introduced widely after the First World War by Southern Railway, which, under the leadership of its brilliant general manager Sir Herbert Walker, electrified almost all the services south of the Thames between the wars. Electrification was advantageous in every respect. Electric trains were far more flexible, as there was no need to move steam locomotives from one end to the other between journeys. By 1912, following electrification, the London, Brighton & South Coast Railway was able to run 900 trains in and out of Victoria station every day, compared with 663 previously. Electric trains had better acceleration and were, obviously, cleaner since they did not emit smoke. Their popularity with passengers meant that the costs of electrification were soon paid off by increased revenues. Gradually, between the wars Victoria, Waterloo and London Bridge stations saw all their suburban and local services electrified.

Despite this, some railway managers remained reluctant to invest in electrification. Liverpool Street had become even busier once the Central Line was extended there in 1912, with more than 200,000 passengers per day. Logically, it should have been electrified, but the ever-penurious Great Eastern could not afford the capital investment. Instead, the company devised a system of using little steam tank engines, which could accelerate rapidly, to operate a very frequent timetable that was dubbed 'the Jazz Service' because of its regularity. The tracks outside the station were reorganized to allow for quicker turnarounds, enabling a 75 per cent increase in services in the morning peak. This ensured Liverpool Street could cope with the ever-rising demand from the swathe of north-east

London that had grown up symbiotically with the rail service. Remarkably, the single line from Liverpool Street to Bethnal Green carried twenty-four trains per hour at peak times; as each sixteen-coach train had 848 seats, the capacity was about 20,000 passengers per hour on those services. Thanks to the efficiency of the Jazz Service, the London & North Eastern Railway, which took over services at Liverpool Street in the 1923 reorganization, could see no reason to spend money electrifying the lines and it was not until 1949 that the first electric trains ran out of Liverpool Street. Fenchurch Street was another latecomer to electrification with its steam services ending only in 1962.

Refurbishment at several other terminus stations accompanied electrification. Victoria, the only other station apart from Waterloo that underwent radical change during the early years of the twentieth century, was partly redesigned to accommodate electric trains. In the last years of the nineteenth century, the London, Brighton & South Coast Railway had demolished its rather dowdy terminus and erected a large station with thirteen platforms, five more than its predecessor. The main feature, apart from a series of five louvred ridge roofs covering the platforms at a relatively low level, was a nine-storey hotel block built across the front as an annexe to the Grosvenor. Jackson describes it as being in 'the so-called free Renaissance style', which blended with the Grosvenor and had a 'red brick frontage, with Portland stone dressings... dominated by an illuminated clock flanked by recumbent figures'.[6] The wood-pan-elled booking hall was impressive, some 115 feet long with a hall tiled in pale green and off-white, with art nouveau motifs.

The South Eastern, which shared the station with the Brighton, was not to be outdone, although its changes were more modest. The company replaced its tatty wooden buildings and the ugly fence with a four-storey masonry block in the French Second Empire style, which was completed in 1908. Its most impressive feature, a huge central arch, survives today. It was originally flanked by an elegant canopy and used as a cab road, which, like all the others, has long disappeared.

After these improvements, Victoria, with its more spacious platforms, became the dominant terminus for Continental services. These included boat trains connecting at Dover to both Ostend and Calais, but also other routes such as Gravesend–Rotterdam and, on the Brighton side of the station, Newhaven–Dieppe.

During the First World War, Victoria played a key role, as many of the trains carrying soldiers on leave ran between the station and Folkestone, and later Dover, and the large cab arch became the site of small groups of soldiers waving goodbye, perhaps forever, to their wives and girlfriends, a scene captured in the well-known photomontage 'The Gate of Goodbye' by F.J. Mortimer. During most of the war years, there was a free buffet staffed by various women's organizations (including the Ladies' Vigilance Society, which prompted Alan Jackson to quip, 'was the vigilance for the ladies or the men?'[7]) that could cater for up to 4,000 men per day.

Charing Cross lost all its Continental services after the First World War and Victoria began to earn a reputation for providing the best trains. Numerous services operating from the station had Pullman carriages and the all-Pullman *Brighton Belle*, with its dining car and tea service, was the businessman's favourite way to reach the south coast. Its service to France via a Channel ferry during the interwar period was its most prestigious. This became the *Golden Arrow*, or *Flèche d'Or*, service to Paris via Dover, which was also all-Pullman and priced accordingly. Partly, this was to ward off competition from airlines, which in the 1920s were beginning to offer a quicker, if rather more perilous, way of reaching the Continent. Just before the Second World War, Imperial Airways, the predecessor of British Airways, inaugurated its London terminal in Buckingham Palace Road next to Victoria; Southern Railways ran connecting trains to the airline's boat planes, which operated from Southampton Harbour to the Far East, Australia and other parts of the British Empire.

These Continental services were the prestige services of the South Eastern & Chatham and the canopies on either side of the cab arch read 'Shortest and quickest route to Paris and the Continent' and 'Sea passage one hour'. The rivalry remained, however, as the Brighton, next door, boasted about its Newhaven–Dieppe service, proclaiming it also – and misleadingly – to be the shortest service. The two stations, indeed, remained separated by the interior wall, but in 1924 a couple of corridors were created to link the two stations, which were now both part of Southern Railway. The platforms were renumbered 1 to 17, removing the duplication and reducing passenger confusion. A joint stationmaster, who oversaw a staff of more than 1,000, was put in charge of both sides but this was little more than a token merger. Effectively, the two sides remained separate with no rail connections until 1938. For a time, too, the electrification systems were different, with the Chatham receiving its first electric trains in 1925, while the Brighton's overhead system survived for four more years until it was replaced by a third rail.

The forward-looking Herbert Walker, the general manager of the Southern, did not overlook the network's other key station, London Bridge, which had become something of a mess. In 1928, a most momentous hole was knocked through between the eastern section, previously home to the South Eastern, and the central section, the platforms used by the London, Brighton &

South Coast. The fact that it took five years for the Southern to do this showed just how entrenched the separation of the old railway companies had been. This new passage was to help the increasing numbers of passengers changing trains at London Bridge, a consequence of the greater frequency enabled by electrification. For operational reasons, this increase in the number of trains meant that more of them terminated at London Bridge instead of continuing on crowded tracks to Cannon Street and Charing Cross. All the platforms were fitted with conductor rails to allow for electrification and were renumbered 1 to 22, north to south. Oddly, however, there were only twenty-one platforms, a consequence of there being no platform 5, one of those mysteries lost in the fogs of railway history.

Many improvements to the terminus stations in the interwar period were extensions to public areas, notably concourses that had often been cramped or even non-existent when the terminuses were originally built. Waterloo, with its long, curved concourse, was a great example to follow in demonstrating the importance of creating space for passengers and offering a wide range of facilities to those waiting for trains. The removal of the cab roads often created space for the concourse and associated facilities, such as newsstands and cafés. The 'throats', the confusing array of tracks and junctions leading to and from the platforms, were, in many cases, expanded and provided with new links in order to facilitate the increased traffic that virtually all the stations, but especially those serving commuters, experienced during the interwar years.

The expansion of Paddington was typical in this respect. A fourth arch was added to allow extra platforms to be created before the First World War and the number of tracks in the station 'throat' was increased to facilitate more traffic. A second round of improvements took place in the 1930s, with the creation of a new concourse for passengers in the area between the station hotel and the platforms still known as The Lawn, even though it had not seen a blade of grass since the completion of the hotel in 1854 – apart, possibly, from the stationmaster's garden. A large art deco office block was built next to the station entrance ramp and the hotel was given what the transport architectural historian Oliver Green calls 'a modish 1930s refurbishment'.[8] The station was never heavily used by suburban services, but it was extraordinarily busy for goods, notably milk and mail. An astonishing 80,000 mail bags were handled in twenty-eight special trains during Christmas 1936.

In the 1930s, Euston and King's Cross were the hosts of the fierce competition between the London, Midland & Scottish and the London & North Eastern on their different routes to Scotland. Each one designed ever-better steam locomotives to outdo their rival and the competition attracted widespread publicity, with the drivers becoming so well known they were featured in cigarette card sets. The London & North Eastern, which managed to cut the journey time from London to Edinburgh to just six hours, eventually emerged as the winner.

The two stations themselves saw few improvements in this period. The frontage of King's Cross was cluttered with what became known as the 'African Village' because it was such a mess; this included a full-size suburban Laing show home, of the type that could be found in the annual Ideal Home Exhibition. It became an increasingly dismal station, described by Jackson as 'neither pleasing nor impressive',[9] with a tiny concourse that was inadequate for passengers and a messy interchange between the suburban and main-line sections. Its best feature, oddly, was the

Gill Sans lettering of the signs that had been introduced as part of the London & North Eastern's design makeover in the early 1930s.

Euston, too, remained largely unchanged between the wars as the London, Midland & Scottish, which boasted of being the largest company in the British Empire, showed little interest in improving its poor facilities. The Great Hall was scrubbed up in 1927 but behind the scenes there were moves afoot to demolish what was a fundamentally inconvenient station. The Second World War intervened, but the station became the biggest casualty of the postwar period when Modernism and its concomitant disdain for Victorian architecture ruled unchallenged. At St Pancras, the closure of the Midland Grand Hotel, which had failed to modernize to maintain standards, marked the beginning of the decline of the station that would result in attempts in the 1960s to close and demolish it.

The continued growth of the City as a major centre for employment led to the expansion of both Fenchurch Street and Liverpool Street. While those two stations eschewed electrification, by the outbreak of the Second World War virtually all Southern Railway's suburban network had been electrified, with both Charing Cross and Cannon Street having had all their platforms fitted with the third rail.

The Depression of the 1930s, followed by war, nationalization and austerity, meant that for the middle period of the twentieth century most of the terminus stations underwent little change, with even war damage being left unrepaired once sufficient patching up had taken place to ensure that services could keep running. Even in the First World War, the terminus stations had been deliberately targeted in the two waves of enemy attacks, initially in 1915 with Zeppelins and two years later with aeroplanes. The worst attack was at St Pancras where a stick bomb hit the cab court just outside the booking hall (which is now the hotel reception area) and killed twenty people who had been sheltering there. Liverpool Street was also the scene of fatalities when sixteen people were killed in 1917 after three bombs fell at the end of the platforms in a daytime raid.

In the Second World War, there were many more raids in which the stations were clearly aimed at. Cannon Street was hit several times, perhaps because its prominent twin towers by the Thames could easily be spotted even during blackout conditions. The terminus stations suffered particularly badly on 10/11 May 1941, the worst night of the Blitz in London when more than 500 German bombers targeted the capital, aiming to destroy the bridges and other key facilities. At Cannon Street, the office block that had replaced the former hotel and the station roof were both severely damaged but, fortunately for train services, the hits on the bridge did little damage. St Pancras, which had already been struck by a land mine in October 1940 that wrecked part of the roof and caused the station to be closed for five days, suffered even more severely that night. A bomb penetrated through to the beer vaults below the platforms and exploded, wrecking the two platforms above and causing the station to be closed for eight days. On the same night, office blocks on the west side of Liverpool Street and the station clock tower were burnt out. Waterloo was the station hit by most bombs that night and a blaze in the arches below burnt for four days after the attack, fanned by huge quantities of spirits kept in the vaults. The station had also suffered previous attacks and was completely closed for a week after raids on the City of London on the night of 29/30 December 1940 that demolished the offices on York Road and the Necropolis station. But the deadliest impact of all was at King's

Cross where twelve people were killed when two 1,000-pound bombs landed on the west side of the station.

London Bridge also suffered badly on the night of 29/30 December 1940 when several bombs gutted parts of the station. Charing Cross was hit numerous times and one of the spans of the bridge leading to it was taken out by a bomb in June 1944, resulting in the closure of the station until December. But such a lengthy period out of action was very much the exception. Thanks to the heroic efforts of railway workers, who sensibly had been accorded the status of a protected occupation in the Second World War, most stations were reopened within a few days. The speed with which services were restarted, even when considerable damage had been caused to the track, demonstrated both the resilience of the railway companies and also the important role the railways were playing in the war effort. Without them, the country would have come to a halt. Indeed, despite all these attacks, none of the terminus stations suffered irreparable damage, though several of them bore the scars well into the 1950s, mainly because British Railways had little money to patch them up and, in any case, its priorities were elsewhere.

In the early postwar years, British Railways, created on New Year's Day 1948, was part of the British Transport Commission, which showed no interest in developing London's terminus stations, a missed opportunity as they were sited on prime locations with enormous potential. Moreover, since British Railways had little money available for investment, the first couple of decades after the end of the war saw few improvements and no major works at London's terminus stations. This changed with a decision by the Minister of Transport, enacted in 1962, to allow the railways to develop their holdings on a commercial basis. This was fortuitous timing given that the reduction in freight transport on the railways was about to release large tracts of land used for sidings and marshalling, some of which was close to London's terminus stations. Many adjoining offices became redundant and schemes for virtually all the terminuses were being put forward by developers as London's postwar boom was beginning.

Redevelopment was the order of the day and virtually every London terminus became, at one stage, the focus of radical plans by British Railways for refurbishment or even demolition. Only two existing stations would be razed to the ground. Broad Street, increasingly neglected as services were moved to other stations, was plainly targeted by the British Railways Board and it was sacrificed to use the land to help pay for the rebuilding of Liverpool Street. Plans to electrify the long-distance services to the North-West meant that Euston, with its short platforms and inconvenient layout, was scheduled for demolition by British Railways. As we see in the final chapter, much has changed at many of the stations after this long period of stagnation. And I have enlisted Sir John Betjeman's help in assessing the results.

THIRTEEN

ROUND LONDON WITH SIR JOHN BETJEMAN

ETJEMAN'S CHARMING BUT not always accurate book *London's Historic Railway Stations*, published in 1972, is suffused with a sense of sadness and indeed loss. Euston's Great Hall and the folly of the Doric arch had long gone, and Betjeman was embroiled in the campaign to save St Pancras from a similar fate. There was a feeling, which also underlies Alan Jackson's book *London's Termini*, published in 1969, that the railway, and therefore London's stations, had had their day. Jackson writes that Paddington, St Pancras and King's Cross deserved to be cherished but in his introduction he appears resigned to losing several others, including his favourite, Marylebone.

Betjeman's book also has an undertone of hopelessness, reflecting the awful reality that most of the London terminus stations were in a decrepit and neglected state, still unscrubbed from the recently abandoned steam age. With the railways expecting further cuts after the politicians had wielded the axe handed to them by Richard Beeching, there seemed little hope of revival. They were at their nadir, although there were signs of revival. The lines out of Euston had been electrified and were attracting many more passengers thanks to the 'sparks effect', a well-established phenomenon around the world. However, across the country parts of the network were earmarked for closure; even in the capital, the North London line appeared destined to go the way of its terminus, Broad Street, which was all but abandoned in readiness for its imminent demolition. This was part of a wider perception of the railway as nineteenth-century technology that, like so many other industrial inventions of the Victorian age, should be scrapped. Yes, there were useful bits carrying commuters and linking a few major towns and cities, but, by and large, people wanted to drive their shiny new cars on the glistening tarmac of the motorway network that was taking shape around the country. Railways were for nostalgics, trainspotters and those poor souls who could not afford to buy their own car.

No wonder that, in writing his short book, Betjeman was in despair, noting in the introduction that ultimately it would only be of historic interest since he expected that 'the architects of British Rail [would] never cease to destroy their heritage of stone, brick, cast iron and wood, and replace it with windy wastes of concrete'.[1] Of Euston, which is relegated to the last few pages of the book in expectation that many people would not bother reading about it, he wrote: 'What masterpiece arose on the site of the old station? No masterpiece. Instead there is a place where nobody can sit [originally British Rail famously did not provide any seating for waiting passengers which caused a major furore]; an underground taxi-entrance so full of fumes that drivers, passengers and porters alike hate it. A great hall of glass looks like a mini-version of London Airport which it seems to be trying to imitate.'[2]

So I thought I would take old Betjeman on a tour round these stations today. I could not expect him to like everything, as he was such a deep traditionalist, but even he, surely, would appreciate how in many cases British Rail and its successors, together with developers and architects, have blended historic and modern features to renew the cathedrals of steam and create some masterpieces in the process. The additions are not 'carbuncles', to quote that architectural reactionary critic Prince Charles, looking out of place amid the century-old heritage. Instead the designers have managed in many but not all cases to meld the old and the new so successfully that the original is enhanced and the experience for passengers greatly improved.

So Sir John, let us do our grand tour, with references to your book, and see how things have changed in the intervening near half a century. It is worth noting to start with that the railways are in far better shape than you might have expected. Passenger numbers had more than doubled in the twenty years running up to the life-changing pandemic of 2020, which turned the railway and its stations into deserts with just 5 per cent of the previous patronage. But even during that disastrous phase, they kept running and passengers will return. New rolling stock is now the norm, and while the seats are not always as comfortable as the old ones, trains are quiet and fast and carriages have sockets to charge one's electronic devices, something that you would find very strange since computers were still huge mainframes and telephones all landlines when you died in 1984.

Let's start at Euston, to get it over with, and from there head in an anti-clockwise direction around London. Euston, it must be said, would still appal you. The problems there are rooted in its intrinsic design faults that were a reflection of the prevailing culture of the time when it was built. Rebuilding the station had been mooted before the Second World War and once British Railways emerged from postwar austerity, a new station was back on the agenda along with electrification of the West Coast route to Birmingham, Manchester and Liverpool. The scheme included the demolition of both the Great Hall, which was in a pristine condition having been recently restored, and the Doric arch.

While the loss of the Great Hall and the boardroom above it was probably unavoidable in order to carry out platform lengthening, the arch could conceivably have been moved elsewhere rather than, as happened, being dumped in the River Lea. The furore over these plans, in which you played a leading role, reached the desk of the Prime Minister, Harold Macmillan, who gave the thumbs down to the arch. He argued that there was neither the funding nor an available site where it could be re-erected. It was later claimed that British Railways had been so determined to dispose of what it saw as a relic of the past that its board turned down an offer from the demolition contractor to reconstruct the arch in the gardens in front of the station. There is no doubt that the arch could have been saved, but the government, British Railways and London County Council all saw it as a barrier to modernizing the postwar railway.

So, Sir John, what we have today is your 'mini-version of London Airport' that you described so disparagingly in your book almost fifty years ago. Well, there are a few seats now, and the entrance has been improved, making it easier to get to the Underground. Upstairs there are more of what we now call 'food outlets', a pub and the first-class lounge. The huge concrete, featureless area that you describe looks even worse when there are few people in it, with the cheap lights and the dark recesses of the roof appearing more prominent. In its favour, there is a sizeable ticket office, a large destination panel that is visible from all parts of the station and getting to and from the platforms is reasonably easy. But, gosh, this is still an unlovable terminus with not a single feature of architectural merit.

The good news is that this station will probably be demolished when HS2 is built, and while no details have yet emerged, one can be optimistic since this will be the gateway to Britain's most important rail line, just as Euston was originally. You may be rather shocked to know that the present station does have its defenders, in the same way that you fought for it. In an article for the Design Council, Thomas Bender, a heritage expert, wrote: 'Euston is a text-book example of a well-ordered station. Everything is efficient, easy on the eye and elegantly designed; from the geometric rhythm of the ceiling to the clear and legible routes to the platforms, and even the layout of the ticket office.'³ So a second battle of Euston may be on the cards.

From the object of your scorn, to one of your favourites, Sir John, Marylebone, which you famously described as looking like 'a branch library in a Manchester suburb'.⁴ It has had a difficult time over the past half century but is now both better used and better kept than in your day. For a time, British Railways was keen to shut the station and ran down services. In 1983, British Rail's then chairman Sir Peter Parker had the crazy idea of turning Marylebone into a coach station, with single-deck coaches running on the track bed. However, the simple step of measuring the headroom quickly revealed that the tunnels were simply too small. You were scornful of British Railways for having 'taken revenge on it for being so new and comfortable' by removing some of the original features, but in truth, Sir John, you would be delighted with how it looks today. Once the coach plan was abandoned, services were expanded, and the station benefited from the British Rail concept of 'total route modernization', which involved new rolling stock and track improvements.

Since rail privatization in the mid-1990s, there has been considerable further investment and expansion but fortunately Marylebone retains a provincial feel and human scale. Your much-loved *porte cochère* between the station and hotel (now reinstated as one of London's finest) has survived intact. You'll be pleased to know, too, that there are once again regular trains to Birmingham and commuter services to places such as Gerrards Cross and High Wycombe are hugely popular. As you came from an era when the bicycle was an accepted part of transport with strong links to rail travel, I think you may also be pleased by the parking space for up to 500 cycles on the west side of the station where two extra platforms have been added, giving it, for the first time, the six that were envisaged when first built. There is, on the same side, a clapboard-covered control room painted in cream that adds to the village feel of the station, which has remained 'durable and well built' as you put it.

Paddington, too, you would mostly recognize, although, like many of the terminus stations, it has been cleaned and greatly improved. As with all the stations, the cab road through the middle has disappeared, replaced with a ramp leading to a completely renovated upper entrance that connects with the Metropolitan & City Line station. Brunel's elegant roof survives, and the station retains a cathedral-like feel, as he intended it to be. Most trains are now electric, which means the glass roof is cleaner, letting in significantly more light than in your day. The concourse has been further extended since you saw it and the area at the back, known as The Lawn, has been glassed over and houses a pub and various food counters. It was designed by Nicholas Grimshaw, whom we will meet again when we arrive at Waterloo and London Bridge, and it is difficult to argue with Oliver Green, who says it is 'a very effective reworking... that has improved the station's facilities but also enhanced its historic features'.[5] My own favourite part is the back entrance that leads directly, via an escalator, to the canal quayside, embellished by the life-size statue of a man seemingly awaiting a train.

The one big addition, unfortunately not yet completed, is the Crossrail station adjoining the main building on the West Side. This has replaced the cab entrance from Eastbourne Terrace where a long ramp used to descend to an archway that led to platform 1. Now a glass roof, oddly decorated with mock clouds that will be difficult to distinguish from the real ones, will allow light through to the Crossrail platforms as the tracks, at this stage, are just below the surface as they head off towards Bond Street, the next stop, and further east. This remarkable new line should have opened in December 2018 but technical difficulties and cost overruns have resulted in a three-year delay. This is architecture and design on a grand scale and fits in with your comment that 'Brunel still dominates Paddington station; it is admirably planned and copes with traffic greater than even he envisaged... It was to be an aisled cathedral in a cutting.'[6] And it is. Both you and Brunel would appreciate the addition of the impressive Crossrail station, as well as the overall feel of the main station that retains its grandeur while feeling modern and light.

Victoria you described as 'London's most conspicuous monument to commercial rivalry'.[7] Other stations could lay claim to that crown but certainly Victoria's origins as two separate stations side by side still screams out. When both stations were rebuilt separately in the early years of the twentieth century, you were right to say that the Brighton had 'maidens cast in stone' only to be outdone by the South Eastern & Chatham, which 'had even bigger maidens carved in stone'.[8] You will be pleased to know the recently cleaned maidens are all still in place. The bus station at the front of the station, which you were rather sniffy about, makes it difficult to obtain a good perspective that does justice to a frontage that consists of three rather different buildings. The huge dividing wall between the South Eastern and the Brighton sections remains, though the concourse is partly unified with a much bigger connecting area than in your day. There are still separate destination indicators and the division between the two sides has been somewhat reinforced by a line of shops with plastic arched roofs built along the northern side of the wall. But much of what you called the 'muddle' of Victoria station has gone, as has its claim to be the 'gateway to the Continent', since all the cross-Channel services have been killed off by aviation with the *coup de grâce* delivered by the Channel Tunnel. The Pullman trains, too, have gone and the only premier service is the Gatwick Express, which is something of a misnomer as it is only a few minutes faster than regular services to the airport and fares are significantly higher. Otherwise, all trace of airport connections is long gone and towards the end of the platforms on the Brighton side there is a soulless and banal shopping centre on the first floor.

Trains from the Brighton side might serve more glamorous destinations, but there is no doubt that the South Eastern section is better designed with the huge arch dominating the frontage. Sir John, you will be pleased to know that the two glorious glazed tiled route maps – one main line, one suburban – of the old London, Brighton & South Coast Railway, hidden for so long by a row of telephone kiosks, have been uncovered since the booths were made obsolete by a device called the mobile telephone. An irksome feature are the ugly-looking automatic ticket barriers that dominate the gateways from the concourse leading to the platforms. Instead of a friendly ticket collector or two, there are these rows of machines policed by a couple of patrolling 'revenue enforcement officers' wearing bright green, high visibility, sleeveless jackets who create a sense of menace. At busy times, queues of passengers jostle around these eyesores that make modern stations look untidy and unnecessarily cluttered. Unfortunately, they are ubiquitous at terminuses today as the railway companies strive to protect their revenue with a minimum of staff.

Next on our tour of the five Southern Railway stations is Charing Cross, which was the first to be affected by changes brought about by the rush to build office accommodation on any available space in central London. Therefore, Sir John, I am sorry to say that while the pleasant frontage of the Charing Cross Hotel survives, below which the cabs still pick up their fares, the 'enormous curved roof nearly one hundred feet above the rails', which you said 'made the station into a cathedral of brick, glass and iron', is long gone.[9]

The huge Postmodern Embankment Gardens development over the platforms built in the 1980s looks good from the other side of the river, with its circular double roof, but inside, the station's oppressively low ceiling cuts out all the natural light. If only the developers had foregone just one floor, the station would still have some breathing space, but instead, Sir John, I'm afraid it is precisely the sort of corporate vandalism that you abhorred. However, the horrible Hungerford Bridge running over the river has been improved immeasurably by the replacement of the old footpaths with cable-stayed pedestrian bridges that share the railway bridge's foundation, and which largely hide it from view. It is, perhaps, a tribute to the authorities that at least Charing Cross has survived into the twenty-first century, having endured a number of attempts to replace it, and today it is still the only terminus directly serving the West End.

Over the bridge now to Waterloo, where there have been changes and additions that mostly have enhanced the basic 1922 design. If it is no longer worthy of O.S. Nock's claim, which you quote, to be 'one of the really great stations of the world', that is more because there are now many more rivals for that crown, both renovated and newly constructed. At Waterloo, the most notable improvement, and I am sure you would like this, is the former International terminal, which was the first terminus station for Eurostar train services to Paris and Brussels via the Channel Tunnel. Built on the western side of the station, it replaced the roof of the Windsor section, which had been retained as a money-saving gesture in the early twentieth-century reconstruction. The renowned architect Nicholas Grimshaw produced a universally acclaimed design, which looked like a modern version of a Victorian train shed running down the side of the station in a gentle curve. It held all the customs and immigration facilities at a level below the concourse and was accessed from the side by a rather inconvenient and narrow road. It was, though, considered a triumph of both architecture and engineering, but was only used for precisely thirteen years as, in November 2007, the Eurostar trains were transferred to St Pancras, which we will come to later. You would have loved the fact, Sir John, that for a couple of years, two of the platforms were used for performances of a stage adaptation of *The Railway Children*, with a steam locomotive making an appearance. However, in a typical railway muddle, it took more than a decade after Eurostar had moved out for those five platforms to be converted for suburban service once again.

There is now a wide ramp up to platforms 20–24 right at the top of the stairs through the Victory Arch that shows off this new roof to great effect and enormously enhances the overall station. The 'cocktail bar of the Surrey Dining Room' that you mention is no longer there, but the view from the floor above the station still gives onto a 'forest of columns' that you describe affectionately. One disappointing aspect is the tacky signage, much of it white on blue, that looks cheap and last-minute. It particularly detracts from the Victory Arch, as there is a sign with the station's name, and then various signposts, that all look very much out of place on this still impressive sculpture with its very moving memorial to the railway personnel who lost their lives in two world wars. Although war memorials feature at all the terminus stations, Waterloo's is the most prominent.

I'm afraid that Waterloo is much changed in character from when you wrote that it 'is associated with fast electric trains taking executives to the coniferous half-world of Woking, with soldiers going to the slippery heather and rhododendrons of Aldershot and with schoolboys and mental patients being drafted off to large institutions on sandy soil'.[10] The fast electric trains certainly still dominate but the schoolboys and soldiers are definitely gone and the mental patients probably no longer so obviously recognizable as you found them. Hordes of executives still swarm onto the Waterloo & City Line below, even if they no longer wear bowler hats, but they are probably outnumbered by software engineers looking after the computers that are the essential part of any business today. Waterloo remains Britain's busiest and largest station, but its users are a more varied group, including suburbanites from south-west London and commuters living in towns further afield such as Woking, Guildford and Winchester.

Nevertheless, I think you would approve of most of the changes, even if the tidying up of the station and the loss of its parcels and milk business have made it feel less distinctive. The Jubilee Line, completed in 1999 to accommodate the seemingly constant growth of passengers (until the pandemic hit), saw the creation of an additional ticket hall on Waterloo Road and a new bridge, over the old one that used to carry the railway tracks, to connect Waterloo East with the main station. Oddly, on Westminster Bridge Road, number 121, part of the old London Necropolis station, survives, and is now called Westminster Bridge House, with the entrance via the roadway that used to lead up to the station still visible. Upstairs, there are far more shops and restaurants than in your day, including a couple of pubs. There is, too, a new link to the South Bank that has become a hugely popular tourist destination after it was closed for four years when part of the Shell Centre offices was demolished.

London Bridge is much changed, thanks to a £1bn redevelopment by, yet again, Grimshaw Architects, the practice created by Nicholas Grimshaw. And it has been a complete transformation, more radical in fact than changes at other terminus stations. London Bridge, Sir John, probably gets the prize as the most improved station since you wrote *London's Historic Railway Stations*, though, as we shall soon see, Liverpool Street, King's Cross and St Pancras are strong contenders for that award. You wrote that:

> London Bridge is the most complicated, muddled and unwelcoming of all London termini. Its platforms are narrow and draughty, it seems to be several stations in one,

and they are connected by toilsome footbridges and mysterious underground passages... at the time of writing the
station is, as it always was, a collection of bewildering signs,
bookstalls, brown and uninviting, bars, shops, one of which
is surprisingly called 'the Hosiery and Underwear Bar'.[11]

This last, sadly now gone, rather confused you since you wondered
how 'one could drink such delicious things'. Alan Jackson was no
kinder, stating 'that thanks to its hybrid origins, subsequent neglect,
and German bombs, it is indisputably the most hideous of all the
termini in its external appearance'.[12]

There were a few changes in the postwar period; the war damage
was patched up, platforms were extended to take twelve-car trains,
and the Jubilee Line was built, which improved connections
between the station and the Underground. Grimshaw, however,
has revolutionized the station and almost completely solved the
messy connections between the upper terminus platforms and
the through ones below. I say 'almost' because it is still not always
possible to know which is the best platform for your destination,
but apart from this lacuna, it is now a station fit for purpose with
a concourse that Network Rail proudly boasts is bigger than the
football pitch at Wembley stadium.

The intricate set of tunnels and passageways under the station,
with their pleasing yellow brick, have been cleaned up and new
shops and food outlets have been added, though it is still something
of a labyrinth to the uninitiated and notably the old section leading
to the Underground has not been refurbished. Nevertheless, the
new entrances from streets on both sides are now far more accessible and the wooden slatted 'acoustic' ceiling is calming, giving the
station a Scandinavian feel.

The only thing wrong with the concourse is the huge lines of gates, barring the way to the platform, as at Victoria and elsewhere, but here they are particularly unpleasing on the eye given the elegant surrounds as they detract from the open and light architecture of spaces like this. The refurbishment has resulted in extended platforms, much better street entrances, three new through tracks and fewer terminating platforms. The upper section, with the terminating platforms, is mostly glass and is rather overshadowed by its neighbour, the Shard, London's tallest building at just over 1,000 feet, and other nearby new buildings. The best view of the impact of the railways on London can be obtained from the Shard, with the busy tracks on London & Greenwich's viaduct that are never seen without a train stretching out far into south-east London.

London Bridge has definitely lost its unwanted reputation as the worst station entrance in the capital, but that award probably now goes to Cannon Street, whose entrance is a set of steps leading from the busy, narrow eponymous road under an office block. You spare no punches with Cannon Street, which you describe as a 'mutilated masterpiece… a contemptible shed' in which 'only here and there could an ecclesiologist looking for a scratch-dial or a pillar-piscina find a vestige of the former station'.[13] The hotel, you wrote, had been replaced by the dullest of office blocks missing 'any human element'. Well, that ugliest of office blocks, designed by the corrupt architect and businessman John Poulson, has gone. While the new one is certainly an improvement, the entrance is hidden under it and lost among the adjoining shops. The lovely train shed, which looked particularly grand from the other side of the Thames, had already gone when you wrote your book but fortunately the two towers survive, even if they no longer have any function. One wishes that the station faced the other way so that the towers could be seen from the street, rather than being hidden behind the new block.

Inside, the station still has the cramped feel that you so deprecated but there is one pleasant addition, a seven-foot-high bronze sculpture by Martin Jennings called *The Plumber's Apprentice*. It was installed in 2011 to mark the 400th anniversary of King James I issuing a royal charter to the Worshipful Company of Plumbers whose livery hall stood on that site until being demolished to make way for the station. It does not, however, make up for the pokiness and claustrophobic feel of the station.

Fenchurch Street is the third of these terminuses to have been squeezed by the lucrative 'air' developments above stations that were the great fashion in the final two decades of the twentieth century. Sadly, your description of how 'the station has been less messed about than any London terminus'[14] is no longer true. Indeed, nothing much happened to it in the postwar period when a scheme to put a huge office block over it in 1959 was turned down by the City Corporation. In the 1980s, however, British Rail agreed to a more sophisticated plan that preserved the façade and paid for the renovation of the station and improvements to the trackwork. You will be pleased to know that the 'zig zag canopy' with its 'fairground charm' survives and opposite the entrance there is now a small pedestrianized area that would benefit from some landscaping but provides a good view of the façade, which remains as you described it.

However, here's the bad news: the 'stairs with attractive cast-iron railings [which] mount either side of the booking hall to the main concourse on the first floor'[15] has, I'm afraid, been replaced with escalators running in rather cramped corridors lined with cold white tiles better suited for a public convenience than a busy stairway.

Even worse, the train shed with its 'crescent-shaped trussed roof of iron, from which depend charming things like flying saucers which hold fluorescent light'[16] has been sacrificed to make room for the office block that is rather cunningly tucked away behind the façade, giving the impression that it is behind, rather than over, the station. The block above is built in a brown-coloured pyramidal structure, which is intended to blend in with the other buildings, on a far larger scale, that are now dotted around the station.

Therefore, as with Cannon Street and Charing Cross, there is a claustrophobic feel to the station that removes any sense of excitement that its daily passengers might have once had when travelling through it. The concourse has lost the light that, as you wrote, came through 'the large round-arched windows on the façade'.[17] It was slightly expanded in the 1980s but remains too small for the number of passengers hurrying through at rush hour. Consequently, there are very few facilities because the clear intention of railway bosses is to ensure that passengers do not linger and cause an obstruction at what remains a busy station, despite the limited number of destinations it serves in east London and south Essex.

The rest, Sir John, is mostly good news. Let's start with Liverpool Street, in a redevelopment that you very much influenced but sadly did not see completed. In your 1972 book you described Liverpool Street very favourably as 'the most picturesque and interesting of the London termini'[18] with the most varied passengers, from blue-eyed blonde Scandinavian tourists fresh off the ferries and Belgians arriving via Southend Airport, to county farmers and agricultural manufacturers. It was, though, a messy labyrinth that was inconvenient for passengers with, as you said, 'a bad connection with the Underground', worse than for any other terminus. I know you liked it but I remember it from my trainspotting days in the 1960s as a cumbersome affair, with a great dividing wall that meant the easternmost platforms were hidden away from the rest of the station, which, in fact, was a hotchpotch of offices and storerooms.

As you know, Sir John, British Rail produced a report in 1975 recommending the complete demolition of both Liverpool Street and Broad Street to be replaced by a single twenty-two-platform station. Much of this would have been underground, like the disastrous developments at Birmingham New Street and New York's Penn Street station. Partly thanks to your efforts, there was a lengthy public inquiry into the proposal, which found that the Great Eastern Hotel and the western train shed of Liverpool Street should be preserved and there should be only eighteen platforms. Broad Street, however, was to be demolished and replaced with an office development, the Broadgate Centre, that would also occupy the space above the Liverpool Street 'throat'. Nothing much happened until Broad Street, which had become something of a ghost station as services were transferred elsewhere, was demolished in 1983 and then a far better plan emerged. Work started in 1985 on what proved to be the best of the station redevelopments, with the design work led by British Rail's chief architect, Nick Derbyshire.

The finest historic features were retained, even if they were at times moved, and the main platform-level concourse is both a coherent whole and easily accessible from the street through a series of escalators and lifts. The entire roof was extended southwards to the new concourse and can only be distinguished from the old one by the colour scheme. Sir John, you should be particularly pleased that some of the old design features have been replaced. You wrote: 'Unfortunately, the capitals of the columns which support this quadruple roof were stripped of their ironwork leaves after the war – some false economy measure – but perforated iron brackets remain.'[19] Well, the good news is that the Corinthian-style tops of the columns have been restored to their former glory, cleaned up and repainted in blue, red and silver, presumably the original colours. There have been losses, of course, like your beloved tea room, where you enjoyed elevenses, but also the odd pleasant addition. Indeed, the oddest is a major piece of architectural deceit. Four brick towers, in an Italianate style, that matched the original 1874 ones were erected in pairs on either side of the station, a homage to the historic railways' love of the Italianate.

Another new feature is a bronze sculpture of five children, which was installed to mark the Kindertransport that saved the lives of 10,000 refugee children from Nazi-occupied Europe, who passed through Liverpool Street after arriving at Harwich in the run-up to the Second World War. There is, too, on the upper floor, the war memorial to the 1,100 Great Eastern staff killed in the First World War, which was moved there following the 1990s redevelopment from its original location in the booking hall. Another plaque explains that the memorial was unveiled in 1922 by Field Marshal Sir Henry Wilson, the former head of the British army, who was shot dead about an hour later outside his home in Belgravia by two IRA men. Liverpool Street is probably the easiest of these stations for passengers to find their way around and reflects a brilliant partnership between the private and public sectors.

At the back of the station, there is a McDonald's whose fare I am sure you would not appreciate. But look carefully: this is the old block known as 50 Liverpool Street that was demolished and relocated here – it is in fact a replica of the listed Gothic three-storey building with a few changes, but essentially the building has been retained. What a contrast with the Euston Arch that British Rail so dogmatically insisted could not be saved, even when there was the opportunity for a compromise. If anything illustrates how the attitude towards our Victorian heritage has changed, a transformation in which you played a key role, it is the story of this station. Liverpool Street was the first of a series of restorations of the major terminus buildings, and as the railway manager Chris Green wrote in an appreciation of your role in railway heritage: 'It is not chance that Network Rail in the twenty-first century is basing the latest redevelopment of St Pancras, King's Cross, Victoria, London Bridge, Paddington – and now Euston – around a careful restoration of the original historic buildings in close association with English Heritage. The Betjeman impact is with us to this day.'[20]

We have left the best to the last, and Sir John, you can claim some credit for this. You and your many supporters succeeded in changing British Rail architectural policy. The arrogant 1960s philosophy, when the Modernist movement was at its peak and rejected anything perceived as old-fashioned, was replaced with a more balanced approach of melding the new and the old, retaining the best historic features while, rightly, bringing the overall space up to modern standards. The contrast between Euston and Liverpool Street marks how that thinking changed and led to even better blends of the old and the new that have characterized more recent redevelopments.

You will be pleased to see, Sir John, that at King's Cross and St Pancras, this approach has succeeded in creating a pair of fabulous stations, standing side by side in contrasting styles. This was greatly helped by your campaigning, along with the Victorian Society, which ensured both stations were listed in 1974. As a result, British Rail and its successors, as well as any potential developers, had to tread extremely carefully. King's Cross had become a dingy, uncoordinated station in an area infamous for being seedy with ever-present drug addicts and desperate prostitutes, one of whom caused the downfall of the then director of public prosecutions, Sir Allan Green, in 1991 when he was cautioned for propositioning her. Alan Jackson singled out King's Cross as the worst of the London stations and described the suburban section as 'a drab untidy mess, mercifully hidden round a corner'.[21] He concluded that the whole 'is neither a pleasing nor impressive station'[22] with a tiny inadequate concourse and a cold breeze constantly running through it because of the openings in the arches. You, Sir John, were slightly kinder, but described it as 'not very practical' and 'narrow and inconvenient', while expressing a preference for St Pancras, which, despite its 'fussiness', you say was 'the more practical station'.[23]

Not so today, Sir John. We will come to St Pancras in a minute, but the transformation of King's Cross is, in many ways, a greater triumph because it started from such a difficult base as described by Jackson. The clever trick of the designers when revamping the station was to extend it sideways. This was the only way of solving the problem of insufficient space for a proper concourse between the buffer stops and the walls of the arches. King's Cross was too small in the north–south axis, and therefore the solution was to extend either westwards or eastwards; west was the only feasible direction.

An initial plan to demolish the Great Northern Hotel was vetoed and instead a modern concourse under a roof of glass triangles and aluminium supports, sixty-five feet high, spreads out from the side wall like a spider's web. Simon Jenkins, the author of a book on Britain's 100 best railway stations, is ecstatic about the roof that covers the large area between the hotel and the station, which previously had been a mess of offices, roads and dirty canopies: 'The roof is exhilarating. The fronds soar and then fall, answering the curved façade of the hotel. They might be considered thick and overpowering, but succeed because, thanks to English Heritage, the old station was never allowed to disappear. The brick wall is dominant.'[24] That was crucial to the success of the new station, the blend of the old and the new. In addition, the ghastly jumble of 1960s buildings, which included a cluttered concourse, was demolished, revealing, for the first time in 140 years, the sheer beautiful simplicity and symmetry of Cubitt's arches.

While the new concourse has plenty of space, and there are no longer dark passages where prostitutes and pickpockets can lurk, there are a few mistakes. There was a plan to encourage most people to enter the platforms via a walkway at the first-floor level, which entailed going both up and down an escalator or stairs, but this was impracticable and was abandoned. The old concourse area beyond the ticket barrier has a very dead feel as no retail or food outlets have been allowed there, giving the impression of the platforms in American stations onto which people are only permitted just before the departure of their train. There is not even a proper destination indicator there, which is a serious oversight. Underneath the station, there is now a new northern ticket hall to cope with the vast numbers using the six Underground lines that connect with the two stations, and the unwary can be sent on very long detours if they follow the misleading signs that are designed to smooth traffic flow rather than offer the quickest route.

These, though, are minor quibbles. The roof and the concourse was a brave blend of the old and the new, with the panache of the British Museum's Great Court rather than the National Gallery's timid neo-classical pastiche Sainsbury Wing. It demonstrated a confidence in the railway's durability and adaptability. As Chris Heather, the author of a book on London's stations based on records at the National Archives, puts it, 'As all passengers now leave the station on to the new King's Cross Square with the heavy functional station wall behind them, the theatrically palatial St Pancras to the right and the historic Euston station a few yards down the road, there must be little doubt in their minds that they have reached the railway capital of the world'.[25] Indeed, where else would one find two such remarkable stations, both modernized in the past couple of decades and yet quintessentially products of the Victorian era?

Therefore, Sir John, we finish with St Pancras, which, and I am certain of this, would give you immense pleasure. Our *pièce de resistance* is sitting down outside the Benugo café next to your very own statue, a playful, larger-than-life representation of you staring upwards at Barlow's magnificent roof that you did so much to save. It is a far cry from the days when there was barely a train or two an hour and the buildings behind us were derelict, inhabited only by pigeons and rats. There are odd-looking trains now, which travel between here and France, Belgium and even the Netherlands, and over there the services to the East Midlands take up four platforms, and on the other side there's another set that go to destinations south of here, such as Dover, Margate and Gravesend. Then below us, two levels down, a floor below where the beer barrels used to be stacked, there are Thameslink trains that go to almost all points of the compass, from Peterborough to Horsham and Cambridge to Brighton.

The Eurostar trains we see waiting to whisk passengers off to Paris, Brussels and now Amsterdam, and hopefully many more destinations in the future, saved St Pancras, through a combination of luck and the forcefulness of a Conservative politician, Michael Heseltine. Originally, the plan had been to run these Continental services on a high-speed line under south London through a long tunnel starting in Bromley to a station below King's Cross, but Heseltine, as Deputy Prime Minister in John Major's government, decided this was a wasted opportunity to regenerate an area of east London as the new route served Stratford. Picking up a plan put forward by the consulting engineers, Ove Arup, he decided a revamped St Pancras, which had a limited number of trains, should be the terminus for Eurostar. The high-speed line was originally envisaged to run alongside the North London line but instead a nine-mile tunnel was built between Barking and St Pancras. Once the line was completed, the Eurostar trains transferred in November 2007 from Waterloo International to St Pancras. This followed a huge £800m redevelopment scheme at the station that resulted in a massive clean-up, the reopening of the luxury hotel, and, controversially, breaking through parts of the floor at track level so that the main through routes connecting the various sections of the station were at the level where the beer barrels used to arrive. The roof, repainted in the original baby blue, has never looked so resplendent and the Dent clock has been fully restored and hung high above the Eurostar platforms.

Again, inevitably, it is not perfect. The station is designed to encourage people to transfer between trains at the lower level, where a wide array of shops have been installed, leaving the upper level, which has an overpriced brasserie and a deserted coffee bar, rather desolate and underused. Bizarrely, it claims to have the 'longest champagne bar in Europe', although there can't be many rivals in respect of that accolade. There is, too, a vast area upstairs beyond the buffer stops that is fenced off by glass security walls; it serves no purpose and forces arriving passengers to take a detour via the crowded downstairs.

But again, these are minor quibbles. The overall impression is of an expansive, beautiful and busy station that surely can claim to be one of the world's greatest, even if my preference is for its neighbour.

St Pancras played a key role in the 2012 Olympic Games, which would never have been held in London had it not been for the new railway and its rapid connection between Stratford and St Pancras via the high-speed line. St Pancras has never looked better, even in its pomp. The lack of steam engines – even the smelly diesels only operate from the northernmost part of the station and therefore their fumes do not sully the roof – the opening up of the vaults and the creation of a series of restaurants and bars mean that it has, as its advertising claims, become 'a destination station'. Next door, by the way, there are now two major institutions on the site of the old Somers Town Goods Depot, both of which you would appreciate as they collectively cover both arts and science: the British Library, which had outgrown its space in the British Museum and is now constantly abuzz with students, researchers, writers and professors; and more recently, the Francis Crick Institute, Europe's biggest biomedical research institute, which opened in 2016. What in all this, Sir John, is there not to like?

Hand in hand with the redevelopment of these two magnificent stations, there has been an equally amazing transformation on the sixty-seven acres of railway land behind them. The biggest redevelopment programme in London outside of Docklands has over the past two decades transformed the crime-ridden and downtrodden abandoned industrial area that once housed huge swathes of sidings, warehouses and other railway-associated buildings. It has now become a largely pedestrian-based development of flats, offices, restaurants, high-end retail and educational establishments. There were inevitable battles with the appointed developers, Argent, seeking at first to produce an environment dominated by offices. However, protests by local people and careful oversight by Camden Council, together with the developers making consummate efforts to accommodate their opponents' demands, have resulted in one of London's great development success stories.

The negotiations resulted in an agreement that, to obtain the planning consent, Argent was required to retain four of the existing gasholders (which it did by removing and rebuilding them), the nature park and canal, as well as to provide considerable social housing. After consent was obtained in 2008, in a clever move, Argent earmarked the large six-floor granary building for the relocation of the world-famous Central St Martins art college, which immediately gave the area a cachet. Several other railway buildings, such as the coal drops and the coal office, have been repurposed, with the former having a remarkable new roof designed by Thomas Heatherwick that overhangs the area between the two rows of former warehouses, and the canal has been well integrated into the scheme, with the creation of a small open air auditorium used for theatre productions and concerts. The success of the development has been underpinned by the retention of the railway features and the emphasis on pedestrian access with very limited road space.

With the exception of Broad Street, and the minor stations such as Holborn Viaduct, Blackfriars and Ludgate Hill – all of which were briefly terminuses on what is now the Thameslink line through the centre of London – possibly the most remarkable aspect of this story, Sir John, is that London still has a dozen terminus stations, all of which are busy and functioning. Moreover, with the exception of three of the former Southern stations that have had tower blocks built over them, and Euston, which is pretty much as you saw it, I suggest that you would be pleased with the developments and improvements at the other stations. Certainly Londoners, when they notice them, like the improved stations and the facilities they offer.

Of course, with rational planning and a strategic approach, London could be better served by its stations. There could, for example, have been some kind of *Hauptbahnhof*, a central station with myriad potential destinations. In a sense, Farringdon, which will serve destinations on all four points of the compass via Crossrail, will be one, though it is not a terminus station. That, too, shows a way London could be better served. If some of those ambitious schemes to link stations south and north of the Thames, such as the plan to join Charing Cross with a rail line to Euston, had materialized, train services would be far easier to use. Through stations are so much more efficient. Whereas a platform that is in a terminal, a dead end as it were, can only cope with two or three trains per hour, a through platform can serve up to twenty-four, as is planned for the Thameslink trains that run under St Pancras to Blackfriars.

Nevertheless, let me conclude on a positive note. Most of these stations are pleasant, well lit, functional, and have retained their traditional features while being far more heavily used than their creators had ever intended or expected. They are not the dirty and dying buildings that you saw and feared. Nor have any, with the exception of Broad Street, been razed to the ground in the name of progress. All have had major refurbishments or developments since you wrote your book, even if some, such as at Charing Cross,

Cannon Street and Fenchurch Street, cannot really be characterized as improvements. However, hundreds of millions of pounds have been invested at all the larger ones, apart from Euston, which is scheduled for redevelopment. Yes, it remains the case that the fact that London has so many stations scattered in a ring around the centre is inconvenient and means that reaching them is not always as easy as it should be. But they represent a fantastic asset that has helped London retain its status as a global city, admired, and indeed loved, the world over. London's dozen, all built in the nineteenth century, have survived and thrived for well over a century and, I predict, will all still be there at the end of this one.

APPENDIX I

Timeline for the opening of London's terminus stations:

London Bridge	1836
Euston	1837
Fenchurch Street	1840
Waterloo	1848
King's Cross	1852
Paddington	1854
Victoria	1860
Charing Cross	1864
Cannon Street	1866
St Pancras	1868
Liverpool Street	1874
Marylebone	1899

APPENDIX II

Passenger numbers in the year to 31 March 2019 at the London terminuses (before the coronavirus pandemic):

	(millions)
Waterloo	94
Victoria	75
Liverpool Street	69
London Bridge	61
Euston	46
Paddington	38
St Pancras	36
King's Cross	35
Charing Cross	30
Cannon Street	21
Fenchurch Street	19
Marylebone	16

Source: Office of Road and Rail

SELECT
BIBLIOGRAPHY

THIS IS A highly selective bibliography focusing on the London terminus stations rather than on the capital's railway system generally, on which there is a vast bibliography. The literature covering some of the stations is far more extensive than for others, and there is a handful of general books, which are either outdated or rather short. The most comprehensive, which is a bit too detailed at times but nevertheless very readable, is Alan A. Jackson's *London Termini* (David & Charles, 1969), but this has not been updated since a revised Pan edition was published three years later. Oliver Green's *Discovering London's Railway Stations* (Shire Publications, 2010) is a short book that gives an overview of each station's history, while Chris Heather's *London Railway Stations* (Robert Hale, 2018) is quirky as it is based on the National Archives and therefore offers some different insights.

There are a couple of major works on stations that provide useful summaries of particular stations. Simon Jenkins's *Britain's 100 Best Railway Stations* (Penguin Random House, 2017) covers half a dozen of London's terminuses, while Gordon Biddle's seminal *Britain's Historic Railway Buildings* (Oxford University Press, 2003) has sections on all of them. I have made heavy use of John Betjeman's charming *London's Historic Railway Stations* (John Murray, 1972). There is a lot of information in H.P. White's *A Regional History of the Railways of Great Britain, Volume 3* (David & Charles, 1971), which is part of a series covering the whole network. The best book on the social history of stations is *The Railway Station: A Social History* (Oxford University Press, 1986) by Jeffrey Richards and John M. MacKenzie.

Most of the individual stations have been covered in a variety of pamphlets and books. The story of the early days of London Bridge is well told in *London's First Railway: The London & Greenwich* (Batsford, 1972) by R.H.G. Thomas. Paddington is covered thoroughly in Tim Bryan's *Paddington: Great Western Gateway* (Silver Link Publishing, 1997) and Steven Brindle's *Paddington Station: Its History and Architecture* (English Heritage, 2004). John Christopher's *Euston Station Through Time* (Amberley Publishing, 2012) is mainly photographs, some of which are terrific, while David Jenkinson's *The London & Birmingham Railway* (Capital Transport, 1988) sets out the station's early history.

There is an extensive literature on both King's Cross and St Pancras. *Change at King's Cross* by Michael Hunter and Robert Thorne (Historical Publications, 1990) is a basic history of the station, and a good account of its recent improvement is *Transforming King's Cross* (Merrell, 2013) by various authors. *Railway Lands: Catching St Pancras and King's Cross* (Matador, 2007) by Angela Inglis, on the history of the Railway Lands that are being extensively redeveloped, has many fascinating photographs and shows the remarkable changes brought about on the land to the back of the stations that was once dominated by the railways. The two best books on St Pancras and both called *St Pancras Station* are by

Simon Bradley (Profile, 2007) and Jack Simmons (George Allen & Unwin, 1968, reprinted 2003 by Historical Publications). Peter Darley's *Camden Goods Station* (Amberley Publishing, 2013) is also mainly pictorial but a thorough and rare account of a freight depot.

The redevelopment of Liverpool Street, together with its history, is covered in a book by British Rail's architect for the scheme, Nick Derbyshire, called *Liverpool Street: A Station for the Twenty-First Century* (Granta Editions, 1991). Anthony Lambert's *Marylebone Station Centenary* (Metro Publications, 1999) is slightly out of date but a good history.

In general, the Southern Railway terminus stations have fared less well with fewer books on their stations. There is *The History of Waterloo Station* by John Fareham (Bretwalda Books, 2013) and the story of the *Brookwood Necropolis Railway* (The Oakwood Press, 4th edition, 2006), which tells the fascinating story of the Waterloo Necropolis station. Otherwise there is much detail of the station developments in the two-volume *History of the Southern Railway* by C.F. Dendy Marshall and R.W. Kidner (Ian Allan, 1963).

Joe Brown's lovingly compiled *London Railway Atlas* (Ian Allan, 2015) is a map of all the lines in the capital, which is useful in understanding some of the intricacies of the system. And last, if you want a history of the London Underground, the third edition of my history of the system, *The Subterranean Railway*, updated to include the story of Crossrail, was published by Atlantic Books in 2020. My history of Britain's railways, *Fire & Steam*, is still in print and was also published by Atlantic in 2007.

I am always happy to help with queries, and can be contacted via christian.wolmar@gmail.com.

REFERENCES

INTRODUCTION

1   Centre Georges Pompidou, *Le Temps des Gares*, La Vie du Rail, 1978, p. 15.

1   STARTING SLOWLY

1   This was kindly calculated for me by Joe Brown, author of the *London Railway Atlas*, and includes the Docklands Light Railway and the Croydon tram as well as the Underground and the national rail network. There are other possible interpretations of, say, parallel running lines and joint stations but this is his best estimate.

2   Peter Ackroyd, *London: The Biography*, Vintage, 2001, p. 574.

3   Simon Jenkins, *A Short History of London*, Viking, 2019, p. 140.

4   Quoted in ibid., p. 142.

5   *Morning Post*, 7 July 1829.

6   For a short period, static engines were used to haul trains up the incline outside the Liverpool end of the line.

7   R. Davies and M.D. Grant, *London and Its Railways*, David & Charles, 1983, p. 22.

2   THE RAILWAY IN THE SKY

1   Quoted in R.H.G. Thomas, *London's First Railway: The London & Greenwich*, B.T.S. Batsford Ltd, 1986, p. 12.

2   The *Quarterly Review* quoted in Frank Ferneyhough, *Liverpool & Manchester Railway 1830–1930*, Robert Hale, 1980, p. 73.

3   Thomas, *London's First Railway*, pp. 140–41.

4   Ibid., p. 133.
5   Alan A. Jackson, *London's Termini*, Pan Books, 1972 (first published 1969 by David & Charles), p. 141.
6   R. Tyas, *The Croydon Railway and Its Adjacent Scenery*, 1839, quoted in Thomas, *London's First Railway*, p. 150.
7   *The Times*, 17 February 1838.
8   *Railway Times*, 4 September 1840.
9   *Kentish Mercury*, 31 March 1838.
10 Thomas, *London's First Railway*, p. 160.
11 Jackson, *London's Termini*, p. 145.
12 Ibid., p. 147.
13 *Illustrated London News*, July 1854.
14 Oliver Green, *Discovering London Railway Stations*, Shire Publications and London Transport Museum, 2012, p. 72.

3   THE FIRST CATHEDRALS

1   Alan A. Jackson, *London's Termini*, Pan Books 1972 (first published 1969 by David & Charles), p. 140.
2   Charles Dickens, *Dombey and Son*, first published in 1848. Available online at www.dickens-online.info/dombey-and-son-page47.html
3   Francis D. Klingender, *Art and the Industrial Revolution*, Paladin, 1968 (originally published 1947), p. 134.
4   Quoted on the Camden Railway Heritage website, http://www.crht1837.org/history/tunnel
5   Gordon Biddle, *Britain's Historic Railway Buildings*, Oxford University Press, 2003, p. 50.
6   Quoted on the Camden Railway Heritage website, http://www.crht1837.org/locations/tunnelportal
7   David Jenkinson, *The London & Birmingham: A Railway of Consequence*, Capital Transport, 1988, p. 29.
8   Samuel Sidney, *Rides on Railways, Leading to the Lake & Mountain Districts of Cumberland, North Wales*, WS Orr & Company, 1851. Available online at https://www.gutenberg.org/files/13271/13271-h/13271-h.htm

9   Augustus Welby Pugin, *An Apology for the Revival of Christian Architecture in England*, 1843, p. 11. Available online at https://archive.org/details/a604881400pugiuoft/page/n25

10 John Betjeman, *London's Historic Railway Stations*, John Murray, 1972, p. 125.

11 Samuel Sidney, *Rides on Railways, Leading to the Lake & Mountain Districts of Cumberland, North Wales*, WS Orr & Company, 1851. Available online at https://www.gutenberg.org/files/13271/13271-h/13271-h.htm

12 John R. Kellett, *Railways and Victorian Cities*, Routledge & Kegan Paul, 1969, p. 4.

13 Francis Coghlan, *The Iron Road Book and Railway Companion; or a Journey from London to Birmingham*, 1838. Available online at https://books.google.co.ukbooks?id=t5g1AQAAMAAJ&printsec=frontcover&source=gbs_ge_summary_r&cad=0#v=onepage&q&f=false

14 Samuel Sidney, *Rides on Railways, Leading to the Lake & Mountain Districts of Cumberland, North Wales*, WS Orr & Company, 1851. Available online at https://www.gutenberg.org/files/13271/13271-h/13271-h.htm

15 Ibid.

16 Jenkinson, *The London & Birmingham*, p. 30.

17 Betjeman, *London's Historic Railway Stations*, p. 125.

18 Jackson, *London's Termini*, p. 29.

19 Ibid.

20 Betjeman, *London's Historic Railway Stations*, p. 125.

21 Jenkinson, *The London & Birmingham*, p. 31.

22 Ibid., p. 31.

23 Steven Brindle, *Paddington Station: Its History and Architecture*, English Heritage, 2004, p. 18.

24 *Illustrated London News*, July 1854.

25 Betjeman, *London's Historic Railway Stations*, p. 108.

26 Jackson, *London's Termini*, p. 326.

27 Oliver Green, *Discovering London Railway Stations*, Shire Publications, 2010, p. 14.

4   A MODICUM OF ORDER

1   Quoted in John Kellett, *The Impact of Railways on Victorian Cities*, Routledge & Kegan Paul, 1969, p. 5.
2   The precise number is the subject of some debate since Euston, Charing Cross and even Fenchurch Street could be deemed close enough for passengers to interchange.
3   Quoted in Gordon Biddle, 'King's Cross and St Pancras: the Making of the Passenger Termini' in Michael Hunter and Robert Thorne, *Change at King's Cross*, Historical Publications, 1990, p. 62.
4   Biddle, 'King's Cross and St Pancras: the Making of the Passenger Termini' in Hunter and Thorne, *Change at King's Cross*, p. 60.
5   Terry Farrell, *Shaping London: The Patterns and Forms that Make the Metropolis*, Wiley, 2010, p. 138.
6   Ibid.
7   D.T. Timins, 'Important Railway Goods Depots, 1', *Railway Magazine*, 6, 1900, pp. 70–78.
8   J. Medcalf, 'Important Railway Goods Depots 4: King's Cross', ibid., pp. 313–20.

5   BREACHING THE CITY WALLS

1   Quoted in Geoff Goslin, *John Braithwaite and the Bishopsgate Viaduct*, London Railway Heritage Society, 2002, p. 5.
2   Alan A. Jackson, *London's Termini*, Pan Books, 1972, p. 99.
3   Ibid.
4   Quoted in Goslin, *John Braithwaite and the Bishopsgate Viaduct*, p. 9.
5   More accurately 5ft ½in though often referred to as 5ft.
6   George, his father, was also involved and it is unclear how much each contributed to the design of the scheme.
7   Quoted in Chris Heather, *London Railway Stations*, The National Archives, Robert Hale, 2018, p. 34.
8   Quoted in ibid., p. 39.
9   John Betjeman, *London's Historic Railway Stations*, John Murray, 1972, p. 46.
10   Jackson, *London's Termini*, p. 129.
11   Quoted in ibid., p. 133.

12 Quoted in ibid.

13 Betjeman, *London's Historic Railway Stations*, p. 46.

14 Wayne Asher, *A Very Political Railway: The Rescue of the North London Line*, Capital Transport Publishing, 2014, p. 10.

15 Betjeman, *London's Historic Railway Stations*, p. 50.

16 Ibid.

17 Ibid.

18 Jackson, *London's Termini*, p. 87.

6   UPSTAGING KING'S CROSS – OR NOT?

1   Jack Simmons, *St Pancras Station*, George Allen & Unwin, 1968, reprinted by Historical Publications, 2003, p. 156.

2   Ibid., p. 19.

3   Ibid., p. 23.

4   C. Hamilton Ellis, *The Midland Railway*, Ian Allan, 1953, p. 35.

5   Simon Bradley, *St Pancras*, Profile Books, 2007, p. 9.

6   From Fredrick Miller, *St Pancras Past and Present*, 1874, quoted in Simmons, *St Pancras Station*, p. 47.

7   Simmons, *St Pancras Station*, p. 55.

8   Some estimates suggest 720 or even 800. A few have been removed in the refurbishment completed in 2007.

9   Bradley, *St Pancras*, p. 70.

10 Simmons, *St Pancras Station*, p. 58.

11 Ibid., p. 19.

12 Ibid., p. 32.

13 Quoted in ibid., p. 45.

14 Ibid., p. 46.

15 Jeffrey Richards and John M. MacKenzie, *The Railway Station: A Social History*, Oxford University Press, 1988, p. 27.

16 Gordon Biddle, *Britain's Historic Railway Buildings: An Oxford Gazetteer of Structures and Sites*, Oxford University Press, 2003, p 55.

17 Ibid.

18 Hamilton Ellis, *The Midland Railway*, p. 34.

19 Biddle, *Britain's Historic Railway Buildings*, p. 55.

20 Hamilton Ellis, *The Midland Railway*, p. 34.

21 *Building News*, 22 May 1874, quoted in Simmons, *St Pancras Station*, p. 74.

22 Alan A. Jackson, *London's Termini*, Pan Books, 1972, p. 59.

23 Simmons, *St Pancras Station*, p. 74.

24 Ibid., p. 91.

25 Michael Hunter and Robert Thorne, *Change at King's Cross*, p. 123.

26 Charles Booth, *Life and Labour of the People in London*, Third Series, 1902, p. 170.

27 Quoted in Malcolm J. Holmes, *Somers Town: A Record of Change*, London Borough of Camden, 1985, p. 22.

28 *Journal of the Royal Institute of British Architects*, 1939, p. 651.

29 *Quarterly Review*, 1872, p. 301.

30 Bradley, *St Pancras*, p. 85.

31 Simon Jenkins, *Britain's 100 Best Railway Stations*, Penguin Random House, 2017, p. 75.

32 John Betjeman, *London's Historic Railway Stations*, John Murray, 1972, p. 126.

7 SOUTHERN INVASION

1 Quoted in C.F. Dendy Marshall and R.W. Kidner, *The History of the Southern Railway*, Volume 1, Ian Allan, 1963, p. 60.

2 Quoted in John M. Clarke, *The Brookwood Necropolis Railway*, The Oakwood Press, 1983, p. 57.

3 Ibid., p. 87.

4 Ibid., p. 25.

5 From *The Globe*, quoted in Clarke, *The Brookwood Necropolis Railway*, p. 29.

6 Quoted in John Fareham, *The History of Waterloo Station*, Bretwalda Books, 2013, p. 33.

7 Alan A. Jackson, *London's Termini*, David & Charles, 1969, p. 225.

8 THE THREE SISTERS

1 J.R. Wilson in *Imperial Gazetteer*, 1869, p. 167.

2 *Punch*, 44, 1863, p. 184.

3 David Brandon and Alan Brooke, *The Railway Haters: Opposition to Railways from the 19th to 21st Centuries*, Pen & Sword Books, 2019, p. 296.
4 *Illustrated London News*, 10 June 1865.
5 Alan A. Jackson, *London's Termini*, David & Charles, 1969, p. 200.
6 Ibid., p. 289.
7 All these quotes cited in Chris Heather, *London Railway Stations*, The National Archives, 2018, p. 95.
8 Quote from an anonymous writer in Edward Walford, *Old and New London*, Vol. III, Cassell & Co, 1897 p. 130.
9 *Railway Magazine*, vol. 75, 1934, p. 159.
10 It moved to its present location in Fulham in 1973.
11 Heather, *London Railway Stations*, p. 99.
12 Jackson, *London's Termini*, p. 177.
13 Ibid., p. 172.
14 John R. Kellett, *Railways and Victorian Cities*, Routledge & Kegan Paul, 1969, p. 72.
15 Ibid., p. 69.
16 T.C. Barker and Michael Robbins, *A History of London Transport: Volume One – The Nineteenth Century*, George Allen & Unwin, 1963, p. 272.
17 Quoted in Kellett, *Railways and Victorian Cities*, p. 74.
18 C. Hamilton Ellis, *British Railway History: 1877–1947*, George Allen & Unwin, 1959, p. 244.

9 THE WORKERS' STATION

1 W.M. Acworth, *Railways of England*, John Murray, 1900, reprinted Ian Allan, p. 406.
2 Quoted in *Great Eastern Railway Magazine*, February 1923.
3 John R. Kellett, *Railways and Victorian Cities*, Routledge & Kegan Paul, 1969, p. 52.
4 Alan A. Jackson, *London Termini*, David & Charles, 1969, p. 104.
5 Oliver Green, *Discovering London Railway Stations*, Shire Publications, 2012, p. 56.
6 Jackson, *London Termini*, p. 104.

7   Ibid., p. 109.
8   Quoted in T.C. Barker and Michael Robbins, *A History of London Transport: Volume One – The Nineteenth Century*, George Allen & Unwin, 1963, p. 217.
9   Nick Derbyshire, *Liverpool Street: A Station for the Twenty-First Century*, Granta Editions, 1991, p. 33.
10 Jackson, *London Termini*, p. 110.
11 Ibid.
12 John Betjeman, *London's Historic Railway Stations*, John Murray, 1972, p. 35.
13 Barker and Robbins, *A History of London Transport*, p. 215.
14 Ibid., p. 216.
15 H.P. White, *A Regional History of the Railways of Great Britain: Volume 3, Greater London*, David & Charles, 1987, p. 178.
16 Kellett, *Railways and Victorian Cities*, p. 63.
17 Quoted in ibid., pp. 97–8.
18 Jack Simmons, *The Railway in Town and Country, 1830–1914*, David & Charles, 1986, p. 83.

10 A TERMINUS TOO FAR

1   Clive Foxell, *The Story of the Met and GC Joint Line*, self-published, 2000, p. 20.
2   Alan A. Jackson, *London's Termini*, David & Charles, 1969, p. 356.
3   Ibid., p. 358.
4   John Betjeman, *London's Historic Railway Stations*, John Murray, 1972, p. 117.
5   C. Hamilton Ellis, *The Trains We Loved*, Allen & Unwin, 1947, p. 38.

11 LONDON'S UNIQUE DOZEN

1   Michael Freeman, *Railways and the Victorian Imagination*, Yale University Press, 1999, p. 122.
2   Terry Farrell, *Shaping London: The Patterns and Forms that Make the Metropolis*, Wiley, 2010, p. 143.
3   John R. Kellett, *Railways and Victorian Cities*, Routledge & Kegan Paul, 1979, p. 244.

4 L.T.C. Rolt, *Lines of Character: A Steam Evocation*, The Branch Line, 1974, p. 19.

5 Freeman, *Railways and the Victorian Imagination*, pp. 16–17.

6 Jack Simmons, *The Railway in Town and Country, 1830–1914*, David & Charles, 1986, p. 35.

7 Freeman, *Railways and the Victorian Imagination*, p. 136.

8 Jeffrey Richards and John M. MacKenzie, *The Railway Station: A Social History*, Oxford University Press, 1988, p. 195.

9 Simmons, *The Railway in Town and Country*, p. 86.

10 From Parliamentary Papers quoted by Simmons, *The Railway in Town and Country*, p. 88.

11 David Brandon and Alan Brooke, *The Railway Haters: Opposition to Railways from the 19th to 21st Centuries*, Pen and Sword, 2019, p. 267.

12 Quoted in Richards and MacKenzie, *The Railway Station*, p. 299.

13 John Murray's publicity material quoted in ibid., p. 300.

14 Quoted by John Betjeman in *London's Historic Railway Stations*, John Murray, 1972, p. 74.

12 SETTLING DOWN AND DODGING THE BOMBS

1 Alan A. Jackson, *London's Termini*, David & Charles, 1969, p. 229.

2 John Betjeman, *London's Historic Railway Stations*, John Murray, 1972, p. 79.

3 John Fareham, *The History of Waterloo Station*, Bretwalda Books, 2013, p. 80.

4 Betjeman, *London's Historic Railway Stations*, p.79.

5 Jackson, *London's Termini*, p. 214.

6 Ibid., p. 301.

7 Ibid., p. 304.

8 Oliver Green, *Discovering London Railway Stations*, Shire Publications, 2010, p. 18.

9 Jackson, *London's Termini*, p. 83.

13 ROUND LONDON WITH SIR JOHN BETJEMAN

1 John Betjeman, *London's Historic Railway Stations*, John Murray, 1972, p. 8.

2   Ibid., p. 125.
3   Available online at https://www.designcouncil.org.uk/news-opinion/
    defence-euston-station
4   Betjeman, *London's Historic Railway Stations*, p. 117.
5   Oliver Green, *Discovering London Railway Stations*, Shire Publications,
    2010, p. 20.
6   Betjeman, *London's Historic Railway Stations*, p. 108.
7   Ibid., p. 97.
8   Ibid., p. 99.
9   Ibid., p. 91.
10 Ibid., p. 74.
11 Ibid., p. 58.
12 Alan A. Jackson, *London Termini*, David & Charles, 1969, p. 140.
13 Betjeman, *London's Historic Railway Stations*, pp. 65–6.
14 Ibid., p. 46.
15 Ibid.
16 Ibid., p. 47.
17 Ibid., p. 47.
18 Ibid., p. 30.
19 Ibid., p. 35.
20 Chris Green, *John Betjeman and the Railways: A Centenary Celebration,
    1906–2006*, Transport for London, 2006, p. 12.
21 Jackson, *London Termini*, p. 67.
22 Ibid., p. 83.
23 Betjeman, *London's Historic Railway Stations*, p. 26.
24 Simon Jenkins, *Britain's 100 Best Railway Stations*, Penguin Random
    House, 2017, p. 56.
25 Chris Heather, *London Railway Stations*, Robert Hale, 2018, p. 69.

INDEX

Ackroyd, Peter, 8

Acworth, W.M., 199

Advantages of Railways with Locomotive Engines, Especially the London & Greenwich Railway, The, 24

Albert, Prince Consort, 67, 79

All Saints Church, Lambeth, 260

Allport, James, 111, 113, 116, 119

Amba Hotel Charing Cross, 254

Andaz London Liverpool Street, 254

Argent LLP (property developer), 301

Arup, Ove, 299

Ascot Racecourse, 252

Ashbee, W.N., 208

Asher, Wayne, 102–3

'atmospheric' railway, 35–6

Bailey, Joseph, 188

Baker, William, 105

Balmoral Castle, Scotland, 79

Barlow, William, 109, 116–19

Barry, Charles, 181, 205

Barry, Edward, 181, 188

Basingstoke Canal, 139

Battersea, 176

Battersea railway bridge, 74, 173–4, 183, 237

Bayswater, 9, 232

Bazalgette, Joseph, 218

Beazley, Samuel, 41–2

Beeching, Richard, 103, 232, 233, 277

Belgravia, 9, 170

Bell, Ingham, 205

Belsize tunnel, 113

Belton Estate, The (Trollope), 123

Bender, Thomas, 281

Berkeley, George, 99

Berlin, Germany, 236

Bermondsey, 26–8

Bethlehem Hospital (Bedlam), 105, 201

Bethnal Green, 10, 201, 206, 268

Betjeman, John, 4, 276, 277–303

  Broad Street and, 104, 106

  Cannon Street and, 290–91

  Charing Cross and, 285–6

  Euston and, 54, 59, 61, 137, 278, 280–81

  Fenchurch Street and, 99–100, 102, 291–2

  King's Cross and, 295–8

  Liverpool Street and, 209, 292–5

  London Bridge and, 288–90

London's Historic Railway Stations, 277–8, 288
Marylebone and, 228–9, 281–2
Paddington and, 69, 282–3
St Pancras and, 277, 295–6, 298–301
Victoria and, 283–4
Biddle, Gordon, 50, 82, 124, 126
Billingsgate market, 58, 130, 177
Birmingham, 44–5, 55, 57
Birmingham & Derby Railway, 111
Birt, William, 207
Bishop's Bridge station, 66–8
Bishopsgate station, 91–5, 99, 200–201, 233, 246
Blackfriars railway bridge, 74, 113, 165–6, 168, 183, 191, 237
Blackfriars station, 137, 164, 166, 191, 234, 301
Blackwall, 95–8
Blomfield, Arthur, 114
Bloomsbury, 9
boat trains, 180–81, 269–70
bookstalls, 254–6
Booth, Charles, 132
Bourne, John, 49
Bow Junction, 103, 105
Braddock, Henry, 227
Bradlaugh, Charles, 153
Bradley, Simon, 114, 117, 121, 123, 135
Bradshaw's, 243
Braithwaite, John, 92, 94–5
Brassey, Thomas, 140, 144, 192

Bricklayers Arms station, 39–41, 42, 233, 241
Brighton Belle, 269
Bristol, 63, 66
Bristol Temple Meads station, 68
Britain's Historic Railway Buildings (Biddle), 50
British Empire Exhibition (1924–5), 232
British Library, 133, 300
British Rail, 106, 136–7, 167, 227, 278–9, 291, 293, 295
British Railways, 136, 160, 229, 275–6, 280
British Transport Commission, 275
British Transport Hotels, 254
'broad gauge', 63–4, 94–5
Broad Street station, 74, 102–7, 174, 200–201, 204, 233, 237, 241, 244, 276, 278, 293, 302
Brookwood cemetery, 150–55, 178
Broun-Ramsay, James, 1st Marquess of Dalhousie, 72
Broun, Richard, 150
Brunel, Isambard Kingdom, 36, 63–9, 174, 177–9, 282, 283
Brunswick Hotel, 97
Brunswick Wharf, 95
Brutalism, 137
Building News, 127, 253
Burton ale, 116–17

cab ranks, 257
cable system railway, 96–8
Camden Railway Heritage Trust, 50
Camden Station, 58
Camden Town, 10, 46–50, 84–7, 103
canals, 83–4
Canary Wharf, 107
Cannon Street bridge, 74, 187
Cannon Street station, 164, 168, 175, 179–80, 186–90, 235, 303
  building costs, 194
  hotel, 188, 253, 290
  modern day, 290–91
  public lavatories, 188–9, 257
  refurbishment of, 273
  World War II and, 274
Canterbury & Whitstable Railway, 21
Capel-Coningsby, George, 5th Earl of Essex, 45
Catch Me Who Can, 16
Cautley, Henry, 185
Central St Martins art college, 301
Channel Tunnel, 222, 284
Charing Cross, Euston & Hampstead Railway 183, 187
Charing Cross Hotel, 181–2, 188, 254, 285
Charing Cross Railway Company, 177
Charing Cross station, 4, 74, 156, 164, 168, 174–86, 190, 237, 265, 269, 302

building costs, 194
clock, 180
Eleanor cross, 182
Embankment Gardens, 285
  hotel, 181–2, 254, 285
  modern day, 285–6
  refurbishment of, 273
  roof, 179, 185–6
  World War II and, 275
Charles, Prince of Wales, 279
Charlton Athletic FC, 252
Chelsea, 8, 10
Chelsea FC, 252
Church land development, 146, 194, 239, 260–61
City & South London line, 159
City of London, 11, 12, 73–4, 91, 93, 100–102, 105, 145, 237
City of London Theatre, 202
City Terminus Hotel, Cannon Street, 188, 253
City Thameslink station, 167
Clapham, 11, 145, 237
Clarendon, Earl of, *see* Villiers, George, 4th Earl of Clarendon
Clergy Orphan Asylum, 224
Coal Drops Yard, 131
Coghlan, Francis, 55–6
Colney Hatch, 155
Continental services, 269–70, 299
Cook, Thomas, 181
Copenhagen tunnel, 77, 82
Corbett's Lane, Bermondsey, 26, 33, 36

coronavirus, 4–5
Covent Garden, 130, 177
    New Covent Garden, 148
Cranborne, Lord, *see* Gascoyne-
    Cecil, Robert, 3rd Marquess of
    Salisbury
Crossrail, 221, 283, 302
Croydon, 14–15, 33, 35, 40
Crystal Palace, 68, 80
Cubitt, Joseph, 80
Cubitt, Lewis, 39, 40, 77, 80–81, 113,
    123, 297
Cubitt, Thomas, 9
Cubitt, William, 39, 80

'Demolition Statements', 193
Denbigh Hall, 55
Dent of London, clockmaker, 80
Deptford, 21–5, 27–8
Deptford station, 25, 32, 37–8
Derbyshire, Nick, 208, 293
Descriptive Map of London Poverty
    (Booth), 132
Dickens, Charles, 48–9
diesel engines, 128, 300
District Railway, 190, 193, 218–21,
    266
Docklands, 10, 74, 84, 95–6, 107
Docklands Light Railway, 97
Dombey and Son (Dickens), 48–9
Dottin, Abel, 30, 140
Dottin Street station, 30
Dover, Kent, 19, 23, 39, 40–41, 298

Early Closing Association, 251
East and West India Docks
    & Birmingham Junction
    Railway, 103
East India Dock, 95
Eastern Counties Railway, 91–5,
    98–9, 101, 199–200
Edgware, Highgate & London
    Railway, 251
Edis, Robert, 205, 228
Edmonton, 10, 206–7, 212
electrification, 259–60, 266–8, 271
Ellis, C. Hamilton, 114, 125, 127, 161,
    196, 229–30
Enfield, 206, 212
Engels, Friedrich, 153
Epsom Downs station, 252
Epsom racecourse, 142–3, 252
Era, The (steam road carriage), 22–3
Essex, Earl of, see Capel-Coningsby,
    George, 5th Earl of Essex
Eton College, 49–51
Etzensberger, Robert, 125
Eurostar, 114, 137, 262, 286–7, 298–9
Euston Road, 73, 130–32, 182
    see also New Road
Euston station, 1–2, 4, 30, 44, 46–8,
    51–63, 64–5, 79, 83–4, 110, 136–7,
    255, 276, 278
    Euston Arch, 4, 51–5, 238, 277,
    280, 295
    Great Hall, 4, 59–62, 277, 280
    hotels, 56–7, 123
    modern day, 280–81

refurbishment of, 272–3, 279–80
Shareholders' Meeting Room, 59, 61
Evening Standard, 160
'excursion' trains, 251–3

Fareham, John, 264
fares, 61–2
Farrell, Terry, 83, 87, 235
Farringdon station, 113, 164, 166, 302
Fay, Sam, 231
Fenchurch Street station, 3, 97–103, 159, 200, 235, 254, 268, 303
   modern day, 291–2
   refurbishment of, 273
Fleet, River, 112
Foch, Maréchal, 172
Folkestone, Kent, 40–41
football, 252
Forbes, James Staats, 218–21
Fowler, Charles, 177
Fowler, John, 170–71, 192
Francis Crick Institute, 300
Freeman, Michael, 235, 239, 245
freight, 57–8, 86, 190–91, 246–50
   coal, 86–7, 130–31, 247–8
   fish, 58, 250
   fruit and vegetables, 58, 130, 148, 177
   meat/livestock, 246, 249

milk, 58, 158, 248–9
Frith, William Powell, 69

Gandhi, Mahatma, 153
gas lighting, 8, 32
Gas Works tunnel, 77, 82
Gascoyne-Cecil, Robert, 3rd Marquess of Salisbury, 202
Gatti, Carlo, 177
Gatwick Express, 284
George IV, King of the United Kingdom, 79
George V, King of the United Kingdom, 261
German Gymnastics Society, 89
Gibson, Reverend Timothy, 93
Giles, Francis, 140
Give My Regards to Broad Street (film), 107
Golden Arrow, 269
Gooch, Daniel, 67
Gothic Revival style, 121–2, 125–6, 134–5
Grace, W.G., 224
Grand Junction Railway, 45–6, 57, 140
Grand Union Canal, 84
Gravesend, Kent, 20, 298
Great Central Railway, 217, 222, 226–32, 259
Great Eastern Hotel, Liverpool Street, 205–6, 293

Great Eastern Metropolitan
    Station & Railways Company,
    205
Great Eastern Railway, 95, 100,
    104, 115, 164, 195, 197, 200–201,
    203–15, 218, 241, 245, 267
Great Exhibition (1851), 68, 77–80
Great Northern Cemetery station,
    King's Cross, 155–6
Great Northern Hotel, King's
    Cross, 123, 125, 296
Great Northern London
    Cemetery Company, 155–6
Great Northern Railway, 77–80,
    82, 84, 86–7, 89, 110–12, 130,
    134, 155–6, 164, 166, 210–11, 220,
    223–4, 241
Great Reform Act (1832), 239
Great Western Railway, 36, 44, 51,
    57, 63–70, 78, 115, 170, 173–4, 213,
    231, 245, 248–50, 252
Great Western Royal Hotel,
    Paddington, 123
Green, Allan, 296
Green, Chris, 295
Green, Oliver, 42, 70, 204, 272, 283
Greenwich, 21–6, 28–9
Grimshaw, Nicholas, 283, 285,
    288–9
Grosvenor, Richard, 2nd Marquess
    of Westminster, 169, 194
Grosvenor Canal, 169
Grosvenor Hotel, Victoria,
    172, 268

Hamilton, Lord Claud, 201–2
Hammersmith, 8, 10
hansom cabs, 12–13
Hardwick, Philip, 52, 54, 123
Hardwick Jnr, Philip, 59
Hardy, Thomas, 114
Harrow, 46
Harwich, 210, 294
Hawkshaw, John, 178–9, 185, 187,
    220
Heather, Chris, 298
Heatherwick, Thomas, 301
Herapath, John, 144
Hertfordshire, 45–6
Heseltine, Michael, 137, 299
Holborn Viaduct station, 166–7,
    234, 301
horse racing, 142–3, 250–52
Hotel Great Central, Marylebone,
    205, 228–9
HS2, 76, 281
Hudson, George, 77, 80, 93
Hungerford Bridge, 178–9, 184,
    285
Hungerford Market, 176–7
hydraulic buffers, 168

Illustrated London News, 42, 68,
    166, 203
Imperial Airways, 270
Importance of Being Earnest, The
    (Wilde), 173
Industrial Revolution, 13–14, 83

International Exhibition (1862), 110

Ipswich, 210

Islington, 10, 46, 84, 103

Islington tunnel, 84

Jackson, Alan, 100, 277
  Bricklayers Arms and, 40–41
  Broad street and, 106
  Cannon Street and, 189
  Euston and, 60
  King's Cross and, 272, 277, 296
  Liverpool Street and, 205–6, 209
  London Bridge and, 30, 43, 289
  London's Termini, 43, 277
  Marylebone and, 228, 277
  Paddington and, 277
  Shoreditch and, 93
  St Pancras and, 128, 277
  St Paul's and, 168
  Victoria and, 173
  Victoria and, 268–9
  Waterloo and, 161, 260, 266

Jacomb-Hood, John Wykeham, 258

Jacomb-Hood, Robert, 171

'Jazz Service', 267–8

Jellicoe, Father Basil, 132–3

Jenkins, Simon, 9, 136, 296

Jenkinson, David, 61–2

Jennings, Martin, 291

Jerome, Jerome K., 159

John Clarke, 153

Kellett, John, 54, 192–3, 203, 213, 237–8

Kempton Park, 252

Kennington, 10

Kensal Green, 63

Kensington, 10, 253

Kent, 19–21, 43–4, 196, 219

Kentish Railway, 19–21

Kilburn, 10

Kindertransport, 294

King's Cross station, 4, 29, 39–40, 62, 70, 76, 79–90, 136, 155, 211, 235, 241, 246, 249, 257
  clock, 80–81
  Copenhagen tunnel, 77, 82
  Gas Works tunnel, 77, 82
  German Gymnasium, 89
  goods station, 86–8
  Great Northern Cemetery station, 155–6
  hotel, 123, 125, 296
  modern day, 295–8
  refurbishment of, 272–3
  St Pancras and, 110–13, 121, 125, 131, 134–5, 137
  World War II and, 274–5

Kipling, Rudyard, 180

Ladies' Vigilance Society, 269

Lambeth, 10, 178, 260

Lambeth Road, 73

Landmann, George Thomas, 21–3, 28, 34

left luggage offices, 265
Light That Failed, The (Kipling),
   180
Limehouse Cut, 84
Liverpool, 159
Liverpool & Manchester Railway,
   1, 7, 13–14, 24, 36, 44–6, 63, 65,
   71, 96, 140
Liverpool Lime Street station, 80
Liverpool Street station, 95, 102–5,
   195, 199–210, 215, 235, 241, 246,
   267–8
   East Side station, 208–9
   Harwich House, 208
   hotel, 205–6, 228–9, 254, 293
   modern day, 292–5
   refurbishment of, 273, 276
   World War I and, 274
   World War II and, 274
Livingstone, Ken, 167
Locke, Joseph, 140–41
locomotives, 48
London
   architecture, 9–10
   cemeteries, 149–52
   cholera epidemics, 112, 115, 150
   diet in, 248–9
   economic stimulus of railways
      in, 245–6
   growth of, 8–11, 244
   hotels, 252
   museums, 252
   poverty in, 11, 92–3, 101, 131–3,
      242

shopping, 252–3
suburban lines, 206–7, 211–13, 244
theatres, 252
see also railway construction:
   slum clearance
London & Birmingham Railway,
   1, 44–57, 63–4, 84–5, 140, 255
London & Blackwall Railway
   and Steam Navigation Depot
   Company, 95–100, 102
London & Brighton Railway, 15,
   35, 38–9, 115
London & Croydon Railway,
   33–9, 75
London & Greenwich Railway, 19,
   21–39, 45, 139–40, 242
London & North Eastern
   Railway, 268, 272–3
London & North Western
   Railway, 57, 59, 67, 78–9, 87, 101,
   103, 105, 110, 112, 156, 170, 173–4,
   183, 213
London & South Western
   Railway, 139–41, 144–50, 153–61,
   245, 258, 261–2
London & Southampton Railway,
   139, 142–4
London and Birmingham Railway
   Hotel and Dormitory, 56–7
London Bridge, 21–2
London Bridge station, 1, 4, 24,
   27–42, 43–4, 74, 139–40, 175,
   177–8, 241, 253, 266–7
   hotel, 253

modern day, 288–90
refurbishment of, 270–71
World War II and, 275
London Central Railway, 183
London County Council, 133, 184,
    261, 280
London Necropolis Company,
    149–54, 178, 260
London Transport, 160
London, Brighton & South Coast
    Railway, 35, 42, 169, 171–2, 175,
    195, 241, 252, 267–71, 284
London, Chatham & Dover
    Railway, 113, 115, 164–7, 170,
    172–3, 175–6, 186–7, 195–6, 203,
    207, 219–20, 241, 245–6, 270
London, Midland & Scottish
    Railway, 133, 136, 272–3
London, Tilbury & Southend
    Railway, 99–100
London Underground, 76, 159–61,
    186, 201, 219, 233, 259–60,
    266
  Bakerloo Line, 160–61, 230–31
  Central Line, 267
  Circle Line, 2, 75, 76, 159, 190,
    217–18, 220–21, 236, 266
  City & South London Line, 159
  Jubilee Line, 285, 289
  Northern Line, 83
  Victoria Line, 233
  Waterloo & City Line, 160
  see also District Railway;
    Metropolitan Railway

London's Historic Railway Stations
    (Betjeman), 277
London's Termini (Jackson), 43, 277
Lord Dalhousie, see Broun-
    Ramsay, James, 1st Marquess
    of Dalhousie
Lord's Cricket Ground, 223–5
Ludgate Hill station, 165–7, 203,
    234, 301

MacKenzie, John M., 123
Macmillan, Harold, 280
Mahon, Patrick, 265
Maiden Lane station, 77–9, 246
Maidenhead, 66
Manchester & Birmingham
    Railway, 57
Manchester, Sheffield &
    Lincolnshire Railway, 219,
    222–3, 226
Maple, John, 228
Marshall, William, 99, 254
Marx, Eleanor, 153
Marx, Karl, 153
Mary of Teck, Queen Consort, 261
Marylebone Cricket Club, 223–5
Marylebone Road, 73, 227–8
Marylebone station, 2, 83, 217, 221,
    223, 225–32, 233, 241
  goods yard, 226
  hotel, 227–9
  modern day, 281–2
McCartney, Paul, 107

Merstham, Surrey, 15
Metropolitan Artizans' and
    Labourers' Dwelling
    Association, 129
Metropolitan Railway, 12, 73,
    112–13, 117, 164–6, 170, 193,
    201–3, 211, 218–23, 230, 266
Midland Grand Hotel, St Pancras,
    122–3, 125–9, 133, 253, 273
Midland Hotel, Derby, 123–4
Midland Railway, 77, 79, 82, 89,
    101, 109–30, 133–5, 166, 213,
    223–4, 241
Mile End station, 91
Mill, John Stuart, 240
Miller, Frederick, 115
Minories station, 97–9
Modernism, 134, 137, 273, 295
Moon, Richard, 183
Moorgate station, 137
Morning Post, 12
Mortimer, F.J., 269
Moxon, John, 75
Murray, John, 256

'narrow gauge', 15, 63
Nash, John, 9
National Olympian Association,
    89
National Provincial Bank, 264
nationalisation of railways,
    240
Necropolis Railway, 149–53

Necropolis station, Waterloo,
    150–55, 260, 274, 288
Network Rail, 289, 295
New Road (Euston Road), 54, 76,
    83–4, 87, 112–13, 125, 227, 241
Newington Academy for Girls, 12
Nine Elms station, 141–5, 148, 233,
    246
Nock, O.S., 258, 286
North London Railway, 74, 102–3,
    106, 113, 164, 200, 241, 244, 278
North Western & Charing Cross
    Railway, 183
North Western Railway, 236
Northern & Eastern Railway, 94–5
Norwich, 92, 210
Notting Hill, 9

Oakley, Henry, 214
Olympic Games (2012), 300
omnibuses, 11–13, 23, 40
Ordish, Rowland Mason, 109
Orwell, George, 265
Ossulston Estate, 133
Outer Circle, 237
Overend, Gurney & Co., 107, 115,
    121, 195, 201
overhead railways, 159

Paddington station, 9, 12, 29, 51,
    65–70, 83–4, 117, 171, 213, 252,
    257

Crossrail station, 283
Great Western Royal Hotel, 123
Lawn, The, 69, 272, 282
milk trains, 249
modern day, 282–3
refurbishment of, 271–2
Palmerston, Lord, *see* Temple,
      Henry John, 3rd Viscount
      Palmerston
Paris, France, 3, 4, 236, 269
Park Lane, 10, 73
Parker, Peter, 282
Paxton, Joseph, 68
Pearson, Charles, 73, 76
Peto, Samuel, 115, 192
Phillips, Samuel, 255
Pickfords, 85
Pimlico, 9, 169–70, 176
Plumber's Apprentice, The
      (Jennings), 291
Portsmouth, 14–15, 139, 144
Poulson, John, 290
Primrose Hill, 47, 50, 52, 103
Primrose Hill tunnel, 48, 50–51
public lavatories, 188–9, 257, 263
Puffing Devil, 16
Pugin, Augustus, 54–6
Pullman trains, 269, 284
Punch magazine, 165–6, 224

Quarterly Review, 23, 134–5
Queens Park Rangers, 252

Railway Clearing House, 196
railway construction, 2–3, 19, 71–3
      building costs, 192–6
      class restrictions, 111, 210
      competition of railways, 239–41
      displacement of people, 32, 104,
         115, 131, 193, 202–3, 208, 225–6,
         244–5, 261
      electrification, 259–60, 266–8, 271
      rail freight, 190–91, 246–7, 276
      railway schemes and invest-
         ments, 20, 24–5, 71–3, 183–4,
         191–5, 211–12
      slum clearance, 10, 26, 101, 129,
         131, 176, 193, 226, 244
      speed of travel, 242–4
      suburban lines, 206–7, 211–13, 244
railway hotels, 56, 123–4, 128, 253–4
Railway Magazine, 144, 180, 263
Railway Station, The (Frith), 69
Railway Times, 94, 97
Ravensbourne, River, 27
Reform Act (1832), 45
Regent Street, 9
Regent's Canal, 46–7, 76, 79, 82–5,
      112–13, 225–6
Regent's Park, 9
Rennie, John, 44–5
Richards, Jeffrey, 123
Richmond & West End Railway,
      145–6
river steamers, 29, 95–6
Robinson, John, 265
Rolt, L.T.C., 238

Rotherhithe, 10
Roundhouse, Camden, 86
Routledge, George, 256
Royal Commission on London
    Traffic (1904), 101
Royal Commission on
    Metropolitan Railway Termini
    (1846), 73–5, 93, 95, 112, 163–6,
    170, 196, 236

Salisbury, Lord, *see* Gascoyne-
    Cecil, Robert, 3rd Marquess of
    Salisbury
Sandown Park, 252
Scotland, 272
Scott, George Gilbert, 109, 120–22,
    124–5, 135–6
Scott, James Robb, 262
Shadwell, 10
Shard, The, 43, 290
Shillibeer, George, 11–12, 23
Shoreditch, 91–4, 99, 104
Short History of London, A
    (Jenkins), 9
Sidney, Samuel, 53–4, 57–8
Simmons, Jack, 109, 111–12, 116,
    128–9, 215, 245, 251
Slough, 67
Smiles, Samuel, 176
Smith, Adam, 240
Smith, William Henry, 255
Smithfield Market, 249
Snow Hill tunnel, 137, 167

Somers Town Goods Depot,
    129–33, 300
Sonning, Berkshire, 66
South Eastern & Chatham
    Railway, 252, 284
South Eastern Railway, 21, 36,
    38–41, 156, 175–8, 180–83, 186–7,
    190–91, 195–6, 202, 219, 222,
    241, 268, 270
South Kensington, 218, 221, 252
South London line, 164
South Western Railway, 252
Southampton, 139–40, 144
Southern Railway, 181, 184–5, 267,
    270–71, 273
Southwark, 26
Spa Road station, 27–8, 36
Spiers and Pond Ltd, 264
Sprye, Richard, 150
St John's Wood, 10, 224–5
St Mary, Lambeth, 178
St Olave's Free Grammar School,
    31
St Pancras Church, 112–14
St Pancras House Improvement
    Society, 132–3
St Pancras Renaissance Hotel, 254
St Pancras station, 4, 29, 62, 82–3,
    109–37, 193, 235, 241, 257, 285
    clock, 81, 122, 299
    hotel, 122–3, 125–9, 133, 136, 253,
        254, 273
    modern day, 295, 298–301
    roof, 117–18, 298

vaults, 116–17
World War I and, 273–4
World War II and, 274
St Paul's Cathedral, 165–6
St Paul's station (Blackfriars), 166–8
St Thomas's Hospital, 31, 38–9, 177–8, 237
Stamford Hill, 207
Stamp, Josiah, 1st Baron Stamp, 133
Stanley Buildings, 132
steam engines, 13, 15–16, 19, 96–7, 128, 130, 179, 267, 300
'steam road carriages', 22–3
Stephenson, George, 45–6, 60, 63, 140
Stephenson, Robert, 45–8, 64, 84, 96–7
Stockton & Darlington Railway, 1, 19
Stoke Newington, 11, 212
Stratford, 299–300
Sunday rail services, 143–4, 152, 250–51
Surrey Canal Company, 139
Surrey Iron Railway, 14–15
Sydenham, 11

Tattenham Corner station, 252
Telford, Thomas, 20
Temple, Henry John, 3rd Viscount Palmerston, 120–21

Terminus Hotel, London Bridge, 253
terminus stations, xi (map), 2–3, 7–8, 42, 74–6, 163, 233–6
impact on local areas, 256–7
see also individual names of stations
Thames, River, 7–8, 10, 14, 24, 73–4, 95, 141, 157, 184
Thameslink, 166–8, 301–2
Thomas, John, 60
Three Men in a Boat (Jerome), 159
Times, The, 10, 37, 142–3, 255
Titbits magazine, 158
Tite, William, 141, 150
Tonbridge, Kent, 39
Tottenham, 10, 206–7, 212
Tottenham Hotspur FC, 252
Trevithick, Richard, 15–16, 27
Trollope, Anthony, 123
'trunk murders', 265
Turnham Green, 10

Underground Electric Railway Companies of London, 160
Underwood, John, 130
Union Jack Club, 261
United States, 14

Vauxhall Bridge station, 7
Vauxhall station, 146, 149

Victoria, Queen of the United
　　Kingdom, 41, 67, 70, 79, 148
Victoria railway bridge, 170–71
Victoria station, 164, 168–75, 181,
　　203, 241, 265–9
　‘Brighton side’, 172–4
　building costs, 194
　hotel, 171, 268
　modern day, 283–5
　refurbishment of, 268–9
Victoria Station & Pimlico
　　Railway, 169
Victorian Society, 295
Villiers, George, 4th Earl of
　　Clarendon, 45

W. & A. Gilbey, 86
W.H. Smith & Son, 99, 255
Walker of London, clockmaker, 81
Walker, Herbert, 267, 270
Walter, George, 24–5
Walthamstow, 206, 210, 212
Walworth, 10
Wandle river, 14
Wandsworth Road station, 41
Wandsworth, 14
Wapping, 10
Waring Brothers, 116
Warrington, 45
Waterloo & City Line, 160, 262,
　　287
Waterloo & Whitehall Railway,
　　147, 160

Waterloo station, 74, 144–61, 171,
　　252, 257–67
　‘Cyprus Station’, 156–7, 159
　‘Khartoum Station’, 157, 159
　‘Village, The’, 265–6
　clocks, 265
　left luggage office, 265
　milk trains, 158, 249
　modern day, 286–8
　Necropolis station, 150–55, 260,
　　274, 288
　public lavatories, 263–5
　refurbishment of, 257–8, 260–64,
　　271
　Surrey Dining Room, 266, 287
　Victory Arch, 261–2, 287
　Waterloo Bridge, 145–53, 159
　Waterloo East, 261, 288
　Waterloo International, 29,
　　299
　Waterloo Junction (Waterloo
　　East), 147, 156, 175, 178, 180, 190,
　　261
　World War II and, 274
Watkin, Edward, 183, 202, 215,
　　218–24, 226, 228, 231, 233
Watt, James, 16
Wembley stadium, 232
West End, 11, 40, 74, 156, 163, 169,
　　175–6, 286
West End of London & Crystal
　　Palace Railway, 169
West Ham Tramways, 102
West London Railway, 237

Westminster, Marquess of, *see*
   Grosvenor, Richard, 2nd
   Marquess of Westminster
Westminster Bridge, 8, 28
Wharncliffe Dwellings Company,
   226
White, H.P., 212
Whiteley, William, 252
Whitstable, Kent, 21
wide gauge, 174
Wilde, Oscar, 173
Wilson, Edward, 205, 208
Wilson, Henry, 294
Windsor, 67, 70

Woolwich, 20
workmen's trains, 202–3, 206–7,
   210–15
World War I, 36, 167, 172, 181, 240,
   260–62, 269, 273–4
World War II, 148, 167, 266, 273–5,
   292
   Blitz, 266, 274–5
Wyatt, Matthew Digby, 68

Yarmouth, 92
Yerkes, Charles, 160–61
York Road, 145, 151, 157, 262, 274

A NOTE ABOUT
THE AUTHOR

Christian Wolmar is a writer and broadcaster specialising in transport. He has worked on several national newspapers, including the *Independent* and *Observer*, and has written a fortnightly column for *Rail* magazine since 1996. He is also frequently on TV and radio, commenting on transport and other social issues.

He has written seven previous books for Atlantic: *The Subterranean Railway* (on the London Underground), *Fire and Steam* (Britain's railways), *Blood, Iron and Gold* (the world's railways), *Engines of War*, *The Great Railway Revolution* (a history of the American railways), *To the Edge of the World* (the Trans-Siberian railway) and *Railways and the Raj* (Indian railways). He has written several other books including *The Crossrail Story* and *Driverless Cars: On a Road to Nowhere?*

He has had a sadly unsuccessful political career, having tried and failed to get the Labour nomination for several seats. He fought the 2016 Richmond Park by-election, recording Labour's worst result in London since 1900. A passionate Londoner, he was also shortlisted to be the Labour candidate in the 2016 London Mayoral election, coming fifth out of sixth in the subsequent vote.

He is always keen to engage with readers and can be contacted through his website, www.christianwolmar.co.uk, or via Twitter: @christianwolmar.